Sacred Path
Cards™

Other Books by Jamie Sams

*Midnight Song: Quest for the
Vanished Ones*

*Medicine Cards™: The Discovery of Power
through the Ways of Animals* (with David Carson)

Sacred Path Cards

THE DISCOVERY
OF SELF THROUGH
NATIVE TEACHINGS

||||

JAMIE SAMS

ILLUSTRATIONS BY LINDA CHILDERS

HarperSanFrancisco
A Division of HarperCollins*Publishers*

FIRST EDITION

Library of Congress Cataloging-in-Publication Data

Sams, Jamie, 1951–
    Sacred Path cards : the discovery of self through sacred teachings / Jamie Sams.—1st ed.
      p. cm.
    ISBN 0-06-250762-1
    1. Fortune-telling by cards. 2. Self-realization—Miscellanea.
    3. Healing—Miscellanea. 4. Indians of North America—Religion and mythology—Miscellanea. I. Title.
BF1878.S26   1990
133.3'242—dc20
                                  90-31856
                                        CIP

90 91 92 93 94 HAD 10 9 8 7 6 5 4 3 2 1

This edition is printed on acid-free paper that meets the American National Standards Institute Z39.48 Standard.

Dedication

The fire that is our essence comes from the stars and to the stars our essences will return. The Earth is our mother who gave us our bodies. After our Earth Walk, our bodies will return to the Earth. Our spirits are from the wind as is our breath. Our words are our breath and therefore are sacred.

With my breath, I speak these words: "I dedicate this book of words and its Medicine to the Children of Earth—all five races, all creeds, all nations—in the hope that together we may heal the wounds we have inflicted on each other. I trust that in unity we will heal our hearts and in so doing we will reconnect to our Earth Mother."

To those members of the Tribe of Two Worlds who have allowed me to call on their personal Medicine when I was in need, I dedicate this book as a continued celebration of life. White Cloud Woman, Carol Morning Dove (La Paloma), Wolf Heart, Linda Amber Fawn, Fire on the Wind, Lloydine, José, Nadia and John York, and my Sisters of the Dreamtime Buffalo, I thank you. We are one.

I have smoked this prayer in the Pipe of the Tribe of Two Worlds and it is good.

Contents

The Cards

Acknowledgments

||||

I would like to acknowledge the sensitivity of the following friends who have emotionally supported me through this project: Sherry and Ken Carey, Wakinya-Ska, Eagle Man, Big Tree, Grey Eagle and Mamma Bear, Brooke Medicine Eagle, Grandmother Twylah, David and Nina, Stephanie Hammer, Judith and Fred Wolf, Sue and Jon Alexander, Katinka Medicine Swan, and Silver Bear.

A big thank you to Colette, Rex, and Gary for reviewing the manuscript and helping me to meet the deadlines with my sanity intact.

Special thanks to the staff of HarperSanFrancisco for their understanding of the Sacred Teachings of the Red Race and their willingness to allow that wisdom to be shared with the world.

Introduction

In my heart of hearts, I knew the time was right to share with the world the Medicine that has brought me through the Void of Great Smoking Mirror. I was concerned about the reaction I might encounter from those who believe that the Sacred Teachings are not to be shared. So I went to the Grandmothers and asked, then I went to the Elders who had been my teachers and asked. They all said, "Yes, it is time."

They also reminded me that the teachings are to be shared through my personal experience and the secret steps of ceremonies were not to be related, for there are those who would defile or misuse the information. So I began with the purpose of assisting those who would not be able to receive the knowledge otherwise. From that viewpoint, I have been able to open my heart and my experience so that each of you may share the journey with me and in turn find and follow your own paths. May those paths be found through your heart's desire and the joy of your own spirit.

Each step of the journey on the Good Red Road is a special experience that warrants attention. Each understanding is a stepping stone toward building the Medicine Wheel, which denotes the continuance of life and Sacred Space. We are here to learn from each other, to live in harmony with All Our

Relations, to express our unique talents, and to heal ourselves and our Earth Mother. In doing all of these things, we trust that we will be able to read the signposts and notice the changes in the Sky Nation.

The signposts are not always as clearly marked for those who have not had the privilege of being taught how to read the clouds or taste the wind. In understanding the beauty of the abilities I have been given, I also know that goodness is to be shared. The gift of how to read the omens and hear my fellow creatures, to see the place where future lives and sing Great Mystery's songs is what I want to share in this book.

If in some small way I can assist my fellow Two-leggeds (humans), I will feel the joy that comes from the rich appreciation of sharing. I do not care if others choose to criticize this work. My answer to them is, "What are you doing to help the Children of Earth to better understand themselves and All Their Relations?" This is my gift. It comes from my heart, and it is good.

I want to make the understanding of the teachings easy and simple to apply. Some may feel that this divination system is a toy, and it can be if you choose to use it on that level. The depth of any teaching has to do with the level the student is willing to explore or has capacity to understand. As always, "Still waters run deep." The use of Sacred Path Cards™ in the silence of a seeking heart allows that deeper understanding to emerge.

It is not my intention to assume that I know all that has ever been taught on any of these subjects. I am merely a fellow traveler who shares the Good Red Road with all of you. I have walked the Medicine Path and learned my lessons through personal experience. I have been taught some of the teachings of the Seneca, Aztec, Choctaw, Lakota, Mayan, Yaqui, Paiute, Cheyenne, Kiowa, Iroquois, and Apache nations. In the spirit of the Wolf Clan, my clan, we share and teach the goodness of wisdom that brings peace to all nations, all peoples. We are pathfinders who share the knowledge of the way through the forest so that the path may be clear for other travelers.

My purpose in reopening these lesson paths for others is to promote understanding and peace between all creeds, all Nations, all Clans, all Tribes, and families. I feel that the more we know about each other and about our universe, the easier it will be to recreate the Uniworld which we came from. When Great Mystery blew the Breath of Life into our physical world and endowed us with gifts and talents that made each life-form a part of the perfect whole, Creation was founded in love. It is now time to remember that the universe may be reunited by that same essence, unconditional love, and become the Uniworld again.

From my Sacred Space and my Sacred Point of View, this is the way I saw and experienced the pathways of initiation and growth presented by my teachers. May these experiences touch each of you in your own unique ways and may your path be joyous and filled with abundance. Da' Naho! (It is said!) Four Winds and Good Medicine—

Jamie Sams–Hancoka Olowampi (Midnight Song)

What Is a Medicine Walk?

In Native American Tradition, Medicine is anything that will aid the seeker in feeling more connected and in harmony with nature and all life-forms. Anything that is healing to the body, mind, and/or spirit is Medicine. To find a special Medicine that would give answers for a personal challenge or problem, our Ancestors would often walk in the forests or on the mesas to observe the portents or signs that would assist them in healing and seeking wisdom. The Medicine Walk was a way to reestablish the link to the Allies, or Medicine Helpers. A Medicine Walk is still possible in today's busy world if the seeker knows how to read nature's signs.

Intuition allows us to maintain Earth-connection through understanding the languages of the Planetary Family. In this system of divination, the Sacred Path Cards™ will present questions to you so you may redevelop your personal intuition. Power is no more than our gifts and abilities and can never be stripped from us by another. It is time for each seeker to acknowledge and use those talents.

For centuries, the Red People have used the omens of nature to arrive at the decisions of entire Nations. All living creatures have their own Medicine messages to share with those who are willing to learn their language. *Hail-lo-way-ain,* the Language of Love in the Seneca tongue, is the way that All Our Relations speak to us. Through *Hail-lo-way-ain,* our hearts can feel the answers received on a Medicine Walk and healing can then proceed.

Two-leggeds (humans) are the only creatures in our world who do not out of gratitude return to Great Mystery the love they have received. The Language of Love can be understood when compassion and mutual respect are allowed to come full circle and are redistributed among those who share our world. To send love to a beautiful sunset, to a Willow tree, to a circling Hawk, by admiring the beauty of each, is one way to begin. Every fellow Creature-being or life-form is a teacher and a potential friend. Each teacher in nature holds a deep abiding love for Great Mystery and will impart messages to those who seek the mysteries of the Void. The unknown is made up of those lessons that instruct us in our roles within Creation as well as the roles others play.

To understand these messages is to become one with the Creature-beings of nature. To seek the peace of the Standing People (trees), to acknowledge the sacredness of all life-forms, and to find harmony with each living thing is to gain respect for Self as a Guardian of our Earth Mother.

The basic premise of this understanding is to acknowledge the Uniworld. The Uniworld is the universal Family of Creation. The Earth is our mother, the Sky is our father; our grandparents are Grandfather Sun and Grandmother Moon. Our Brothers and Sisters are the Stone People, the Standing People, the Creature-beings, the Plant People, and other Two-leggeds. We are never alone. When our human family is separated or moves onto the Blue Road of Spirit through physical death, we have nothing to grieve if we remain connected to the universal Family of Creation. The Medicine Walk is one way of reclaiming those connections.

In our modern world, the understandings of the Language of Love, *Hail-lo-way-ain,* can be understood only through an open heart, for it is a way of living life rather than a system to be mastered. We must be willing to use the feelings and the inner senses to "hear" the tender teachings of our fellow life-forms.

Imagine walking through your favorite forest, rolling hills, mesas, or green valley. See yourself surrounded by those crea-tures who are your Totems, or favorite animals. Notice which direction the Wind is blowing. Look to the Cloud People; do they take the form of faces or animals? Feel the warmth of the Earth Mother nurturing you in her gentle arms. Look at Grandfather Sun, see how his light plays upon the Earth Mother's breast. Taste the breeze and drink in the promise of rain. Respect and admire all that surrounds you. In this way, you are ready for the Language of Love to penetrate your senses in the silence of a quiet heart and mind.

Each flower or rock can be your teacher. They wait to be acknowledged by you as you walk through the land you share. The Medicine they hold is freely and abundantly given, if you allow yourself to feel it. The Wind is the forerunner of any lesson, for all spirit comes on the Wind. If it comes from the South, it is offering a teaching on faith, trust, innocence, humility, or the child-within. If Wind blows from the West, it offers lessons on inner-knowing, seeking answers or goals through introspection. When Wind blows from the North, it beckons you to be grateful and to know the wisdom being offered as well as acknowledging the wisdom you hold per-sonally. The East Wind brings breakthroughs, new ideas, and freedom through illumination. The East Wind will assist you in casting aside doubts or darkness by opening the Golden Door that leads to new levels of understanding.

Once we understand which type of lesson is coming our way on our Medicine Walk, we can then proceed by noticing which Allies call to us. When something catches our eye, it has called our attention and is speaking to us through the Language of Love. In caring for that messenger we establish a link that will allow the message to be received. In observing each Medicine Helper, whether it be Dragonfly or Ponderosa Pine, Petroglyph or Stone Person, we learn the lessons of nature.

In the way of my Ancestors, I have chosen to create a teaching system known as the Sacred Path so that you have the basic principles and can use them in the wilds or your favorite spot on the Earth Mother to reestablish your Earth-connection. The Sacred Path Cards™ are a bridge to the ancient understandings of our Native Knowing Systems. All that is necessary from the seeker is an open, feeling heart, a desire to learn, and a willingness to feel the Language of Love.

Our Native way of life can bring a change in consciousness that opens new doors of expression and expansion. To understand the Red People is to reach out to another culture and share the beauty of our common paths. In doing so, we trust that our common goal will be attained: peace, truth, and healing for Mother Earth's children. When the Children of Earth are healed, we may welcome the Rainbow of Peace into our hearts and trust that each Medicine Walk on the Sacred Path will bring new connections and Good Medicine that can be shared. In this way, we become the living prophesy of the Fifth World of Peace.

How to Use the Cards

In this deck of Sacred Path Cards™ there are no contrary cards. The reason for this is that you are viewing the steps of initiation that your Earth Walk contains. The purpose of the cards is to show you the steps of your spiritual development in a way that allows you to come to your own personal truths. Therefore, if you read the individual lessons and apply them to your present situations, you may come up with some specific answers that will shed light on your present path.

It is best to shuffle the cards side to side so that all cards are upright. Then place them in front of you and spread them like a fan so that you can easily choose any card from the deck. By approaching the cards in a receptive state or in silence, you may better understand what the messages are and how you are to use them. It is of utmost importance to recognize the power of your own understanding. Everyone has intuition and this system is designed to allow that personal talent to be used.

We are all growing and developing at a rapid rate due to the amount of understanding that is being sought. The more we understand about life, the more information is made available. Every life-force is offering assistance if we will only stop to listen. The Sacred Path Cards™ are doorways to the worlds of information and wisdom that can be accessed by Two-leggeds. These Medicine Symbols are intended to offer an opening for those who seek to Walk in Beauty with All Their Relations. By All Our Relations, we mean the Creature-beings, the Stone People, the Standing People (trees), and Sky Nation, the Earth Mother, the four Chief Spirits of Air, Earth, Fire, and Water.

To understand all the aspects presented by these cards, you also need to go forth into nature and gather experiences on your own. The cards are merely a tool for opening the door to a way of thinking, a way of living, a way of being. The growth and manner of expression is open to the individual. You should never expect to receive the lessons in the same manner or in the same order each time the cards are used. That is the beauty of our uniqueness; we each will express our learning in a different way that represents our personal creativity.

Many of you have asked, "Why forty-four cards?" As many of you know, four is the sacred number of the directions and also the number of the Earth Chiefs—Air, Earth, Water, and Fire. You may not be aware that forty-four is a sacred number in Native Tradition. The reason is there are forty-four secret Sisterhoods and Brotherhoods. These circles are divided into twenty-two societies on the physical plane with members who walk the Good Red Road (physical life) and twenty-two in the Other Side Camp or spirit world that are comprised by the Ancestors. In the physical life, there are eleven Sisterhoods and eleven Brotherhoods, the same number as dwell as complements on the Blue Road of the Spirit World. These secret organizations comprise the Guardians of the Sacred Hoop of all Native Nations.

These Sacred Path Cards™ can be used with the Medicine Cards™ that I coauthored with David Carson. You can use the spreads in this book with the Medicine Cards™ or the other way around. For further clarity you can use these cards with their spreads. If you want to know which Totem will assist you, pull a Medicine card to go with the Sacred Path card. These Sacred Path cards are the teachings and the Medicine cards are the lessons of Totem Animals.

For example, if you pulled the Council Fire card (decisions), and wanted to know what decisions you need to make, you could then pull a Totem from the other deck. Let us say you pulled Buffalo. The decision would be about abundance and would reflect your ideas about jobs, income, scarcity, or the comforts you wish to give yourself. Then for further clarity you could pull another Totem and discover which Creature-being would be your teacher during your decision process.

The decks assist one another but are not necessarily used together unless you want to go deeper. The fun comes from using your own intuition and discovering the multitude of messages that apply to your present pathway.

The Sacred Path Cards℠ are self-oriented in order for each individual to reflect upon the roles, gifts, and self-reliant abilities that can be gained on this Earth Walk. This growth process is limitless and like each spirit is eternal.

The Card Spreads

Each of these card spreads gives you a different viewpoint of the path you are following in life. They are intended to allow you to reflect upon the varying ways you experience the lessons you have chosen to learn on your Earth Walk. The power of truth is the force behind the lessons in the cards. The magic is the way they simply relay the messages that you need to hear coming from your own heart.

These spreads are different from the spreads in the Medicine Cards™ book, but both sets of cards may be used with all card spreads. The energy of truth is always interchangeable; therefore, I devised a way that both sets of card spreads would reflect different aspects of the total picture and could be used in tandem.

Daily Lessons

The Sacred Path Cards™ can be very effectively used as a daily form of guidance by choosing one card and allowing that teaching to be applied to life. Each time a card is read, the lesson will enhance the living of that day. Every time a card is drawn and the lesson reviewed, the application will change with the growth process of the individual. Seeking new ways to walk the Sacred Path is a skill that comes through introspection and discovery of the Self. In allowing the Self to be the adventurer, life will continue to be magical and fulfilling.

As always, the quietness of the seeking heart will allow you to penetrate the subtle levels of these Native Teachings and enter the world of deeper understanding. The Knowing Systems that evolve will be your own and will be founded in your personal truths. I trust that your journey will be wonder-filled and that your growth process will be graced with new understanding.

Corn Stalk Spread

The Corn Stalk Spread

Corn has been the daily staple of our people for hundreds of years. We believe that corn pollen is sacred and that we are fed by the fertile earth whose gift is our corn.

A wise Medicine Man once said that if a philosophy did not "grow corn," it had no value. Corn is the symbol of goodness, abundance, and fertility to our people, and these are the things that feed us daily. We may feed the body, the mind, the heart, and the spirit if we seek beauty in our daily lives. For it is the beauty of living in balance that "grows corn."

The Corn Stalk spread is a way to receive the life Manna that comes from sacred corn pollen. It is a gentle daily reminder of the beauty to be experienced if you are open to it.

1. The first card is the Root card, which denotes the beauty that can be experienced today by connecting to the Earth Mother. This card can also speak to you about the "root" of the problem, if you are in turmoil about some life situation. The Root card can also allow you to see the resources available through connecting to Mother Earth.

2. The second card is the Stalk card, which expresses the attitude needed to Walk in Beauty and balance. The Stalk card

can also denote the lesson you need to learn, so you may be a bridge between the path of understanding and the crooked trail. This human bridge is the peacemaker, true witness, or healer. You may be called upon to take one of these roles at anytime. The courage, talent, or ability needed to be a human bridge is supported by the Stalk card.

3. The third card is the Kernel card, which tells you what the fruits of your labors will provide for you. The lesson of this card should be fully digested so that the ear of corn can give energy to the body, mind, or spirit and support your present path. Kernels of corn represent the seeds of the future to Native People. These kernels also provide food for the present; through learning present lessons the future will be assured.

4. The fourth card is the Corn Manna card, which denotes how your "corn silk" is catching the sacred pollen and bringing abundance to your life. If you are feeling the fear of scarcity, the Corn Manna card will present the lesson that you need to learn to realign with the Field of Plenty. If your life and personal philosophy are "growing corn," this card shows how to continue the growing.

NOTE: Attitudes change daily and depend on the events you are experiencing. To change your attitude, you may wish to acknowledge the resources available (root) and the harvest that may be coming your way through the Corn card. Notice that the integration of these two clues to what you are creating are supported by your stalk. The stalk is the attitude that will bring the abundance into physical form.

The Grandfather Sun/Grandmother Moon Spread

In the Grandfather Sun, Grandmother Moon spread we are looking for the balanced nature of our male and female sides. Both aspects of our personality allow us to draw upon the

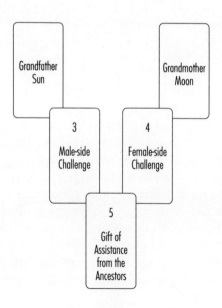

strength of male and female characteristics that will allow us to be balanced in all life situations.

We must acknowledge that it does not make any difference what gender our bodies are or what sexual preferences we have, all life-forms have three aspects, male, female, and Divine.

By attuning ourselves to the needs of our male and female sides, we can recognize our inner desires or conflicts and then work toward healing the parts of Self that need assistance. From that "balanced Self," we may then seek alignment with Great Mystery's divine energy.

1. The first card represents the lesson your male side is learning now.

2. The second card is the lesson your female side is learning now.

3. The third card is the challenge found in the lesson of your male side.

4. The fourth card is the challenge found in the lesson of your female side.

5. The fifth card is the assistance you are receiving from the Grandfathers and Grandmothers while you learn these lessons. This fifth card is a gift from the Ancestors that walked the Good Red Road before you. This gift may be received or ignored by you. It may come through your dreams or in a material way. A Creature-being (animal) or another person may come to you as a messenger, a leaf may fall in your path to be a reminder, a Standing Person (tree) may give you shade and a quiet space for learning. Accept the gift. In accepting this gift of wisdom you are giving yourself a way to overcome the challenges set in your path by your male and/or female sides. It is time to face the growth movement inside you and then move on to your next lesson of self-discovery.

The Four Directions Spread

The Four Directions spread is a broad overview of how you are balancing your Shields. Each Shield is a part of your basic Medicine, or makeup, that allows you to be who and what you are. In using the term Medicine, once again we are expressing the unique healing properties that every living thing has been endowed with since before the beginning of the physical world. Everything in our universe has the potential to be healing rather than harmful. Each flower, bird, tree, person, plant, and cloud has a message that can express something that will allow another creature in nature, if it is wounded or seeking wisdom, to grow and heal.

(To understand what your personal Shields are, you need to evaluate your strengths and weaknesses with a "cold eye," without letting your ego get in the way. Do this by using the lessons in the Shield cards of the Four Directions in the deck. Note that this is a separate lesson and is not a part of the Four Directions spread.)

The following is the layout for the Four Directions spread:

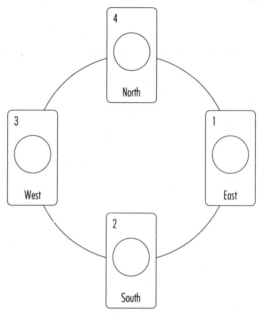

1. The East card expresses the spiritual door you are now opening in your life. This card is the spiritual seed that needs fertile ground and nurturing. How you accept the role of nurturing depends on your present situation and/or state of mind.

2. The South card expresses where your faith should be placed or where a loss of faith has caused you to feel weak. You must determine which application touches the child within you. That child knows the truth due to its faith and innocence.

3. The West card represents how to find the inward answer that introspection brings. To reach our goals, we must seek our own truths as to what we desire, how we plan to fulfill that desire, and what our purpose is in meeting that goal.

The West card gives the tool that may assist in finding those truths.

4. The North card expresses the wisdom you will gain if you follow a true course and apply the knowledge of the other three cards. The North is also the place of the Elders, gratitude, and healing. The North card may be a tool you may use for seeking personal healing and/or for discovering what blessings you should give thanks for.

Tipi Spread

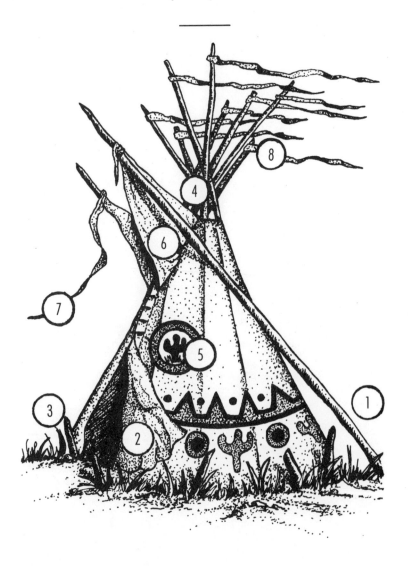

The Tipi Spread

The Tipi spread gives an overall view of the life lessons you have created and reveals the future impact of how you are handling those lessons. In the Tipi, we find the home that lodges us and the familiar things that nurture our sense of Self. The conical shape of the Tipi allows the Wheel of Life's energy to spiral to and from the Great Star Nation. The Tipi is also a movable lodge, demonstrating the flexibility of our people and reflecting the continued need for such flexibility in the changing world. The Tipi spread clarifies one's position in an often confusing world.

1. The first card represents the Past, or the lesson just completed.

2. The second card represents the Tipi door, which is the Present. This door represents the lesson we are learning in the present moment.

3. The third card is the Future that lives on the other side of the present moment. That future is totally dependent on our living the present so the future will be supported.

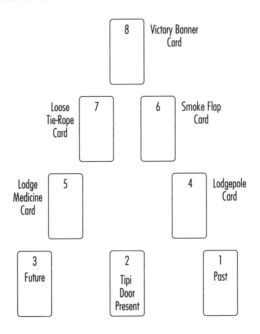

4. The fourth card is the Lodgepole card, which is the structure that holds the canvas or hides of the Tipi in place. This card expresses the structure needed to sustain your present activities.

5. The fifth card is the Lodge Medicine card. Each Tipi has symbols of protection painted on the hide covering that represent the dweller's personal Medicine. This card denotes the Medicine that will assist you and the strength you can call on.

6. The sixth card is the Smoke Flap card, which represents the hole at the top of the Tipi where the hearth fire's smoke

leaves and returns to Father Sky. This card symbolizes the needs met and the prayers being answered in this situation.

7. The seventh card is the Loose Tie Rope card, where the second smoke flap rope has come undone and is loose, blowing in the wind. If the smoke flap is not secured, snow, wind, and rain can come into your lodge. So the seventh card represents the unexpected challenge in this situation.

8. The streamers at the top of the lodgepoles denote the purpose of the Tipi and the owner's function in the Tribe. These streamers are Victory Banners; therefore, the eighth card is the Victory Banner card, which reflects the ability gained by the successful completion of your present pathway.

Peace Tree Spread

The Peace Tree Spread

The Peace Tree spread should be used if you are feeling at odds with your environment or aspects of the Self. The Peace Tree is the White Pine, which symbolizes the end of strife and the union of the Original Five Nations of the Iroquois Peace Confederacy. We, of the Wolf Clan, hold peace as our guiding light.

In understanding the role of peace in the Fifth World, on which we are now embarking, we must first seek inner-peace. The serenity that comes from a clean conscience, a humble heart, a smiling face, a twinkling eye, a gentle touch, and a positive outlook is the goal. In the modern world where the serene forests are not always available, confusion, worry, hurry, and noise take their toll. The Peace Tree lives in the hearts and minds of those who seek the silent places of the spirit.

1. The first card is the Buried Talent card, which represents the gift or ability you are not acknowledging because you have not sent your roots deep enough into our Earth Mother. This talent will directly apply to your seeking inner-peace.

2. The second card is the Root card, which represents the strength to be gained. This card gives you the tool needed

to earth your confusion and replace it with substance or strength. When looking at the lesson presented by this card you may wish to imagine this card as the root of your new understanding.

3. The third card is the Trunk card, which signifies the lesson you need to apply to your physical body and your sense of Self. To walk tall, in health and in balance, you should apply this lesson to your life.

4. The fourth card, the Branch card, tells you what lesson is needed to reach the light of Grandfather Sun's love and understanding. This card is also a clue to mental attitude. If your attitude is limiting the amount of joy you experience, it will be evident to you. That is, if the card reflects something you are not doing, it reveals the mental attitude that could use an adjustment so that you may reach farther and touch the peace you seek.

5. The fifth card is the Father Sky card, which indicates the personal freedom that you can gain. Knowing you may attain personal freedom whenever you find inner-peace, you may also find the courage to lay aside judgments, conflicts, or doubts that keep you from the freedom of flight in Father Sky. The winds of change live in Father Sky and can also be your Allies when letting go of old habits that create stagnation.

The Sacred Mountain Spread

Sacred Mountain is the place of inner-knowing and proper perspective. The Sacred Mountain of our Ancestors is not a physical place; it is a place of balance that exists within the Sacred Space of each individual. To reach this place of wisdom and enlightenment balanced with faith, trust, innocence, and courage, you must climb the mountains and hills of your own limitations and conquer the fears that keep you from knowing.

When the challenges are many and the path is crooked, you may feel confused or temporarily lost. In such times, the Sacred Mountain spread is the tool that will aid you in seeing the truth from the perspective of the Eagle. In freedom and from above, the overall significance is clearly put into perspective.

This spread is what I call a "working spread," because you must climb to the top using your own courage and strength rather than being carried by someone else. If the going is getting tough and you are willing to confront the limitation you have set in your own path, this is the spread to use.

The first four cards represent the areas of creativity open to you where you have set a limitation or denial. The Sacred Mountain card is the reward at the end of the climb or the gift you will attain by completing the journey.

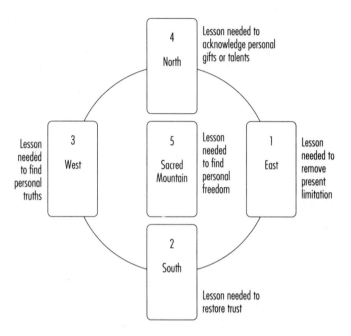

1. The first card appears in the East and signifies the lesson needed to remove any present limitation. This is the place of the Golden Door that leads to all other levels of awareness. No matter what card appears in this position, you are being asked to look at what you feel you cannot achieve in the card's lesson, hence your limitation is made clear for you.

2. The second card appears in the South and represents the lesson needed to restore your trust. The South card is also where you limit the faith you once had as a child, where you need to handle your ego, or where you need to heal the hurt of being betrayed after you trusted. The second card may also reveal if you have become a whining childlike victim instead of the courageous child that saw the world as an adventure.

3. The third card appears in the West and points out the lesson needed to find your personal truth. This West card may also imply that there is a limitation you have put on yourself regarding your ability to know what is right for you.

4. The fourth card is in the North and represents the lesson that will assist you in acknowledging your personal talents or gifts. If you are taking your gifts, talents, abilities, and material possessions for granted, you may be limiting the future gifts from the Field of Plenty because you shun the beauty of the ones you have.

5. The fifth card, the Sacred Mountain card, represents the lesson needed to find personal freedom. In letting go of the limitation you may have placed in your own path, the choices are now clear. The place of inner-knowing and balance high on top of Sacred Mountain is now accessible because you have confronted your fear and self-limitation. Now it is time to bask in the beauty of the unlimited view.

Kiva Spread

The Kiva Spread

Imagine yourself standing on the high desert surrounded by blood-red mesas and yellow-ochre castlelike rock formations. Far off in the distance is the purple haze of the sunset, graced with bright pink clouds and the reflections of Grandfather Sun's radiant russet form. Before you is the entrance to the sacred Kiva. The opening is on the ground in front of you. The hole in Mother Earth supports a ladder that leads below to the inner-space of prayer, reflection, and ceremony.

At the bottom of the ladder is the earthen floor with a small ceremonial fire burning just east of the Kiva's center. The walls are laced with the fire's reflections. The shadows appear like phantom forms of ancient Kachinas dancing around the circular walls of the Kiva.

This is the place of inner reflection. This is the place where the Sacred Hoop of all nations is made whole. As you near the fire, you are shown the Medicine that allows you to know your place in the Sacred Hoop. Your relationship to All Your Relations is made clear. How you relate to each set of Great Mystery's creatures and life-forms is revealed in a set of visions brought before your eyes in gusts of smoke from the ceremonial fire.

Imagine again, that you sprinkle bits of dried Cedar over the fire and the smoke from the Cedar brings each vision. The messages you receive from these visions are the gifts that each set of your relations is giving. All Your Relations will show you how to better understand your relationship to them.

The first cloud of smoke brings the vision of how you relate to the Stone People, the keepers of Mother Earth's records. The vision of the East Shield glows before you in the muted light of the Kiva's fire. It tells you that your pathway to illumination will be aided by the records the Stone People carry. When you need direction and spiritual strength, you may call upon the Stone People as Allies. Using your intuition, you begin to understand that the three pathways to illumination are presenting you with a Medicine Helper. You will know when to take a Medicine Walk, and you may hear the Stone Person's voice call to you. That Stone Person will be a part of your Medicine Bundle and will assist you in seeking the truths of the East Shield. That Stone Person's voice may sound like your own voice speaking to you through your thoughts, or you may just feel what it wants you to know.

The second cloud of smoke brings a vision of the Standing People (the trees). You see in the depths of the billowing clouds, a vision the Pipe reaching out to you. The Pipe is singing a sweet song that brings inner-peace. The Pipe brings the message that you are to seek the silence of the forest and listen to the Standing People, so they may show you the type of Tree Person who will teach you serenity. They may also be saying that the altar stand for your Pipe of peace should be made from a certain wood. The type of wood should be from your peace tree. Deeper in the vision you see that the roots of that species of Standing Person can be an earthing force for you. The earthing force will allow you to stand in your truth and maintain peace in your life. An earthing force teaches you Earth-connection and how to feel the power of strength and courage that Mother Earth so freely offers all her children.

Each of these visions brings you a sense of belonging and you must use your intuition, which is a part of your personal power, to determine what the message is. The Kiva spread is to be done *only one time* and will give structure to your pathway of seeking on the Good Red Road.

1. The first card is the Outer World card, which will give you a clue to the way you present yourself in the world of modern life. This attitude will aid you in maintaining balance in the work-a-day world so that you may stand in truth in your Sacred Space among your fellows.

2. The second card, the Entering card, tells you which attitude to assume every time you enter the silence of ceremony, vision seeking, or nature. It speaks to you of the tool you need to maintain at-oneness with the Sacred Space you are entering. The Entering card is represented by the Kiva ladder and may also speak of the steps of your inner journey.

3. The third card is the Floor card. When you reach the dark inner-space of the Kiva, you may need to adjust your senses. The Floor card is the tool that will hone your intuitive senses so that you may better understand the messages life will present in your Earth Walk. You are here to seek answers. In the void of Great Mystery, all answers await the person that seeks them with a humble heart and an open mind. Altered states of awareness can be achieved through the help of the card you pull in this position.

4. The fourth card, the Stone Person card, will be the gift you are given by the Stone People to aid you in your Earth Walk. This card may also speak of your relationship to the Stones and the records they hold. The truths of this card are deep and will bring many revelations of how the mineral kingdom is aiding you in your journey.

5. The fifth card is the Standing People card, which denotes the relationship you have to the Tree Nation, what assistance they offer you, and on which steps of your Red Road path you will need their peace and earthing influence. They also aid in finding your roots, the root of a problem, and the branches of your creativity. Another aspect of their gifts of wisdom is the fruits of their limbs, which are the truths of those who seek the light of Grandfather Sun.

6. The sixth card is the Creature-beings card. It speaks of the tool you need to relate to the animals of Mother Earth. The Four-leggeds, the Finned-ones, the Winged-ones, and the Creepy-crawlers are our teachers and wish to aid in the progress of the Children of Earth. This card speaks of the tool needed to make that connection strong as well as the area of your life where they may be of the most assistance.

7. The seventh card is the Sky Nation card, which denotes the relationship you have to Grandfather Sun, Grandmother Moon, the Thunder-beings, the Cloud People, all planets, galaxies, stars, and solar systems. These are the family of the Sky Nation, and each member carries a Medicine of its own. Each may speak to you in a different way and assist you on different trails of your Earth Walk. The Sky Nation card will denote which areas of your life this heavenly family may aid, the tools you need to connect to their energy, and/or the path you need to honor in order to "reach the stars."

8. The eighth card is the Subterrainiums card. It represents the race called Subterrainiums that live in the inner-Earth. Our Ancestors have carried one-hundred thousand years of oral history in their hearts, and we have been told through that history that we came from the inner-Earth at the beginning of each of the four preceding worlds. The Earth changes that ended each world were known by those that

listened to the voices of nature. The cavernous tunnels that lead to inner-Earth were opened to some Two-leggeds because of their faith and balance. Many of our people still live in the interior world as Guardians of the seeds and Creature-beings that will emerge in the Fifth World. This family is in constant contact with the creatures that burrow, the roots of the Standing People, and the Stone People that make up the body of the Earth Mother. This eighth card reflects how you may relate to the members of inner-Earth family and what they can teach you. It also reveals how to hear the voices of nature within the Earth. The inner sun of the Subterrainiums exists at the north pole and is the Great Mystery's gift of the Aurora Borealis. These northern lights are a Rainbow of Peace that the family of inner-Earth sends us as a reminder of our goal in any Earth Walk—peace.

9. The ninth card, the Ancestors card, symbolizes all of those who walked the Red Road before you. These Grandfathers and Grandmothers who now walk the Blue Road of Spirit in the Other Side Camp are always here to aid you. They carry powerful wisdom and ancient knowledge that can open many new trails of initiation and growth. The ninth card gives clues for approaching the Blue Road of Spirit and discovering the areas where the Ancestors may assist you, the gifts of knowledge they wish to impart, and/or whether your present path is the one that you originally chose or not. They may present alternative routes or merely show you the bypass that will allow you to correct a crooked trail.

10. The tenth card is the Kachina card, which speaks of your relationship to the Kachinas. The Kachinas came to our Hopi, Tewa, and Zuni Brothers and Sisters from the Great Star Nation. They are the teachers from other planets and solar systems who have brought much wisdom and knowl-

edge to our people. There are many types of Kachinas and all are teachers and helpers. They may assist you in seeking the vision of future, protection for your household, personal truth, universal understanding, and/or where you came from in the stars and where you will return after this Earth Walk. Whatever area the Kachina's wish to address in your life, you may be assured that this card will give you the tools to relate to the lessons of the Kachinas. The insight to understand, the courage to see beyond the physical illusion, or a broader outlook based in wisdom are among the gifts given to any seeker by the Kachinas.

The Initiation Spread

As each lesson and act of life has its own initiation, so each of these activities has a power animal or Totem that will best assist us in learning that particular lesson. This Totem is our guide, our protector, our teacher, and our friend. Often the lessons are hard and we may be blind to the things that are blocking our further progress. In calling on a Creature-being for assistance, we are opening our awareness to the growth potential afforded by each Totem. These Creature-beings have naturally learned the lessons we seek to understand. They can show us, through their actions and instinct, the pathways to successfully completing our chosen lessons.

The initiation spread helps us tune in to the lesson we are now learning in life. There may be millions of applications for each lesson learned and many levels of understanding as we learn and relearn the same lessons. It has been said that there are seven levels to understanding any teaching. As we view each lesson from the Seven Sacred Directions that surround our Sacred Space (card 44)—East, South, West, North, Above, Below, and Within—we can see every level of our total being.

If a mountain were viewed from each of these directions, each face of the mountain would be different, but it would be

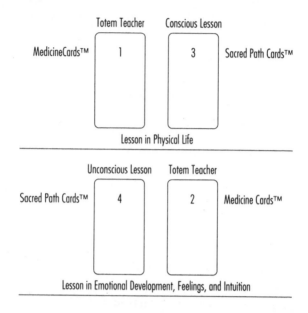

the same mountain. So it is with all initiations. Different people will experience very different lessons because the lessons will apply to their personal experience. The Totems teach the key to finding how the lesson applies to a present life situation.

You must use your gift of intuition to see your personal situation and application. The use of intuition is the initiation into each approaching lesson of awareness. It works best if you hold a specific question or situation in your mind while you are asking the Totem-teachers and the Sacred Teachings to come forward.

To use this spread, you will need the deck and book of *Medicine Cards*®: *The Discovery of Power through the Ways of Animals*. Using the Medicine Cards,® you can choose the Totem-teachers for these two lessons, which you are learning on the conscious and unconscious levels. Pick two Totem cards and place them face down in positions 1 and 2.

The lesson cards are in your Sacred Path™ deck. Choose two cards and place them face down in positions 3 and 4. Read the teaching portion of each card only. How to learn or apply these lessons will be taught through reading the Totem cards you chose for positions 1 and 2.

Turn over the first card in position 1 so that you can see your Totem-teacher. Read this Power Animal's characteristics all the way through. Both dignified and contrary positions will give you a clue to the strengths and weaknesses you may need to acknowledge in your present situation. Then turn over the lesson card in position 2.

Read the teaching only and see how this teaching can best aid you in understanding the present course you have charted in your physical life. Will it aid you in expanding your understanding of why you have chosen your present situation to learn from? Does it point out something you have forgotten to include in your life? If you are in doubt about moving forward, does this teaching show you where to look for courage or strength?

Your guide will be the Totem you pulled as your first card. Look and see what Medicine and strengths that Creature-being willingly offers you in achieving the understanding of the lesson card. Then picture that animal walking by your side as you experience life for the next few days.

Turn over the next two cards and repeat the process. On this level we find our dream teacher or the Totem who guards our hidden goals, dreams, and desires. The beauty of understanding our hidden feelings is that these feelings regulate how we will react to future events.

If we are trying to understand life from a feeling or intuitive point of view, we will see that in the lesson card. If we are bulldozing our feelings or ignoring the things that will give our hearts the greatest joy, we will see that in the Totem card's contrary meaning. Each person must answer the questions presented to find if it applies personally.

Look at the Totem. Is the essence of that teacher a personal talent that you are ignoring? Do you feel you can use that same gift to meet the unconscious lesson about to emerge and understand it? Have you been denying the careless part of your nature, the part that refuses to live in harmony? If so, the teaching of the lesson card will show this. This teaching reveals the improvement in attitude that may be needed for you to conquer your next challenge in life.

The top two cards of this spread offer the guidance needed to understand life situations you already know about and the bottom two cards give the guidance needed to understand the emotions that can inhibit *or* assist your personal growth. Each person will have to look deeply, recognize and own the aspects of Self they would like to keep or change. Remember that the heart is the Within direction, and truth must live inside the heart or living becomes a lie.

≡ The Cards ≡

≡ Pipe ≡

Pipe of my Forefathers
Teach me to sing praise
For all of the gifts that
Great Mystery gave.

Allow me to know
My spirit's release
And bring to my heart
Eternal peace.

1

Pipe

PRAYER/INNER-PEACE

The Teaching

From the moment that Great White Buffalo Calf Woman appeared to the Sioux nation, the Pipe has been a Sacred Medicine shared by the Brothers and Sisters of Native America as a way to pray, speak truth, and heal wounded or broken relationships.

We were given the Pipe to send our prayers and gratitude to Great Mystery and to signify peace among all Nations, Tribes, and Clans. The bowl of the Pipe represents the female aspect of all living things and the stem is the symbol of the male aspect in all life-forms. When the stem is placed in the bowl, this act signifies union, creation, and fertility.

When the Pipe is loaded, each pinch of Tobacco is blessed as each branch of Our Relations is asked to enter the Pipe in their spirit-forms to be honored and smoked. We honor Mother Earth, Father Sky, Grandfather Sun, Grandmother Moon, the Four Directions, the Standing People (trees), the Stone People, the Winged-ones, the Finned-ones, the Four-leggeds (animals), the Creepy-crawlers (insects), the Great Star Nation, the Sky Brothers and Sisters, the Subterrainiums, the Thunder-beings, the Four Chief Spirits (Air, Earth, Water, and Fire), and all other Two-leggeds in the human family.

In smoking the Pipe, it is of utmost importance to smoke every pinch of Tobacco that was loaded into the bowl. Each flake of Tobacco has taken spirit into its body and is honored as having the essence of All Our Relations in its form. If the fire, which is a part of the Eternal Flame of life, does not touch and ignite the Tobacco, the spirit that is inside cannot be released in smoke. If the smoke is not taken into the body, the spirits of Our Relations and our Ancestors cannot come into communion with us. To empty out a bowl that has not been fully smoked is to commit a grave error and dishonors those spirits who have come to smoke with us. The reckless use of the Sacred Pipe can stifle the willingness of spirits to assist us in our quest for wholeness.

The smoke from the Pipe represents visualized prayer and reminds us of the spirit in all things. We understand that all life comes from Great Mystery and will return to that original source. Due to this understanding we know that we are all walking the same path, stepping on each spoke of the Sacred Hoop or Wheel of Life.

We find union with All Our Relations when we share the Pipe. The essence of every living creature enters us when we smoke them and we carry their spirits inside our bodies. We are reminded that harmony is attained through sacred union with all our fellow beings. We never place the spirit of any life-form outside of ourselves since through the Pipe, we have asked them to enter our being and share our Sacred Space and life experience.

To be a Pipe Carrier is an honor and a calling. The Pipe Carrier can be called on to smoke at births, deaths, marriages, rites of passage, contractual agreements, councils, special purification ceremonies, moon meditations, or when anyone needs comfort, prayers, or wishes to give thanks.

It is through visions or dreams, usually from long preparation and purification, that one is called to serve our people as a Pipe Carrier. The path of the Pipe Carrier is not a fad or a trend, it is a way of life that comes from the heart. The Medicine Way is a long and narrow trail of discovery with constant rebirth. It should never be treated in a frivolous manner. Pipe Carriers are guardians of Sacred Tradition and ceremony. They serve the people, as a pastor or rabbi serves in a traditional church or synagogue.

The aspect of the teaching of Pipe that has to do with peace is multileveled. In the modern world, we often look at peace as the absence of war, but peace represents more in the Native way of thinking. Peace is a way of acting, knowing, creating, listening, speaking, and/or living. In all instances, peace comes from within our own beingness. This peace is the balance of recognizing and honoring male/female, teaching/learning, humility/pride and every other aspect of living in harmony. It is not something that can be weighed except by the Self. If there were to be a measure, it would be measured by the capacity of the heart to remain open, serene, and unafraid.

My grandfather took me to the fish pond on the farm when I was about seven, and told me to throw a stone into the water. He told me to watch the circles created by the stone. Then he asked me to think of myself as that Stone Person. "You may create lots of splashes in your life but the waves that come from those splashes will disturb the peace of all your fellow creatures," he said. "Remember that you are responsible for what you put in your circle and that your circle will also touch many other circles. You will need to live in a way that allows the good that comes from your circle to send the peace of that goodness to others. The splash that comes from anger or jealousy will send those ugly feelings to other circles. You are responsible for both."

That was the first time I realized each person creates the inner-peace or discord that flows out into the world. We cannot create world peace if we are riddled with inner-conflict, hatred, doubt, or anger. We radiate the feelings and thoughts that we hold inside, whether we speak them or not. Whatever is splashing around inside of us is spilling out into the world, creating beauty or discord with all other circles of life.

So sacred is a person's word and honor that it is to be upheld even if the cost, paid dearly, is that person's life. Anytime the Pipe is shared, the words spoken and agreements made are based upon the Indian idea of honor, truth, and mutual understanding stemming from each person's inner-peace.

The Application

The Pipe card speaks of inner-peace that can be found through the balancing of the Self. It is now time to honor both sides of your nature, male and female, and to acknowledge the Eternal Flame of Great Mystery that lives inside of you. How you influence the lives of others depends upon this balance.

Inner-peace can be found through prayer and the understanding of your role in the whole of Creation. World peace begins in the heart of each individual. It may be time to make peace with others or with any inner-conflict that keeps you from seeing the beauty of your true potential.

In all cases, the Pipe card asks you to honor the blessings given by Great Mystery. It asks you to honor who you are and why you are here. It asks you how you can assist our world. In making peace with the Self, these questions will be answered and the Sacred Path will become clear.

≡ Sweat Lodge ≡

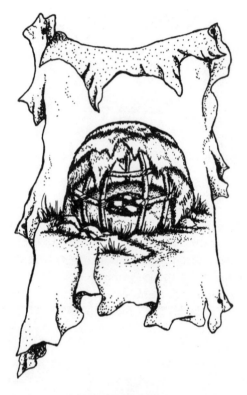

Fire of purification,
  Steam from sacred Stones,
Prayer ties and tobacco,
  Meld with spirit songs.

≡ 2 ≡

Sweat Lodge

PURIFICATION

The Teaching

The term Sweat Lodge has been used for a long time and doesn't truly express the purpose of this ceremony. The purpose is to purify the body, mind, and spirit so that a new sense of Self may be present on the path. Sweating is one of the things that you do in the lodge but is not the reason that you enter the ceremony of the lodge.

For centuries, the Native American people have understood the purpose of purification. The spirit can pick up some "rust" along the way when the experiences of physical life run amok. Since the beginning of the Fourth World, which was the World of Separation beginning approximately sixty thousand years ago, the polarization of all nations, creeds, and races has ravaged the Children of Earth. We have been taught to hate anyone that looks, acts, or believes differently. At the very least we have been taught to be suspicious of others and to demean other customs and attitudes due to the threat they represent to our belief systems (no matter which race or creed we are). The knowing systems of Native Americans are different. If we believe something, those beliefs may be changed, but to *know* is to have a gift that is a part of our total Self and is as much an extension of who and what we are as is our leg. Our beliefs, however, can be filled with misconceptions or others' opinions, which may create impurities. They may be filled with confusion and/or a sense that because someone else said it was so, it is. As the Family of Humankind, we have long forgotten that these are impurities that need cleansing. If we forget to pray for love and peace to enter the hearts of all races, nations, and creeds, we destroy the pure intent of those prayers and praise.

Before any Native American ritual or ceremony can be performed, all participants must purify the body, mind, and spirit. To enter ceremonial space carrying impurities is to lessen the potential of the ceremony's outcome. The purification may be done with Sage or Cedar smoke, a Sweat Lodge ceremony, "feathering," or a variety of other ways. Sabotage of ceremonial space occurs when participants in that ceremony neglect to purify themselves prior to taking part in the ritual. There cannot be an at-one-ment among the participants if someone is carrying resentment, hatred, jealousy, envy, or other negative emotions. In understanding this idea, our Native Ancestors made a ceremony to allow each person to let go of the "rust" that would keep them from shining and contributing their talents.

The Sweat Lodge is made from Willows and is circular. The number of Willows used depends on the purpose of the lodge. The Willow is the Tree of Love in our Seneca Tradition. It bends with grace and does not break easily. The lodge's door may be placed at the East, so illumination and spirit from the Blue Road may enter and join the ceremony, or the door may be placed in the West so healing and female receptive energy may enter. The door to the Purification Lodge is built low so we have to enter on our knees, a reminder for us to be humble and to understand that we are no greater or lesser than other life-forms.

The Stone People heated in the fire pit are volcanic so their bodies do not shatter or break when water is poured over them and steam is released. These Stone People are the carriers of Earth-Records and release ancient lessons through the steam. We need to reconnect with these ancient lessons in order to aid in the continuation of life on this planet. As our perspiration returns to the Mother Earth in the form of water, the Earth is again nourished. When the door to the lodge is opened in between endurances, or rounds, the steam travels to Father Sky to take our prayers home to Great Mystery.

Some purification ceremonies begin or end with a Pipe ceremony and others do not, depending upon the purpose of the Sweat. The Purification Lodge is covered with tarps (originally with animal hides) that block out all sources of light. This evokes a feeling of returning to the womb of our Earth Mother and provides a safe space to let go of all the things that have created "rust" in our lives. The songs and prayers are a way of filling the spirit as purification occurs. There are four rounds of songs and prayers that honor the Four Directions. These rounds allow the participants different viewpoints of the purpose for purifying themselves. Each round, or endurance, addresses different segments of Creation and allows the participants to reconnect with All Our Relations through prayer.

When I learned to make my first Tobacco ties, I learned the art of prayer. These ties are praise and gratitude we send to Great Mystery during the ceremony. Each tie is a tiny pinch of Tobacco bundled inside of a small square of colored cloth then looped with cotton string. An inch or two later a loop is placed around the next bundle. In this ceremonial way of making prayer ties, we never tie our prayers with knots, which would stop the results. The loops allow our prayers to flow freely.

Most Nations use six colors for the Tobacco ties, and each color has a special meaning. Each prayer tie invites the spirit of its color into the lodge and asks blessing from that Relation. Yellow is the Eagle, male energy, and the illumination of the East. Red is the energy of the child, the South, faith, trust, innocence, and one or more of the animals of the South Shield. In the Eastern Tribes, it is Porcupine; with the Plains Tribes, it is Mouse or Coyote. Black represents the West, female energy, the Bear, and the place of introspection and goals. The white Tobacco tie signifies the North, the Elder, gratitude and wisdom. For the Eastern tribes, it signifies the Moose and for the Western Tribes, the Buffalo. The blue tie carries the energy of Father Sky, the Great Star Nation, and all things above. The green prayer tie contains the energy of Mother Earth, the plant kingdom, and all things green and growing. The ritual involved in making the Tobacco ties and the number of each color used varies depending upon the Tradition and the purpose of the prayers being sent.

In humbling ourselves and crawling through the opening to the Purification Lodge, we are asked to check our egos at the door. Since sacrifice originally meant "to make sacred," approaching every act of life in a sacred manner is the Indian way. The circular form of the Purification Lodge reminds us not to assign blame to others if they falter or fall but rather to gently teach in loving-kindness so that the circle of the Sacred Hoop may remain whole. Willow is our reminder of the cleansing love necessary for that growth to occur.

The Application

The Sweat Lodge card speaks of a need for purifying some aspect of your life. This cleansing can be gentle and healing if you are willing to approach it in a sacred manner. It may be time to cleanse negative thoughts or attitudes. From another point of view, if you have people pulling you down and stopping your forward movement, cleaning away the barriers is called for here.

Whether the purification is of body, mind, emotions, attitudes, or spirit is for you to decide. The constant rule of the Sweat Lodge card is that humility and purification always make way for new life-force to enter. Remember that once the "rust" is removed, you may shine in your own right.

≡ Vision Quest ≡

High upon Sacred Mountain,
  With unrestricted view,
The clarity of vision,
  Comes to us anew.

Direction with purpose,
  Great Mystery will bring,
Strong Medicine Allies,
  To grace our Medicine Dreams.

≡ 3 ≡

Vision Quest

SEEKING/FINDING

The Teaching

The Vision Quest is one of the oldest tools used by Tribal People to seek direction for life. Under the guidance of a Medicine Person, the seeker is sent to a remote location to fast and pray for three to four days. The result of this activity, which is called Going On the Hill by the Sioux, is a fuller understanding of your place or pathway in the world.

Great Mystery gives the Sacred Medicine Helpers permission to come in vision-form to the person who is Vision Questing. The spirit of the animal, tree, stone, Moon, stars, or Ancestor who appears will be an Ally, or guide, during that seeker's Earth Walk and will protect that person's Sacred Path. Another aspect of the vision involves harnessing the energy presented to the seeker in the form of personal talents. If these gifts are used properly, they may allow a new type of growth potential throughout the seeker's life. The path that should be followed to develop these talents may also be revealed during the Vision Quest.

On my first Vision Quest, Joaquin, my beautiful Yaqui/Aztec/Mayan teacher in Mexico, took me to the mountains high in the state of San Luis Potosí. I walked for many hours until I found the place that "spoke" to me. When we had agreed that we would meet at a certain place in three days, he left me. I had time to reflect on my reasons for being On The Hill as I prepared to stake out my Questing Circle.

I decided to do the Vision Quest because at twenty-two, I felt as if all of the directions I had intended to take in life had ended in detours. I was singing in a Mexican rock band and studying with Joaquin. Living in Mexico had brought its hardships, particularly in my relationship with my father, and it was now time to release all of the emotional upset so that I could be "still." The inner-turmoil around my family issues had limited my ability to Stop the World, so I needed help understanding who I was and where I needed to go.

The place I chose was near a tiny trickle of water. A rock overhang provided a bit of shade, but there was little vegetation, as San Luis is meager high desert. Apart from a few desert grasses and herbs and an occasional cactus, the russet body of the mountain was my only companion. I built my circle of Stones that would represent the Medicine Wheel of my Sacred Space for the next three days. The last Stone to be put in place was the Eastern Door. The moment the Eastern Stone was in place I was not to leave my Sacred Circle. I had arranged the Stone People so they would encompass the trickling stream of water. I would not be allowed to drink the water but I could wash or cool my face. Grandfather Sun's heat was fierce in this high canyon, so the running Water was my Ally.

The first day was rough and I battled my body's urges and needs. The days were hot and the nights were very cold even though it was late spring. The second day was hell and I was mumbling prayers faster and faster, hoping that I would find the strength to make it just a little longer. I was still focusing on using my stubborn streak and my strength of will to get me through, but still no vision. I had seen spots in front of my eyes and was in fear of fainting but a vision did not come to me.

By the third day in the thick of the heat, I was sure I was going to die. My tongue was swollen and my face was burned, my body was aching from sleeping on rocks and my eyes were so dry they could not create tears even when I needed to cry. I had to handle a great deal of personal fear due to the "fear of dying alone syndrome," which had plagued me since I was a small child. Finally, I reached sunset on the third day. I was sure that something touched me deep inside as the colors of Grandfather Sun's rays lit the valley below and sparked the love in my heart. I felt a wave of trust envelope me and give me strength to meet the night with courage, but still no vision.

Around midnight I cried out to Great Mystery and finally let go. I let go of the pride, the stubbornness, the self-impor-tance, and the pain all in one breath and was sobbing like a little girl. I knew that I could not make it through this Vision Quest or life alone. Without the connection to Great Mystery, I was nothing and nothingness. I had watched the mountain Creature-beings for three days. They had ignored me totally. I then realized they were showing me I was no more or less important than the Spiders and Lizards. They were right.

I gave away the "I" and begged to be consumed by the eternal "We." I felt as if I was exploding and melding with the indigo night, as if all the Star People lived inside as well as outside of me. I looked up to the heavens, which were covered horizon to horizon with star-filled wonder, and let my tears flow unchecked. Suddenly, in the Sky Nation, I saw all of the Stars turn colors, many of them colors I had never seen before. Each Star was a different shade, tone, or hue. The Star People started to sing to me and I began to repeat the song, letting my spirit become the music.

Much later I learned that the words to my personal power song were Seneca and a part of my roots. It was through my power song, given to me by the Great Star Nation that I received my Medicine name, Midnight Song. Through a vision that followed, I was shown the truth of my personal pathway that would lead me to further growth on the Good Red Road.

When I came off the mountain, I felt reborn. I was totally exhausted, sunburned, dizzy, and very happy. When I reached Joaquin at the bottom of the canyon wall, he presented me with a paper cup full of the sweetest water I had ever tasted. After I drank half the cup, I poured the rest of the water on Mother Earth in gratitude, as an offering for the life she so richly had given me and the new one I was beginning. Joaquin tied an Eagle Plume into my hair as a reminder of the new freedom I had discovered through my union with all life-forms.

Vision Quests are one tool used by those seeking direction in life. Every time anyone Seeks the Silence of a balanced heart, the intuitive process can allow the truth to come forward. Truth is the final destination of any seeker's path. When the truth is found inside of the Self, there is no need to look further. Since we Two-leggeds are here to grow and experience the Good Red Road, we find that the path changes many times and can include many shifts in perception. The vision created from truth is the heart's desire to Walk in Beauty. A vision created from the need to control others or from greed is based in lies about the natural order of Creation. A vision of the Sacred Path is always clear.

Every aspect of life and every state of awareness is accessible to those who seek the serenity of the Silence. It is not necessary to go on Vision Quest once this natural balance has been achieved within the Self. The original purpose of Vision Quest was to assist the seeker in finding a way to contact this state of inner-knowing so truth would be present in that person's life every moment. Learning how to Stop the World at will is a talent that comes through working on the Self. The more a person is connected to the Earth Mother and Great Mystery, the easier this balance becomes.

It is not a good idea for anyone to try to do a Vision Quest without guidance from a trained Medicine Person. Each person lives a Vision Quest on a daily basis. The key is to be aware of it. To seek the signs and omens that allow humans to make proper decisions, then act upon those signs is a part of the Quest for life. On the physical journey, the Good Red

Road affords the seeker hundreds of lessons that lead to inner-knowing. The goal is to reach that place of inner-serenity so that the inner-world is equal to the outer world. When the two worlds are one, we become the living dream.

The Application

The Vision Quest card speaks of a time of new directions or strengthening of the present path based on personal truth. Sometimes to find this truth it is necessary to Enter the Silence and remove personal confusion. In other instances it is necessary to actually go on a Vision Quest.

This card tells you that the course of your life needs to be clarified through vision. It is now time to ask for assistance from the Allies and/or Ancestors so that your choices will be reinforced with their wisdom and assistance. Seeking your personal answers is the keynote. Trusting those feelings and following them with action is the way to find the truth. To accomplish this you must release confusion and doubt, then proceed by allowing your truth to emerge. Remember: in seeking you are asking for answers; be willing to accept and recognize the truth when it comes to you. Recognition and acceptance always precede inner-knowing.

≡ Peyote Ceremony ≡

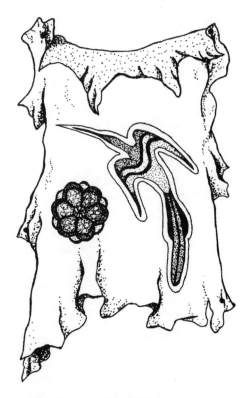

When the people's spirit was broken,
When the Buffalo no longer roamed,
When all our lands were taken and
We no longer had a home.

The Water Bird's reflection
Of the universes within
Showed us new abilities
And gave us hope again.

≡ 4 ≡

Peyote Ceremony

NEW ABILITIES

The Teaching

The Native American people had been robbed of their land and virtually stripped of their customs when the Trail of Tears ended in the late 1800s. Forced to move and live on reservations, separated from teaching their own children by mission schools and red tape, they struggled to save the last vestiges of personal freedoms.

Joaquin, my Medicine teacher, told me a story from the viewpoint of the Brothers and Sisters south of the border. The beginnings of the Native American Church were a Medicine gift that has brought our people a new perspective on life. Freedom came to the Red Race from a dark time that seemed to imprison the very spirit of the Red Nations north of the border.

It was a cool, crisp day in San Luis Potosí, Mexico. We bundled ourselves against the wind that cut down the mountains from the old silver mines. Joaquin was taking me on a Medicine Walk across the arroyos, down a dry river bed, and then up a canyon. As we walked up the path, I looked at all of the healing herbs and plants that Joaquin used in his *curandero* (healing) work. We always located the Chief Plant to

ask permission and offer Tobacco before we gathered anything. The red rocks gave way to patches of Chamisa and
other native grasses along the trail. The Wind was not as
biting behind the canyon wall and the enormous turquoise
sky made a happy canopy as we continued our climb.

Joaquin stopped for a minute and motioned for me to make
a wider berth around one of the cacti. "That is Mescalito, the
deity of the Peyote," he said. "He is the Chief cactus in this
area and we treat his Sacred Space with reverence," he continued. "Mescalito has served our people well and the other
nations to the north have also benefited." "Joaquin," I asked,
"when did the Peyote Ceremony come to our people in the
north?" He replied, "We will sit on the ledge over there," he
motioned, "since this story takes a while."

When we were seated among the saffron and rust-colored
Stone People, he continued. "Before my Grandfather was
grown, the Yaquis had visits from the Apache Warrior Clans
and Medicine Clans that wandered northern Mexico. Now
their reservation is near Ruidoso, New Mexico. These Brothers were fierce fighters who had watched their people harmed
by the White Eyes who had fenced the land and killed the
Buffalo. The spirit of the people had been broken. These braves
reported to our Elders that they had been stripped of everything but their souls. Their fear was that the White Eyes would
steal their spirits too if they found a way to get to them."

Joaquin seemed lost in thought as he reviewed the past in
his mind. Then he began again, "You see, Midnight Song, it
was a new kind of Medicine that was needed then. It was in
1882 that my great-grandfather's brother gave the Apaches
the Medicine of Mescalito." He smiled, then his bass voice
moved to a whisper. "No one can trap the souls of our people
now, they have no fear of death. Through Mescalito, they
have seen beyond the Void and have visited the Other Side
Camp. We know that we always continue to live in one form
or another. That is the new kind of power that we gave the
Apaches, who shared Peyote Medicine with other Tribes and

Nations of the north. These Apaches are honored and from that time, they were called Mescalero Apache."

I was very touched. I began to understand that death in body or death to the ego was still the first step to rebirth. I stopped my musing as Joaquin continued. "The Peyote Ceremony is a sacred ritual that propels the spirit into the crack in the universe where there is no time, no space, just the raw energy of Creation coming from Great Mystery. All that lives inside you is free to give you joy or to haunt you until you face it," he said. "Once people see truth and touch eternity, there is no way to strip them of their dignity or their knowing. Many people think that the power substances that are ingested are narcotics that make us crazy Indians, so we let them think what they want to think. The truth is that we gather our plants in a sacred manner, honoring the life-force of each plant and making our prayers of gratitude as we go. We always leave an offering of Tobacco for the Earth Mother in gratitude for the Medicine she has supplied. Each plant is strung on a dream string behind the bed of the person who will be taking the Medicine and is allowed to dry for a long time. Each Peyote bud is cut in the ritual of the Four Directions and whether it is powdered or made into tea, each part of every bud is used, never wasted."

Joaquin then instructed me in the ritual of the gathering and stringing and cutting. The songs and prayers were to honor the preparation. The ceremony itself is never revealed and is a part of the most private ritual of the Native American Church. Although Joaquin's songs are different from those of other Tribes to the north, the meanings are the same. All songs are sung to the glory of life and in gratitude for the "look beyond" the physical illusion.

The crack in the universe puts us in touch with pure creativity and allows us to see our abilities and talents, confront our fears, and to move into who and what we are becoming. The raw potential that is the true Self is the knowing that brings freedom to every person. The Peyote Bird, or Water Bird, is the Totem of the Peyote Ceremony. This sacred Medicine Bird sees the pond and observes its own reflection in it. The gift of self-examination allows the seeker to see those aspects of Self that lay below the surface of the physical reality and to discover universes of consciousness. The fears that do not surface due to denial can be accessed and handled through prayer and singing. The reconnection to Great Mystery in sacred ceremony is the mainstay of the Peyote Ritual.

In understanding that this ceremony has become one facet of the Native American Church's religion, one must look at how the Red Race has kept faith with the Earth Mother throughout centuries. The Native People have used the herbal Medicines that the Earth Mother has provided for all kinds of healing. Whether the healings are of body, mind, or spirit makes little difference. If any substance is used properly, it can become a healing agent. If it is abused, it will be toxic and can kill.

The ritual of the Peyote Ceremony is not a regular occurrence. The Medicine Men who run the ceremony have to travel great distances to attend to the church members, and therefore the ceremony only occurs when they come to that area. The Road Men of the Native American Church, the equivalent of ministers in organized religion, carry out the duties of leading ceremony, prayer, teaching, counseling, and comforting the People in times of need.

Although the Peyote Ceremony is not Traditional among the Sioux, the Seneca, and many other Tribes, it is used by those who have joined the Native American Church. Many Medicine People do not use this ceremony because they have not lost the ability to reach this place of understanding. Many can travel to the crack in the universe alone without the aid of Mescalito or the spirit of the Water Bird. Those who do not need the assistance of Peyote still honor the right of others to practice their own rites and ceremonies because it is the proper tool for some Native People.

There are thousands of Traditions among Native Americans, and even though the United States Government only acknowledges about 276 tribes, there are in truth over 387 Tribes and Traditions on Turtle Island. These Traditions are finally beginning to trade information and teach others outside their Tribes the Medicines, rituals, customs, and understandings of their Ancestors. In this time of the White Buffalo, it is time to share what we have learned from our Sacred Points of View without trying to alter the opinions of others. This understanding is becoming a new ability in itself. Honoring all abilities in the Self and in others marks the pathway of peace.

The Application

If the Water Bird has flown your way and brought you the Peyote Ceremony card, you are being asked to recognize your immortal spirit. Look to the crack in the universe for new ways to develop the abilities that can enhance your growth. Remove any denial that keeps you from developing new skills and use the talents you have to the fullest.

The Peyote Ceremony card puts you on notice that opportunities to discover the Self and for expansive growth are now possible. You are never as limited as you believe you are. The resources of the true Self are filled with potential. Conquering limitation created in the mind will allow you to discover these new abilities and know that all goals are possible. Remember that the decision to attack your fears is the beginning of the Sacred Path.

≡ Standing People ≡

Aho Sacred Tree of Life,
  The root of every tree,
Thank you for giving
  The gifts you give to me.
Aho Standing People,
  From you I will learn,
To keep my roots well planted,
Yet reach for Grandfather Sun.
Aho Willow, tree of love,
  Teach me to bend,
Til I come full circle,
Each relation as my friend.

≡ 5 ≡

Standing People

ROOTS/GIVING

The Teaching

The Standing People, the trees, are our Sisters and Brothers. They are the Chiefs of the plant kingdom. The Standing People provide oxygen for the rest of the Children of Earth. Through their trunks and branches, trees give shelter to the Winged-ones. In their roots, trees provide burrows for smaller Four-legged creatures. Materials for building homes for their human relations are another gift of the Tree Nation.

The Cherokee teach that the Stone People hold energy for the Earth Mother and hold specific records of all that has happened in a place. They teach that the Standing People and all others of the plant kingdom are the givers who constantly provide for the needs of others. The Stone People and the Standing People balance each other as holders and givers.

The Standing People see the needs of all of Earth's Children and apply themselves to being providers. Each tree and plant has its own gifts, talents, and abilities to share. For instance, some trees bear fruit and some provide healing on the emotional or physical level. The White Pine is the Tree of Peace and can bring serenity into the life of a person sitting in its shade. The rain forests are full of trees that carry curative properties and substances such as rubber that can be used to assist humankind in making useful items. The world is full of gifts that the Standing People have provided. Furniture, chewing gum, rayon fabric, books, paper, pencils, kitchen matches, spices and seasonings, fruit, nuts, rope, tires, herbal remedies, and grass-roof homes are just a few of the gifts from the Standing People.

Each Standing Person has a special lesson to give humankind as well as physical gifts. Birch gives the essence of truth and the lessons of being straight with ourselves or being deceived by forked-tongue lies. Pines are peacemakers and peace bringers. Pine teaches the lessons of being in harmony with ourselves and others as well as the lessons of a quiet mind. Rowen, or Mountain Ash, brings protection from harm and teaches the lessons of seeing through deception as well as the lessons of how to protect our Sacred Space. Sycamore teaches the lessons of how to reach our goals and make our dreams come true. Walnut teaches us clarity or focus using our mental gifts and how to use our intelligence properly. Oak teaches us strength of character and how to keep our bodies strong and healthy. Willow is the wood of love and teaches us the give-and-take or bending that is necessary for love to be fruitful. Cherry teaches us the lessons of clearing the pain of the heart or relating to others in a compassionate manner.

Mimosa is the tree that teaches us the lessons of our female side and the loving heart. I learned many lessons from the Mimosa when I climbed her branches as a child. She taught me the beauty of feeling feminine and her sweet flowers made perfume for my hair. She told me the secret of the Fireflies and how they had unborn stars in their tails. Mimosa told me these stars would grow inside each person with an open heart. Then they would take their place among the Great Star Nation when they had loved and been loved on the Earth. Mimosa told me that the pain and betrayals each heart would endure were like water tossed on the fire of these tiny stars to see if they could continue to grow in spite of the hurt. Those that continued to love would one day become big stars and would send the love they had gathered to everyone in the universe as a reminder of the open heart of Great Mystery. Mimosa reminded me to open my heart and to love, no matter how deep my pain, every time I saw my star light up in a "lightning bug" that flew by to be my reminder.

Native people from all parts of our world have lived in harmony with the plant kingdom of their areas and have used the plant kingdom's gifts to assist them in survival. The indigenous people of Mother Earth have only used what they needed and have not hoarded, out of fear of scarcity, the offerings the trees have given. In our Native American Tradition, we gather all plants in a ceremonial and sacred manner. In my Tradition, we approach the largest plant of the species we are going to gather from, then we offer Tobacco and ask permission. This is the Chief Plant or Tree of that species since it is the oldest and largest. When we receive a feeling or message that it is all right, we pass the first seven plants or trees we could gather from so that the next seven generations of humans will be provided for. In honoring our children and our children's children we ensure a future for all creatures as well as the plant kingdom.

If we receive a "no" when we ask permission from the Chief Plant, we move to another area to gather and ask permission once again. If we are gathering pine nuts, for example, we only take a little from each tree so that our Brothers and Sisters of the creature kingdom will also be provided for. How do we know when we have gathered enough from one plant? It is easily recognized by those in tune with our green Sisters and Brothers. The plant will not let go of its fruit, herbs, or nuts when we have taken enough. The plant will strengthen its limbs and refuse to let go. This is the way in which the giving nature of the plant says, "You have taken enough, move on."

The Senecas say that each tree has more roots than branches. This is a teaching on how each Standing Person is connected to the Earth Mother. As with the Standing People, we Two-leggeds have a spine like a trunk, arms like branches, hair like leaves. We reach for light as the tree's branches reach for Grandfather Sun. We receive understanding through our antenna, which is our hair, just as the trees receive light through their leaves. Each human has a different body as do the Standing People; no two are alike. We walk on two legs and see many things whereas our tree relations stand in one place and receive nurturing from the Earth Mother constantly so that they may give to others all they have. As Two-leggeds, we also give and receive if we are Walking in Balance. Walking in Balance can be achieved through remembering our roots, the only physical tree-part we are lacking as humans.

The Standing People teach us how to run our roots deep into the Earth to receive spiritual nurturing as well as the reconnective energy that keeps our bodies healthy. Without these roots we lose Earth-Connection and can no longer Walk in Balance. In my Tradition, we are taught that humankind is the bridge between Earth and the Sky Nation and like the Standing People, we are of both worlds. To accomplish this balance, we must live in harmony with All Our Relations, be rooted in this world through our Mother Earth, and allow our spirits to fly through the other worlds and be at one with those realities as well. Without being rooted in this world we cannot fully understand the purpose of our visions, dreams, potentials, or the Dreamtime reality.

As we return gratitude for the gifts we have received from others, we acknowledge the root of each blessing. The root of anything is its source. If we return our gratitude to the Source of our blessings, we will balance our world through acknowledging the gifts we receive. We are also reminded that the Ancestors who rode the Wind before us are a part of our roots and that we are here to respect the value of their gifts and their lives by living in a balanced manner. The taproot of all civilizations to come lives in each of us in the present. To nurture the future is to honor the seeds of the present by allowing them to grow. The Standing People are asking us, as Guardians of our Earth Mother, to look for the root of every blessing, acknowledge the truth in it, and use that blessing for the highest good so that the giving is not in vain.

The Application

The Standing People card speaks to us of roots and giving. We must nurture ourselves through connection to the Earth in order to give freely without exhaustion. The root of the Self is where strength is gathered. This root should be firmly earthed in the soil of our Mother Planet. Without this connection, dreams cannot manifest and our giving cannot be compensated by the Earth Mother. If you are spaced out, stop and reconnect.

Be still and become the trees in order to observe what is growing in your forest. The root of every answer for physical life is found in the Earth. Look to your family tree for the strength offered by your Ancestors. Lift your branches high, seeking the light of Grandfather Sun and you will see how your roots make you of the Earth and yet a bridge to the Sky World.

The Standing People are asking you to give of yourself. Ask yourself if you are willing to give and receive. Count the root of every blessing with gratitude. Find any blockage that limits your root system or ability to go deeper. Then remove that feeling and go deeper once again for the answers you seek. Remember that we are also the root of the future and through our lives, future generations are nurtured. Weed out anything that will inhibit future growth and you can stand proud among your Tree Relations.

≡ Sun Dance ≡

Within the sacred arbor,
   The warriors dance the sun,
      Tied to the Tree of Life,
         Until the dancing's done.

They feel the pain of woman,
   So the people may live,
      Seeking Medicine Visions,
         As of their pain they give.

≡ 6 ≡

Sun Dance

SELF-SACRIFICE

The Teaching

The Traditional Sun Dance is the Sacred Ceremony or ritual that allows Warriors the right to give of their pain, of their blood, of their prayers, and of themselves, sacrificing for the good of all the People. The Sun Dance is usually held once a year by each Tribe. It is a four-day ceremony that honors the Four Directions and the sacred Tree of Life, and gives the Warriors an opportunity to prove their worthiness to be protectors of the People.

The Sun Dance is called by its name because Grandfather Sun is known and honored as the source of love and warmth on the Earth Mother. The male aspect of Grandfather Sun demonstrates how Warriors can be the protective and loving force that allows all members of the Tribe to grow and flourish under their protection. As Grandfather Sun gives light to all green and growing things on the Earth Mother and protects us from darkness of thought, heart, or total night, so must the Warriors of the People protect their Nations from enemies, loss of courage, and the dark night of the soul when fears take over.

The area for the Sun Dance is prepared in a sacred manner. A circular arena that has been prepared by the women is set up and an arbor of brush is built around the center where the

Sun Dance Tree will be placed. This Standing Person (tree) will be carried, never touching the ground, from the site where it was cut to the center of the circle where it is planted into the earth. The Sun Dance Tree represents the Tree of Life. The actual Warrior's ceremony with their sponsors is secret. However, I will say that it is very beautiful and gives respect to the Standing Person, the dancers, Mother Earth, Native Tribal Tradition, and Grandfather Sun.

When the tree is in place, a Sun Dance Bundle (see card 28) is placed high on the Sun Dance Pole, which is the new Medicine identity of the Standing Person (tree). In the Sioux, Kiowa, and Crow Traditions, the honor of climbing the tree and placing the bundle was given to a Ma-ho, a person considered to have two souls in one body. The "Two-souls" person was a man with female traits or a female with male characteristics. In Native America, this was considered the third sex and was a rare and beautiful gift. The Ma-ho could represent the men and women equally. Since only one person could climb the Sun Dance Pole, it was good luck to have that person be of both sexes.

The Sun Dance Bundle is a leather pouch that carries the Sacred Medicine of Totems. Through these bits of fur, teeth, feathers, bones, and claws, the essence and Medicine of those Creature-beings is felt. The Sun Dance Bundle also carries special items created for that particular year to bring about a specific desired outcome. The ancient items enclosed can be a Pipe, a Sun Dance doll, or an Eagle-wing Whistle. These items ensure the protection of the various Totems and benevolent spirits. Each Sun Dancer looks for a Medicine Vision in order to know his place in the further growth of the Tribe as well as in the Tribe's destiny.

Traditionally, each Sun Dancer must be sponsored by a Warrior who has Danced the Sun before him. The sponsor vouches for the dancer's worthiness and strength of character. The members of the Warrior Clan who choose to sacrifice for the good of the people must prepare for three days prior to

the dance with fasting and praying and instruction from the
male Elders. On the third day, the dancers are pierced through
the connective tissue at the pectoral muscles, first with an
awl, then with a sharpened Cherry wood stick. Then thongs
are attached to the small stakes that have been run through
their breasts to the Sun Dance Tree or the Tree of Life creating
a special umbrella or carousel-like effect.

Many early agents for the United States government saw
the Sun Dance as self-torture because they did not know the
purpose of the ceremony. Consequently, it was banned in
1941 by the Department of the Interior. Only in recent years
have the Sun Dances begun again to give the spirit back to
our people. The purpose of the Sun Dance is to allow young
Warriors to share the blood of their bodies with the Earth
Mother. It is understood that women do this through their
Moontime, or menstrual cycle (see cards 17 and 21). Women
give of their pain through childbirth and the men through the
Sun Dance, so the people may live. Women nurture the seeds
of the future generations and the men commit their lives to
the protection of that future through the ceremony of the
Dancing the Sun.

During the last two days when the piercing ceremony and
final dance take place, many women make small cuts on their
forearms or pierce their biceps or wrists. They allow their
blood to drip and touch the body of our Mother Earth to
show respect for the dancers and to once again recommit their
lives to the guardianship and the preservation of all living
things. This is an act of self-sacrifice for the women as is the
Warrior dancers' piercing of the flesh in the chest. Traditionally, women do not Sun Dance since they have already proven
their faith and constancy through the acts of childbirth and
nurturing established by their gender.

These Mothers of the Creative Force have acknowledged
the fact that any liquid from our bodies is a female element
as is the Water Clan Chief. Our tears, our urine, our blood,
and our saliva are water elements that when given back to the

Earth Mother may be recycled as moisture for the fertilization of future growth. The Sun Dance acknowledges the female aspect, and the dancers honor both sides of their nature through this Sacred Rite. Just as the water element travels to Father Sky to take the form of Cloud People, a Warrior's heart travels to Grandfather Sun to be illuminated during the Sun Dance as his blood nourishes the body of the Mother Earth.

The stamina and courage that it takes to dance without food or water for four days is a true test of the fabric and character of the dancer. The months of preparation before Dancing the Sun include fasting, Vision Questing, Purification Ceremonies, Dog Soldier training (see card 12), and much personal prayer. To fall down at the Sun Dance brings dishonor to the sponsor of the brave who fell and can portend a time of misfortune for the Tribe or Nation. The first to bear the dishonor is the sponsor who did not properly prepare the brave by rigorous methods prior to the event.

In past times, if a Warrior received a vision during the Sun Dance it was considered Good Medicine. The vision could be of a coming battle, a Coup, a wife, new horses, or other things. In many Plains Tribes, the men were not eligible for marriage until they had Sun Danced. In this way, the Warrior would have greater respect for the woman who would bear his children. He could also then come to the marriage lodge with honors and proof of his courage. If he had received a vision during the Sun Dance of some Ally or Medicine Helper, he was assured that his life would be long and fruitful. If no vision was received, the dancer might feel as if he had not completed the Sacred Ritual in some way. For some, the unwillingness to surrender to the messages of the Allies was mixed with their unwillingness to fall or bring disgrace to their Clan. So they danced year after year to help the People and to once again pray for vision.

In the vision, a Warrior might see which symbols to place on his shield while Dancing the Sun. In some Traditions, the dancers carry smaller versions of their personal or Clan Medicine Shields made especially for the Sun Dance. Every dancer is equipped with a Sage wreath for his head and an Eagle-bone Whistle that is blown at intervals to meet the drumbeat and build and retain the energy of the ceremony.

The Cherry wood spikes must be ripped from the skin as each Warrior pulls against the Tree of Life to which he is connected. In so doing, each man is giving of his pain so that the people may continue to flourish. My Blood-Brother, Eagleman of the Ogalala Sioux, has Danced the Sun six times and has told me that it takes many months for the connective tissue to heal. I have seen many other Brothers that carry the scars of the Sun Dance and all bear them with pride. These brave men have known a small fraction of the pain that women have in childbirth and they have come to respect the role that women carry in Great Mystery's plan.

The Sun Dance is in operation again and the spirit of our people has been restored. When the sacred rights of spirituality of any people are taken from them, the spirit of life can wane. The Sun Dance is not for everyone to experience but the lessons learned are a beautiful way to understand the balance between male and female, courage and pain, vision and stubbornness, and loyalty and love. To sacrifice of oneself is to bring a knowing that the sacrificer is loyal to the People. This ancient ritual is considered a strong act of love. It teaches us how to Walk in Balance and let go of the parts of ourselves that are only interested in the personal "I."

The Application

The Sun Dance card asks us to look at what needs to be sacrificed so that the sacredness of our lives may be restored. It could be that doubt or fear are trailing our dreams and need to be sacrificed so that our dreams may live. On the other hand, if some bad habit has limited our capability, that habit needs to be conquered. Recklessness and overindulgence can thwart the abundant life we seek if we do not rid those parts of the self that represent our shadow.

Your shadow is always ready to be sacrificed. If you have learned from dancing with the darkness of ignorance, you will learn what is no longer sacred in your life. Then the sacrifice becomes your truth. If you use less paper in order to save the rain forests, you make them sacred. In all instances, you are being asked to give up something in order to stand in the truth of your convictions. Giving up aerosols, apathy, bitterness, greedy friends, or too much sugar can change the worth of your life.

Remember, self-sacrifice is not denying your needs, but rather the Self's decision to willingly sacrifice limitation through action.

≡ Medicine Wheel ≡

Stones that border Sacred Space,
  The hoop of life made whole,
Eagle, Coyote, Bear come sing,
  With great White Buffalo.

Here we greet the winds of change,
  We praise Grandfather Sun,
Here we honor the wholeness of all,
  Coming together as one.

≡ 7 ≡

Medicine Wheel

CYCLES/MOVEMENT

The Teaching

The Medicine Wheel is sometimes called the Sacred Hoop. This symbol of all of life's cycles has given the People of Native America an evolutionary blueprint for centuries. Each cycle of life is honored in a sacred way, giving us a way to see the value of each step of our pathway and a new understanding of our growth patterns.

Just as all people and their gifts are honored as living treasures of the Tribe, so are the life-lessons they learn. When Tribal Members share the wisdom gained from actual experience, the whole Nation benefits from the stories that are passed among different bands or Clans. The understanding of each person's unique experience is a way for the other members to see varied themes on the same lesson.

The Medicine Wheel is the circle of lessons that each person must pass through to complete their journey on the Good Red Road of physical life. Physical life begins at birth, which is the South direction on the Sacred Hoop. Each of us will travel through the circle on that South-to-North path until we reach the place of the Elder, which is in the North.

Our Spirit is made of Wind, which is one of the Four Clan Chiefs of this world. Our Spirit can travel around the rim of the Medicine Wheel and send us urges to learn certain lessons.

The East is the home of the Golden Door, the entry point to all other levels of awareness and consciousness. Spirits of the Ancestors who have finished their Earth Walks, leave at the North of the Wheel and follow the rim of the Hoop to the East. This allows them to pass through the Golden Door and enter the Blue Road of Spirit, which crosses the Wheel East to West (see diagram). We also return to new physical lives via the Blue Road. Once again we come through the Golden Door in the East as spirits and travel the rim of the Medicine Wheel to the South where our spirits are born again into physical bodies.

The powers (talents and lessons) of the Four Directions can be immediate answers when sent by the Wind Spirits. Traditional Native American teachers always teach the children of

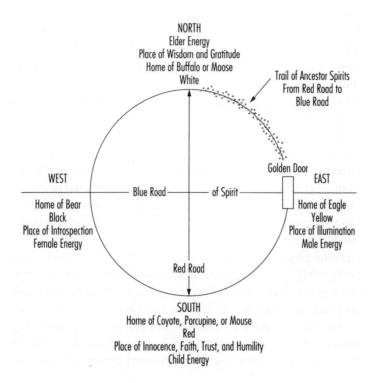

NORTH
Elder Energy
Place of Wisdom and Gratitude
Home of Buffalo or Moose
White

Trail of Ancestor Spirits
From Red Road to
Blue Road

Golden Door

WEST

Home of Bear
Black
Place of Introspection
Female Energy

Blue Road ———— of Spirit

EAST

Home of Eagle
Yellow
Place of Illumination
Male Energy

Red Road

SOUTH
Home of Coyote, Porcupine, or Mouse
Red
Place of Innocence, Faith, Trust, and Humility
Child Energy

their Tribe to feel the Wind so that they will know what to do if they are lost or afraid. If Wind blows from the West, they would sit and look inside their hearts for courage or an answer. If Wind came from the South, they would stop pretending to know all the answers and find humility, perhaps listening to another child who knew the way home. If Wind caught them in a whirlpool of motion, they would wait until help arrived. If Wind came from the North, the children would know that the Elders, in their wisdom, knew where to look for them. When Wind came from the East, they were to use their good sense or logical ideas that would bring an answer to their predicament.

The Medicine Wheel is the blueprint for all situations and can be used in a multitude of ways. To build a physical Medicine Wheel for Sacred Ceremonial use, twelve Stone People are needed. The first is placed in the South, the beginning of life. The second and third Stones are placed in the West and the North. No Stone is placed in the East; the door is left open. Following the circle, the fourth Stone is placed at the four o'clock position and the fifth at five o'clock. South is the six o'clock position and is filled with the sixth Stone. Stones fill each empty position until you reach the East once more.

Before the East Stone Person is placed to close the circle, the Medicine Wheel is blessed and the Spirits of the Four Directions are asked to enter the circle through the Eastern door. Then the Spirits of the other three sacred directions— Above, Below, and Within—are asked to balance the Sacred Hoop. When the energies of these directions have entered, the Medicine Wheel is dedicated to the honoring of Sacred Ceremonial Space. The Stone People are thanked for their Guardianship and for holding the energy of the circle. At this time, the East Stone is put in place closing the Golden Door. Celebration and feasting follows the Dedication Ceremony.

The Stone Circle of the Medicine Wheel is a symbol of Sacred Ceremonial Space that has been honored by our people for centuries as a place to come and experience the beauty of the cycles of physical life. These cycles of planting, gestation, birth, growth, change, death, and rebirth are the life lessons of the Sacred Hoop.

In seeking the answers of the Void where future lives, life becomes extraordinary, exciting, and filled with beauty. The mundane awareness of daily living melts away when we pause to sense the adventure offered by the constant messages brought by the Four Winds of Change. Everywhere we look, life is calling. Each moment is packed full of the life-forms that seek to align with us as Two-leggeds. We are the only creatures who have lost our sense of belonging to the total Creation of Great Mystery. In understanding the lessons of the Sacred Hoop, we learn to touch life in a deeper and more gentle way. The understanding comes from a way of living, being, and thinking.

To live the path of the Medicine Wheel, we are asked to see the gifts of growth that each direction offers. If only by noticing the obvious around us and asking our inner feelings and knowing what those feelings mean, we begin the seeking. Associations with the Four Directions are made through using the connections of the Totem Animals in those directions. In connecting with the lessons of Eagle, Coyote, Bear, and Buffalo, or their counterparts in those directions, we may see the lessons they offer. In asking what answers they may bring us and by giving permission for them to come to us in dreams, we may come to the place of inner-knowing. (The beginner may start by using the four Shield cards in the deck as a guidance system for working with the Four Directions.)

In many writings on Native American Tradition, the mention of the Sacred Hoop becoming whole again has left a question in the reader's mind. How was the Hoop broken? The Hoop was never broken. The faithful of all Nations have kept the Eternal Flame alive in their hearts since the beginning of time. The Sacred Hoop is growing stronger because those who were Red People in other lives are now remembering their roots and are coming together from different pathways to preserve the Earth Mother and reconnect with the spirits of nature. When we as Children of Earth lose our sense of where we fit into the Medicine Wheel of life, we lose sight of the unified circle and how to live in a sacred manner.

Our Native Nations are gathering the Teachings and preparing the way for the Fifth World of Peace by returning to ceremony, ritual, and using the wisdom of the Ancestors to heal any old wounds and bitterness. The Spirit of the People is returning and the Whirling Rainbow of Peace is mending our hearts.

The Application

The Medicine Wheel card portends a time of cycles and/or movement. You are asked to notice which stage of the cycle you are presently experiencing. Is it the beginning, the creation, the growing time, and developing or end of a cycle? How you look at where you are will assist you in clarifying what it is that you need to do next. Any retreat, hesitation, or stopping has now ended.

With this card you are being put on notice that the stagnation is over and new beginnings have taken root in the present. Don't get caught in old patterns. Notice which direction on the Medicine Wheel will assist your forward movement and apply that lesson to your life. Your choices are illumination and clarity (East), faithfulness and humility (South), introspection and goals (West), or wisdom and gratitude (North). It is now time to decide for yourself which type of movement will keep the Wheel turning. In all cases, the Medicine Wheel card assures you that life continues. The quality of the new cycle depends upon you, your actions, and attitudes toward growth.

≡ East Shield ≡

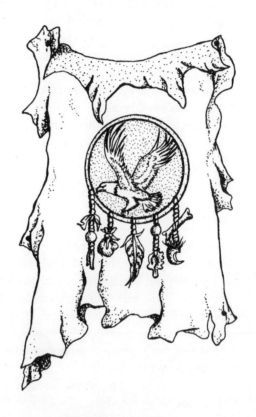

Shield of the East
Illuminate my path
So I may fly with Eagle
To the home of Grandfather Sun's first light.

≡ 8 ≡

East Shield

ILLUMINATION/CLARITY

The Teaching

The ancient Medicine Man, Yellow Three Fingers, parlayed his way into my morning silence and sat before me, carefully removing his red bandana headband. He looked deeply into my eyes. A faint smile, barely perceivable, moved across his weather-worn face. He touched my mind. His words fell like Prayer-lances in the fertile earth of my memory.

"I have come to teach you your East Shield," he said.

I watched as he dipped the first three fingers of his left hand into a bowl of sacred Corn pollen and gently drew them across his forehead creating three yellow lines. West to East they traveled across the rocky crags of his time-worn, wood-grainy brow. I observed in silence, knowing that each movement was a dance step of the Eastern Shield.

"The Eastern Shield is the place of illumination where Eagle lives. In this place you will find the Golden Door that leads to all other levels of awareness and understanding. The East is where Grandfather Sun greets us each morning. There are three pathways to the wisdom of the Eastern Shield," he said. "Here at Tsankawi where my forefathers grew tall, you will find the symbols of those three paths. Follow me on a Medicine Walk and we will share the goodness of this day of falling leaves."

As we walked, I came upon an ancient Anasazi pottery shard and Yellow Three Fingers told me to offer Tobacco and take it with me. We continued around a small mesa and he called to me to mind my step. I stopped and looked down. There in front of my feet was a Bull Snake nesting on her eggs. I offered her Tobacco and gave her a wide berth as we continued. I continued below the backside of the mesa and came across a copper penny waiting for me, proudly sitting on a mound of red earth. I picked it up and offered Tobacco. Yellow Three Fingers nodded and motioned to a large boulder down the hill.

We sat quietly before he began to speak. "The three paths are found in these symbols," he began. "The pot shard is the symbol of the artist's creativity. The first path is to use any talent or creativity you have and you will know illumination."

He continued. "The second pathway is guarded by our Sister, Snake. She sheds her skin and we see this shedding as a way of letting go of old habits. The Snake Medicine People transmute poisons to change and heal. The second path to illumination is healing and transmuting poison."

He paused then spoke once again. "The third pathway to illumination is like the symbol of white man's money. It comes in knowing how to properly use and exchange energy. Energy exchange can be barter, trade, or pay. It can be give-away, IOU, or simple greed. Exchange is performed by givers and takers who know that money and energy are the same. People fear not having money and energy (health). They fear being taken and they fear wrestling with their own greed. Illumination's third path is rugged, but the proper use of energy exchange will bring understanding of all material and non-physical forms of energy. The greatest lesson of the third path is that true energy exchange is sharing."

So I was taught and I share with you.

To further examine the lessons of Yellow Three Fingers, I would like to address the yellow paint of the three lines across his forehead. When Native People had dreams about this Medicine, their Allies showed them how to paint their faces to represent their personal Medicine. Anytime a yellow line was used above the eyes, it denotes a Seer, someone who was able to see beyond the physical illusion. The color yellow is the color of the East on the Medicine Wheel and the home of visionaries on most Medicine Wheels. (Black Elk, due to his vision, used red in the East and yellow in the South.) Most Traditions, however, use yellow, which is the color of Grandfather Sun when we greet him in the morning.

In our Seneca Tradition, the East is also the home of the Golden Door. This door leads to all other levels of imagination and awareness. To pass through the Golden Door is to see beyond the mundane and to touch Father Sky. Riding on Eagle's back to the freedom of true knowing often occurs when one Journeys through the Golden Door. On the other side of the Golden Door there is no limitation, no hesitation, and no fear. Fear cannot exist in the presence of the golden love of Grandfather Sun. Truth abides with us when we challenge our limitations and move through any set of negative thoughts into the expansiveness of lofty ideals, allowing ourselves to see the Golden Light of Understanding.

The East also holds the energy of the male side of our nature, which has the ability to go forth into uncharted areas of life and seek new ideas. The beauty of our demonstrative nature is that we have the courage to tackle our limitations, which may hang back and wait for others to test the waters. Independence is the keynote to our East Shield. It allows us to seek the ideas that bring further enlightenment. It is in the East that we challenge and conquer our greatest lessons in forward movement.

Since the East Shield is the Traditional home of the Eagle on the Medicine Wheel, all three paths to the illumination of the East Shield are graced by Eagle's Medicine and protection. Eagle is the symbol of freedom from all forms of ignorance and bigotry. Eagle guards the place of lofty ideas. Eagle is closest to Grandfather Sun and bathes in the love of that golden light. To understand the East Shield is to invite Eagle into your heart. The heart that is free to soar to the heights above Sacred Mountain and view all of creation is one that knows the lessons of the East Shield

The Application

The East Shield card represents a need for clarity in some part of your life. It may also mark a time of illumination when suddenly things begin to fit together and make sense to you. If you have been confused, now is the time to ask for order in your life. Order can be restored through making lists of things to do, cleaning up your living space, or finishing old projects. When order is restored, you are then more receptive and can find the clarity you need.

The illumination of the East can also be asking you to assist another in finding clarity. Sharing your ideas may bring illumination as others give you feedback. It may also be a time to heal old wounds or negative thoughts so that there is room for clarity to enter your life. Be creative and daring in order to stretch your concept of who you really are and venture into new realms of understanding.

In all cases, the East Shield marks a time of new freedoms that come from wiping the mud from your eyes and seeing with the eye of Eagle. Observe which thoughts keep you in blinders and clear that blindness through summoning your courage and taking flight.

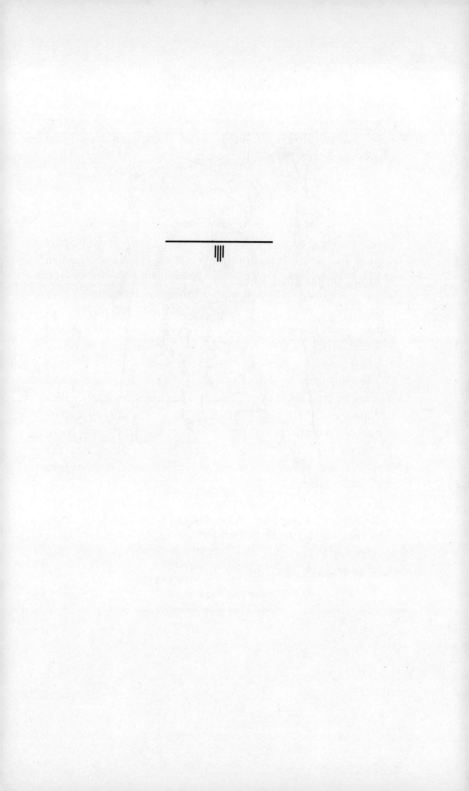

≡ South Shield ≡

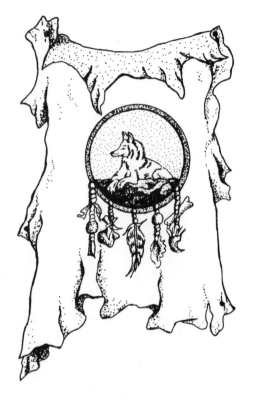

Red Earth, South Shield,
Child filled with wonder,
Teach me to yield.
Laughter is your Give-Away,
In innocence and joy,
Tricking me into the place,
Of little girls and boys.

≡ 9 ≡

South Shield

INNOCENCE/INNER CHILD

The Teaching

The South Shield is the Shield of the child within as well as the place where physical life begins. Red, the color of faith, is the color of the South on the Medicine Wheel, or Sacred Hoop. From South to North, the Good Red Road of our Earth Walk leads us to the experiences that give us understanding of living in harmony. In the Western Tribes, the Coyote or Mouse sits in the South and in the Eastern Tribes, the Porcupine is the Creature-being that holds the energy of the child.

In our day-to-day lives, the adult Self often forgets to allow the wonder of life's beauty to enter the heart space and sarcasm takes over. It is during these times that the ego begins to fear the loss of self-esteem and wrecks the best laid plans for using creativity in a positive way. Fears can destroy the sparkling synchronicity of our internal timing and lay waste to the perfection of our beautiful uniqueness. Great Mystery created all people in their own Sacred Spaces, with their own gifts, talents, and abilities. The child of the South Shield knows this and is more than willing to allow others to share in the co-creation, using all talents to better the whole. It was during a time when I had become too serious that I was given the teaching of the South Shield.

I was sitting on a hill on the side of a canyon high above the noise of the city, looking to the South and Entering the Silence of a quiet heart. On my right was the far canyon wall covered with giant bushes of green Sage, Nopales Cactus, and fragrant Larkspur. It was early spring and the place where I was sitting was the perfect vantage point for viewing the whole canyon. The headiness of the early morning dew on the Sage and Larkspur was filling my senses with rich perfume. I closed my eyes and reveled in the glory of being alive.

Grandfather Taquitz's voice filled my head and he guided to me a place inside myself that held the understanding of the South Shield. He had reached out from the Blue Road of Spirit to touch my heart and introduced me to a little girl that was riding the back of a Coyote. I watched her in my mind's eye as she wound her way up the canyon trail, giggling as she petted the Coyote that served as her transport.

Grandfather Taquitz told me to notice her gentle way of being. He said, "She may look like a child who is ordinary, but look at her connection to the Coyote. There is no fear in her. The Coyote has no desire to trick her and run far and fast so that she would fall off."

I began to understand why Coyote was called the Trickster. Coyote teaches us the beauty of our trust and our innocence until we become too serious, then backtracks to trick us out of the pompousness that masks our fears and seriousness. If we forget to be children and take life with laughter and ease, Coyote is there to pester us until we let go of the inner pain that keeps us from knowing the joys of life.

The little girl rode up to the big rock where I was sitting and handed me a basket with three items in it. She began giggling and the Coyote rolled his eyes and then laughed in a howling sort of way. Grandfather Taquitz's voice filled my head as he instructed me to look at the gifts in the basket. "These gifts are the symbols of the three paths to understanding the South Shield. Touch them and listen to their meanings."

I picked up the first gift. It was a Heyokah doll. "The first path to understanding the wisdom of the child is the spirit of playfulness," he said. "If you can laugh at the events that strip you of your ego-centered pride, you will return to innocence and humility. It is from that place of new beginnings that all things become clear and filled with truth. The seriousness of the adult cannot wreck your relationships with others if you honor the child's wisdom of balancing the sacredness with the irreverence. All things have their place and time. They allow laughter to bring balance to the sense of Self."

Grandfather Taquitz then told me to hold the next gift as he explained the meaning. It was a shiny red ball. The moment I touched it, it darted out of my hand and bounced down the canyon wall with the little girl and Coyote bounding after it, laughing as they chased it. "Physical fitness is the second path to the South Shield," Grandfather began. "To know the joy of using your body, developing the skill and grace that comes with play, allows the body to rid itself of the tensions of the adult world. In this way, it is easier to trust yourself to walk in balance. The skill of knowing what your body can do, what its needs are, and how to give it the freedom of its own expression is the second path to having faith in yourself."

I questioned Grandfather, "But isn't the South Shield also having trust in others, in life, and in Great Mystery's plan?"

The old Medicine Man smiled and said, "You learn quickly, little one. Of course it is. You must now see the value of trust. Know that you may always trust every living thing to be exactly who and what they are at any given moment. Your friend, Carol Blue Dove, told you that long ago. It is only when you forget to observe what the essence of each truly is, that the projection of what you want them to be brings Coyote to trick you out of the illusion." He paused, then continued, "Balancing the body is the key to observing the truth in all things. If you use the body for work only, it gets tired and knotted up. If you balance the body with physical play, it can release those ideas of being a slave to work. In doing this, you find that there is no need to hold resentment. If your body has no resentment your thoughts become clearer. There is no tension that would stop you from trusting yourself or others, or the beauty and balance of Great Mystery's plan."

I understood and took the knowing of the second pathway into my heart for safekeeping. Then I reached into the basket for the third gift, which was a mirror.

The little girl and Coyote came galloping up the trail to hand me back the red ball and pretended to throw the ball into the basket. It slipped and shattered the mirror. I was horrified as the image of my face shattered, then I was suddenly looking deep into Grandfather Taquitz's obsidian eyes.

"Don't worry," he chuckled, "that is a part of the lesson of the South Shield. When you can destroy the illusion of who you are to others and be yourself, you will have restored your innocence."

Looking into the mirror I saw thousands of tiny reflections of my face. Each broken piece held a whole picture. I began to realize there are many faces or sides of ourselves that we show to others. This was almost always what we want them to see based on which face would bring us approval and acceptance. I knew that the way to regain the truth of who I was would be found in the little girl. That child within was the essence of my personal beginnings and carried none of the adult fears. She would be my teacher, helping me to learn to shatter the mirrors of self-importance and to laugh at the expectations or projections that others sent my way. It was OK to be me once more.

Grandfather Taquitz smiled and said, "Yes, you have understood that the third path to the South Shield is through being who you are and understanding the beauty of that original essence. You need not alter that innocence and childlike precociousness for anyone. It is a gift for others to see that reflection so that they may drop the masks of their fear and see that they also hold that beauty in their inner child. Through knowing the child-within, you will restore faith in life and capture the wonder of being alive."

I thanked my three teachers of the South Shield and offered Tobacco to the Four Directions, Mother Earth, and Father Sky. It was a good day to be alive, a good day to laugh, and a good day to begin again.

The Application

The South Shield card marks a time of returning to the child-like parts of Self that need no support from the ego. Look at how you can be humble in the present situation. Balance work with play and sacredness with irreverence. In other words, you'll need to lighten up and drop the uptight parts of Self before you can continue.

This may be a time to get some physical exercise to loosen up tight muscles or to laugh to loosen up your sophisticated garbage. Stop holding on so tight and remember how to trust. How can you trust anything or anyone when the image in the mirror is not really you?

In all cases, the South Shield card insists that the child-within is trying to teach you something about how to handle the situation. Listening and trusting the little tike might restore some of the lost magic of life. Remember, playfulness heals a world of woes. The more serious you take the game, the less chance any of us have of winning.

≡ West Shield ≡

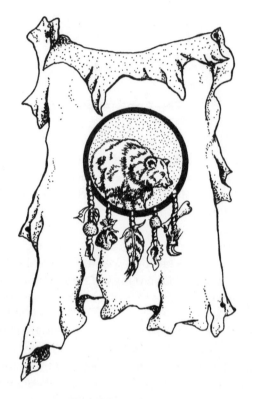

West Shield
Power of woman to seek answers.
Place of Bear's cave,
In the fading light
of Grandfather Sun,
The horizon of tomorrow
brings the strength
to meet my goals.

≡ 10 ≡

West Shield

INTROSPECTION/GOALS

The Teaching

The West is the Traditional home of Bear on the Medicine Wheel. The color of this direction is black, which represents the Void where the answers live within the dark cave of Bear. The ability to go within and to introspect is the female energy, which is receptive. The womb of woman is the place where all ideas, as well as babies, are nurtured and given birth. The darkness of the fertile womb is the place where each of us on the Good Red Road of physical life had our beginnings. We were the future generation to our parents. What Future holds is always in the West, the place of our tomorrows.

To understand the West, the "looking-within" place, we must first understand our natures. Unless we are connected to All Our Relations, the Standing People (trees), the Stone People, the Creature-beings, Mother Earth, Father Sky, Grandfather Sun, Grandmother Moon, the Four Chief Spirits (Air, Earth, Water, and Fire), the Creepy-crawlers (insects), and all other life-forms from atom to Great Star Nation, we feel that the answers live outside of us. If we understand that the spirit of all of these other life-forms dwells inside our bodies, we begin to understand that we can look within to feel and know the answers. In our earthly bodies, our cells carry memory of all that has ever been. Answers live in our spirit's knowing potential.

The Bear came to me in a Dreamtime waking state several years ago and lumbered through my awareness to take me on a Dreamtime Medicine Walk. I found myself in a forest high in the Rocky Mountains by the old burial ground near Creede, Colorado. The Bear wandered up to the spring above Moonshine Mesa and drank deeply of the cold, pure water coming from the Earth Mother's breast. Then Bear turned to me and spoke. "We used to use words like you Two-leggeds," she said. "We retreated into our silence at the end of the Second World. When the Earth was cleansed by the great ice mountains your people had finally come together in clans and families. They had heard the tundra Wolf's song and started to use words of their own. We knew that you humans would not be alone and that humans would survive if they could communicate with one another. We Creature-beings had to leave the Two-leggeds alone so they could learn their own sounds and how to use communication. Unfortunately, that was also the time that Two-leggeds shared so many of the opinions of others that they started to judge their personal truths. They began to worry about what others thought and failed to find their own answers within their hearts."

I understood that Bear was trying to show me how we Two-leggeds sought approval, entangling ourselves with the fear of being different. If new ideas presented a threat, it could be hard for individuals to follow their personal truths.

Bear continued, "It was during those days of the ensuing cold that humankind learned to eat meat. In the first world, the Two-leggeds had been vegetarian. Fruits, berries, roots, and wild vegetables were plentiful until the cleansing of the First World. When the great ice mountains moved across Mother Earth's face, the plants, which had sustained all creatures, vanished. The Two-leggeds were starving until they learned to eat meat. The Creature-beings, who understood the need for balance and sharing, offered their bodies as food to the Two-leggeds. My Creature Ancestors gave the warmth of their bodies' fur and the instinct of survival to the Two-leggeds. Then through consuming the meat of Bear, the West Shield's lessons were learned."

"I have memory of the way our gift was received by a female Two-legged," Bear said. "She was called Alona. Alona ate of the meat of Bear and sank into a fulfilling, deep sleep. She saw the memories of our Bear Clan and learned the three paths of the West Shield."

I listened as Bear continued. "In the dream, Alona watched Grizzly as she ate all that she could find in the way of berries, honey, and fish from the stream. This giantess was filling up for hibernation time when she would have to live off her stored fat. Then Alona saw Grizzly go into her cave to sleep through winter's white robe. In her dream Alona followed Grizzly and slept at her side. In the Spring when Grizzly awoke, Alona followed her into the deep green forest. Grizzly seemed very intent on rediscovering the forest and noting the changes in her favorite hollow logs. The deep winter sleep had propelled Grizzly into a new state of awareness."

"Mama Grizzly had left Alona to her thoughts and had gone to forage through the forest continuing her routine," Bear said. "It was only when Alona was left to her own devices that a tiny, still voice spoke to her silent heart, and showed her the value of Grizzly's lessons. Alona saw that in tasting the fruits of all ideas, you could expand one's outlook on life, just as Grizzly had done by eating all manner of foods. Then Alona remembered the retreat into the cave. Grizzly had taught her to go into the silence of her own Sacred Space to digest her ideas. The ideas that did not sustain her could be eliminated and the others would nurture her during the time of looking within. Alona realized that she could best meet her goals when she acted on the ideas that were most nurturing to her."

I looked at Bear's big brown eyes and smiled. I was beginning to understand the West Shield in a new way. "So the three pathways to understanding how to look within and reach our goals are like the actions of Grizzly in Alona's dream, right?" I asked. "Right," Bear replied. "Now you tell me how you see those paths."

I thought for a moment and then spoke. "The first path is to enter the stillness of our Sacred Space. Basically, it is being willing to receive the answers made available to us through the experience of daily life. That is, allowing our female-receptive side to come forward to magnetize or receive in the silence. So it is Entering the Silence." "Correct," said Bear. "And the second path?"

"Well, I suppose the next step is digesting the answers that come and learning to feel which ones apply. So the second pathway is integrating the information and discerning what our personal truth is," I replied. "Right again," said Bear. "It is in the second step, which nurtures the answers received, that the third path becomes evident."

"Oh, I understand," I said. "It is because the third path is structure based on personal truth. If we have a knowing about our digested ideas, we may then formulate a plan on how to attain our goals, that's the structure. If our goals are based on our personal truth and desire, they will be approached with joy. They will be goals we want to nurture because they are truly our own, not ones that others have expected of us. That's right, isn't it?"

Bear chuckled and rolled over scratching her back on the boulder next to the spring. "You have the idea," she mused. "All of the actions of Grizzly will allow each person to tap their inner-knowing and like Alona of long ago, my Clan can give the strength necessary to meet each tomorrow with joy. There is no need to fear the unknown that future holds if you follow Grandmother Grizzly and digest the knowing of your personal truth."

I thanked Bear for the lessons and began the journey of understanding my personal West Shield. May this sharing also aid you in your joy-filled sojourn to the land of Bear and the lessons of the West.

The Application

If the West Shield has appeared in your spread, Bear is asking you to look at your present goals and discern how they affect your future. Are the answers you seek from your own inner-knowing? If not, it may be time to Enter the Silence and digest the questions so that your personal answers can emerge.

Bear also reminds us that the West Shield is the place of all tomorrows. If you are afraid of the unknown, it may be time to clear away the fear. Strength to accomplish this clearing is Bear's greatest Medicine. Call on Bear and feel the courage to meet the Future fill your spirit.

In all cases, the West Shield speaks of the ability to complete our goals, the acknowledgment of our inner-strengths and the power to find and know our own answers. Remember that the opinions of others become mixed with our own doubts and become limitations when we forget to Enter the Silence.

≡ North Shield ≡

North Shield
     Sacred place of the Elders
          In gratitude I sing your praise.
    Sacred Buffalo
        White as driven snow,
   Hold my heart
       Until the end of my days.

≡ 11 ≡

North Shield

WISDOM/GRATITUDE

The Teaching

As I was Entering the Silence one winter's eve many years ago, I was taken into the Dreamtime and whisked away to an ancient forest filled with newborn snow. The bare trunks of the Birch and Aspen were stark against the emerald green of the Peace Trees, the Pines. Giant flakes of crystalline snow were falling around me as I came to the edge of the forest.

Below me was a vast meadow, deeply drifted in blue-white powder where not one blade of grass could peek above the blanket of snow. Far across the meadow, in front of another stand of trees was a Sacred Spirit Buffalo asking me to come nearer. I walked down the hill into the meadow with the fringe from my buckskin dress leaving soft impressions in Mother Earth's new cloak of white. The only sound was the gentle crunch of my moccasins against tiny ice creatures that made the threads of the snow robe.

As I approached, I noticed that steam was rising like Pipe smoke from Buffalo's nostrils and her giant brown eyes held me as we joined minds. This Sacred Buffalo of the Dreamtime had me sit cross-legged in the snow at her feet and feel the warmth of her breath so that I would not be cold. In a flash of lightning her hooves turned white and I raised my eyes to see all the color drain upward out of her body. Her eyes turned the color of summer sky, a cornflower blue. Her horns became silvery-white and she spoke my name.

"Midnight Song, follow my horns skyward to the Council of Elders for the teaching of the North Shield," she commanded. "There you will be given three trails that lead to wisdom and you will know the lessons of the Sacred White Buffalo."

I turned my eyes skyward and the scene suddenly changed. I was sitting in the South of a great Council Fire. This circle of Elders numbered over two hundred. In the center of the wheel was a blazing fire that lit the faces of the ancient ones so that I could see the expressions in their sparkling jet-black eyes.

One of the Grandfathers in the North of the wheel told me to walk to the fire and stand in the center of it. I obeyed and was not burned. Then that Grandfather spoke to me. "All three roads to the North Shield are walked many times and each path is tempered by the fire of experience," he said. "Come to my seat in the circle and receive the three symbols of the paths to the North."

I stepped out of the fire and walked to the seat of the wise old man. There were three Elders waiting for me. The first Grandmother handed me a great conch shell. She smiled and then spoke. "This shell is the power of listening to Mother Earth, her Creature-beings, and her children. Through listening you may come to know wisdom."

The second elder, a Grandfather, placed a tomahawk in my arms and said, "This tomahawk represents the Peacemaker who knows when to bury the hatchet and forgive and when to defend with truth. It is through proper use of truth, forgiveness, and humility that you may also know wisdom."

The third elder was Great White Buffalo Calf Woman. She presented me with a Pipe. Her voice was grave, but her eyes were twinkling as she spoke these words: "The Pipe is the symbol of balanced shields, male and female, Red Road and Blue Road, and of being grateful for the beauty of Great Mystery's perfect plan. The third path is gratitude and prayers of thankfulness. Through this path you may also know wisdom."

I thanked the Elders and returned to stand in the fire as the blue-orange flames spun me in a vortex of silver smoke that propelled me into the sky far above the Elder's Council Fire. I was suddenly aware of being in a totally different setting.

I was sitting in the South of an enormous table made of a slab of pewter colored stone. The Council that sat at this table numbered over four hundred. The shock of seeing their faces nearly sent me crashing back into my body on the physical plane. They were the races that came from the stars. Some appeared to be earthlike, but most of the others were races that I had never imagined possible before. I understood for the first time how the Kachinas must have looked to the Hopis who greeted them.

The Sky Brothers and Sisters were an odd assortment of races who enveloped me with warm feelings of goodwill and caring. Despite the love being emitted, I was still aghast at their appearances. Some appeared to be over seven feet tall with golden hair and very blue eyes and were very much like Earthlings, others were three to four feet high with enormous eyes that were all jet black with light-bulb-shaped heads and weblike feet. Some of the others had copper-colored skin with tall human bodies and oriental eyes that were sky blue. Still others reminded me of hammerhead shark faces with flat-topped heads and eyes at the outer edges of the flat top. All together, there must have been over seventy-five species of extraterrestrials.

It took me a while to adjust to being looked at and I was trying not to ogle back. A being with blue-gray skin, bald head, and pointed ears was sitting in the North of this gigantic round table. He rose and spoke to me, giving me information about what I was to accomplish during this Earth Walk. He told me things about my personal records in times past and why I was to release the records that held the understandings of the Red Race.

I looked around the table and smiled at each being, seeing past the outward appearance until I understood the inner beauty of this variety of races. The Sacred Path of universal wisdom also has to do with our ability to accept the unusual or bizarre with grace and understanding. I was stunned to see a few faces that were a part of Earth's history.

It was an astounding vision, and I was endowed during that time with a profound understanding of what it is to be a universal being rather than a limited identity. I found that beauty is in the eye of the beholder and that all races of our universe are ready to assist us. I committed the wisdom I had been given to memory and bid the Spirit Council good-bye as I was engulfed in the whirling smoke of silver energy that returned me to my body.

The revelation of the teaching of the North Shield is that North is the top of our Medicine Wheel and beyond that is the South or beginning of a new Medicine Wheel that is the place of the Ancestors. Beyond the North of that wheel is the South or beginning of the Universal Medicine Wheel. Like giant links to the chain that connects all of Great Mystery's creatures, we transcend the links one at a time and travel each wheel, constantly evolving in unified oneness. Remember that there is no limitation when you reach the place of wisdom. The secrets are no longer meant to be kept from those with ears to hear and eyes to see.

The Application

Some type of wisdom is coming your way if you have chosen the North Shield card. You are now being asked to show gratitude for these new understandings in order to continue the growth process. Wisdom is one way in which you can experience the natural order of the universe and how it applies to your life.

Wisdom is an inner knowing that cannot be traded, sold, or stolen from you. Knowing is truth that has been experienced in your life. The North Shield tells you that you have learned a lesson and derived from it a sense of Self that will serve you for the rest of your life. The successful completion of this lesson should be marked by prayers of thanksgiving or acknowledged in gratitude. In so doing, you will have completed the circle of the Sacred Hoop and honored the source of that truth. Remember that the gift of wisdom is in the heart of the recipient and remains alive as long as it is honored as a blessing.

≡ Arrow ≡

Warrior Clan, your arrows,
Fly straight and true.
Bold of heart,
Proven faith,
Protection lives through you.

≡ 12 ≡

Arrow

TRUTH AS PROTECTION

The Teaching

The Warrior Clans of Native America were the protection of the People. The spirit of the Warrior Clan is represented by the Arrow. The Arrow is straight and true, quick and deadly if aimed to kill. The Braves earned their right to be called by that name through many tests of leadership and agility. Courage was the main ingredient in the making of a Warrior, but it had to be tempered with truth, common sense, physical prowess, integrity, and connection to spirit before the right to be Warrior Clan was earned.

After Rites of Passage (see card 21), which occurred around a young man's thirteenth year, the slow and arduous process of learning how to be a man was begun with a father, an uncle, another Warrior Clan member, or a Chief. These lessons included hunting and tracking, going on a raid, Counting Coup, Vision Quest, Sun Dance, and leading a hunting party. The nightly dancing of these activities, reenacted for the Tribe, celebrated each of these victories.

Honors were bestowed upon each young man who honored his Clan with acts of bravery. Each step of the path to Warrior Clan was purposely hard and grueling since the leadership of the Tribe and sometimes the Nation would fall on the shoulders of the next Warrior Clan generation. A man's skill in making Arrows could show how much care he would take in leading his people. The best of the best would be chosen as Chief after they had honored themselves for fifty or more years. A Warrior was never considered an Elder and wise enough to be the main Chief until his life was rich with experience. He was considered a full grown adult at fifty years.

In Sioux tradition, after puberty, a young man could become a Dog Soldier, learning service and loyalty to the people while acting as sentry and protector for the camp. If these lessons were well learned by the Braves, some would be eligible for the Strong Heart Society, which was considered to be very elite and the mark of those that had distinguished themselves in battle and had earned many Coup feathers. The Warrior Clan was very honored when one of its members made it into the Strong Heart Society.

Many young men that married at an early age were not eligible for the Dog Soldier Society because they had to provide for a family. These men were scorned a bit and called "hang-around-the-Tipi." They often wanted to be a part of the Dog Soldier's Lodge but were not allowed. All members of the Dog Soldiers lived in the same lodge and women were never allowed to enter. The mothers of these braves would bring their food and only place one hand into the Tipi, up to the wrist, to give the son his food.

From the Warrior Clan, the best hunters and trackers emerged. Many times, these men would never be Chiefs but would hold places of honor in the Council of Men, which included all the leaders of the various Clans. Some of the Warrior Clans of Native Americans were called Fox Clan, the protector of the family. Others were called Coyote Clan because they could trick the enemy by knowing how to double back on the unsuspecting. For their Warrior Clan each Nation had a different Totem. The Totem held the attributes of the animal in their area that taught them the value of being a Warrior or Brave. The Warriors who had completed Dog Soldier training had earned the right to marry and move up the ladder in status based upon continued service to the People.

Men of the Warrior Clan could belong to other Clans as well depending on how well they distinguished themselves. From the age of seven all of a child's gifts or talents were in place. The grandparents had earned a rest from the heavy work of daily activity and were the ones to discern which talents each child could offer the Tribe. These gifts determined which teachers the children would go to among the Tribal members after their Rites of Passage. The female children would learn from other women and the male children would be taught by the men in the Clans those tasks which the children showed an aptitude for. This gave each child the best possible role models so that they could develop their gifts in a way that would bring honor to the Tribe.

Upon being bestowed the honor of the title of Chief, a man could never again raise his voice to a woman or child. This was the unspoken law of Warrior Clan. They were the protection of future generations and the living treasures that the women as Mother-Nurturers represented. The bravery and constancy of these Warriors kept them above petty arguments, but they were truly tested time and again by the bickering among those that had not developed the character of the Warrior. For a Chief to be balanced and compassionate, he would always put the good of all his people before his own feelings. The Warrior-nature within him was tempered by years of silence in listening to the Elders who had come before him. He had to see the value of the Arrow in its true form.

The Arrow was quick to protect and quick to act in crisis. Straight and true, weighing all future possibilities, each Chief aimed for the highest good and remained totally responsible for the actions of each decision he made. The Bow of Beauty was the joyful expression with which he viewed his task of leadership. Even in times of great sorrow, the ability to bend without breaking was remembered through the Bow of Beauty, the arch of inner strength that gave flight to the Arrow. The Bow of Beauty was said to have been made of finest gold, which represented the golden light of Grandfather Sun's love, and was inlaid with pearls, which represented the essence of

Grandmother Moon's nurturing. At the core of the Warrior Clan's principles was the balanced male/female within each Brave. This balance was found through the willingness to bend like the Bow of Beauty and send the Arrow of Truth into the world.

For any Warrior to carry special Medicine, he had to dream it or have a vision on a Vision Quest. If he could not reach the female receptive side of his nature through fasting and Vision Questing or Sundancing, he would buy a copy of another Warrior or Medicine Man's Bundle (see card 28). This individual had little chance of becoming distinguished enough to become a Chief due to the lack of balance afforded in his makeup. This was no dishonor, but it was a difficult road to follow. Again and again, the Brave in this situation worked to overcome his dominant male nature so that he could receive understanding from his Medicine Allies or the Ancestors.

The frustration of being unable to receive his own Medicine Dreams often created problems in the Council of Men. The inflamed young bucks of the Warrior Clan could become hot-headed and lead the Tribe's good fortune down the crooked trail. If order was not maintained within the natural balance created by the Chiefs, all could be lost. To lose face was the final agony among the Braves of the Warrior Clan and often was followed by exile from the Tribe. If the infraction was big enough, the entire Nation would no longer welcome the offender to their fires. Brotherhood was the common law of the Warrior Clan.

The Blood-Brother Ceremony of Native America is the undaunted connection of man to man that has produced the union of heart, body, and strength that creates a support system for the balanced Warrior Spirit within each man. Much has been lost in the World of Separation that needs to be regained. By exchanging blood through a small cut on both men's hands, the two pledge to allow their blood to run as one. The undying loyalty of a friend made Brother is promised in this Blood-Brother Ceremony. That type of commitment is rare in any culture of today's world.

Remember that the Arrow's path is straight and narrow and that its target is the heart. At the heart of every Warrior is the compassion of the Chief and the legacy of leadership for the good of all the people. All races of the Earth Mother depend upon the Rainbow Warriors of the world to reform the Warrior Brotherhood in order to accomplish the fulfillment of the Fifth World of Peace. For this to occur we must use the teaching of the Arrow, that is, using total truth as our weapons and our protection.

The Application

If the Arrow has found its target in your cards today, you are being asked to find the truth of your present situation. You can protect yourself from uncomfortable situations by using the truth as a protection. It does not matter what others think of you. You know the truth. When you honor that truth, you cannot be hurt by the lies of others.

Arrow also speaks of the ideas of Brotherhood. This is to say that you must armor yourself with the good intent and truthfulness of those you wish to associate with. Drop those who would no longer honor your path or truth. Remember: Arrow is straight and always says, "Stay on The Sacred Path."

≡ Coral ≡

Red Coral please remind me
  of the blood of all my kin.
Each of us has feelings
  that reflect the joy within.

May I nurture my own needs
  Then learn to share in turn,
The love that is my essence
  The heart that in me burns.

≡ 13 ≡

Coral

NURTURING

The Teaching

Coral is often used in Native American silver jewelry along with Turquoise. Coral is from the seas of the Earth Mother and is a symbol of the blood of our planet. As we have blood in our bodies, the waters of Mother Earth are considered to be her blood. Native Americans see the Earth Mother as a living being with consciousness and free will of her own. She is the true Mother of all living things.

Turquoise on the other hand is from the soil of the Earth Mother and represents the Sky Nation, which protects those who act as Guardians of the Earth. Turquoise is a male element, which can be worn for protection. Just as the Warrior Clans protect the People and all future generations, Turquoise protects the wearer from bad Medicine. This protection is needed so that the nurturing can occur in a safe space. It is for this reason that Turquoise and Coral are worn together. Our parents, Mother Earth and Father Sky, work hand in hand to protect and nurture all creatures that are connected by the family ties of red blood. The Silver settings of Turquoise and Coral jewelry carry the symbol of purity and truth that is the marriage of Earth and Sky.

Each human Two-legged has the need to be nurtured. From birth to death, humans seek comfort and nourishment from others of their kind, from pets, from possessions, from careers, and other aspects of the Earth Walk. Many Two-leggeds feel that they are alone, that the needs they have are not met by the parents they choose, the work they do, the relationships they make, or the lifestyle they lead. These dissatisfied people have forgotten their true Mother, which is the Earth.

Red blood runs through the veins of every creature on the Earth. From mammal to reptile, from bird to fish, from human to insect we all are a part of the Planetary Family. Our Brothers and Sisters in this enormous family seek to live in harmony with us. It is through this understanding that we begin the reconnection process with All Our Relations. No matter how much we would like to believe it, we are never alone.

The Water Nursery of Creation gave birth to all things. In our Seneca Tradition, our oral history tells us that after the Earth Mother was created by Great Mystery, the waters of the Earth came from the Field of Plenty (see card 38) and that all life-forms were nourished in the blood/water of Mother Earth. As seeds washed to the shores and rooted in the soil, plant life began. Creatures crawled from the oceans, rivers, and lakes, and began their lives on land while others chose the waters to live in.

In the womb of woman, all humans are nurtured in watery warmth until they are delivered through birth. So it was that the Earth Mother birthed life-forms from her Water Nursery of Creation. Since the Coral used by Native Americans is red and comes from sea water, it is used as the symbol of our birth and our connection to the Mother Of All Things. Every life-form is sustained through its connection to the Earth Mother and All Our Relations.

Using Coral can allow us to reconnect to the blood in our bodies and to the waters of the Mother Earth. As our feelings and intuition are connected to the Water Clan, we may once again feel the needs of our bodies as well as our spiritual needs. Once we reconnect with our feelings we can develop a communication with our physical form that is not based upon addiction, compulsion, fear, gluttony, or selfishness. The spiritual aspect of understanding the body's need for air, food, physical activity, and sexual coupling is sacred. The gifts we are endowed with cannot be used properly unless we have a vehicle to accomplish those Earth Walk Missions. The body is that vehicle. The way we view life is dependent, to a certain extent, on how we feel and how we respect and care for our bodies.

In the Second World, the Ice World, a Tradition began among many Tribes and Clans that won them the name Red Earth People. These humans understood that the Earth was their Mother. They understood the concept of life cycles and that when they finished their Earth Walk, their bodies would return to the womb of the Earth Mother in preparation for rebirth. When members of the Clan died, their bodies were rubbed with red ochre soil and placed in the fetal position along with all of their Medicine and possessions, then covered with herbs and flowers. The womb of the Earth Mother accepted them again and the grave was closed. The Red Earth People of the Brown and Red Races understood that the circle must come together in wholeness. As we came into this world with the blood of our mother's womb on our tiny bodies, we should leave this world in the same manner, to be nurtured again by our true Mother, the Earth. In this way we are preparing for a new birth of our spirit and a new set of lessons.

Many times when Coral was not available, a shell was placed in the grave of Red Earth People to insure reentry into the Water Nursery of Creation. The leopard shell and the cowry shell are shaped like the vagina of woman and represented the birth/rebirth element of the life cycle. These shells are still used by Black, Red, Brown, and Yellow Tribal People. Many times these shells are used along with pieces of Coral, stones, and bones to divine the future of a seeker. Today a Seer, a Holy Person, or Black Lodge Woman will throw the Bag of Bones (stones, bones, and shells) into a Medicine Circle marked in the Earth. The manner in which they fall determines the future events in the seeker's life. There are only three fates: Past, Present, and Future. Every event in a person's life is influenced and decided by choices made in the Present. To change what the future holds, we must seek guidance as to the proper decision and trust that we will create Beauty in our lives. Red Coral is one of the tools that will reinstill that faith. Knowing we are nurtured by our Earth Mother and that she will meet our needs is one method of destroying fear and affecting healing.

All nurturing comes from the ability to pay attention to our needs and our feelings. If we don't know what we need, how can we nurture ourselves? If we don't know what others need or how they feel, how can we give comfort? If we are out of touch with our own bodies, how can we keep them healthy and strong? Our Earth Mother supplies many teachers who can aid in the discovery of answers to these questions. Mother Earth can only supply comfort and nurturing if we are willing to listen. Then through these new understandings, our Knowing Systems teach us to trust that we are taken care of. If we are willing to nurture ourselves through connection to our Earth Mother, then we will learn how to nurture others.

The Earth Mother loves and nurtures All Our Relations equally. This form of unconditional love is the basis of Beauty. Beauty is a form of nurturing that is an accepted Native American understanding. To Walk In Beauty is to walk gently with a twinkle in the eye and loving thoughts in the mind and a smile in the heart. Coral also speaks of this message as the original intent of the Mother Of All Things. Coral is a very special teacher who allows us to connect to our feelings, the Planetary Family, the Water Nursery of Creation. Coral helps us to listen with open hearts and to understand that to feel is to heal.

The Application

If Coral has appeared in your cards today, you are being asked to look at the idea of nurturing. It may be time to nurture yourself or another. If you refuse to be nurtured it may be time to drop that superhuman attitude before you get sick. Coral tells us that our bodies have needs too. Pay attention and be good to your body.

Coral also speaks of the Planetary Family. If you feel lonely or alone, it may be time to have a reunion with the other creatures that share the Earth with you. Listen to All Our Relations and cut the "I'm the only one" refrain out of your thoughts.

Coral always tells us to listen to our feelings. If you have been ignoring how you feel around certain people or how your body feels, Coral is insisting that you reconnect to those feelings. Remember: to feel is to heal.

≡ Kokopelli ≡

Kokopelli play for me,
So my heart may sing,
Magic flute of mystery,
Fruitful dreams you bring.

Song of Aztlan,
Fertile Fire,
Canyons of my mind,
Sacred union,
Heart to heart,
Speaks of the Divine.

≡ 14 ≡

Kokopelli

FERTILITY

The Teaching

Kokopelli was a proud Toltec who came to Aztlan from deep in the heart of Mexico. Aztlan was the origin point of the mighty Aztec Nation before they built their capital in the middle of a lake, on an island now known as Mexico City. Aztlan's uppermost border was in southern Colorado and covered all of the Rio Grande Valley in New Mexico. The inhabitants of Aztlan were the peaceful Pueblo Nations. These Pueblos were farmers and cliff dwellers who depended upon the Thunder-beings and the Whirling Rainbow to feed the Three Sisters—Corn, Squash, and Beans—so the People could live.

The name of Kokopelli carries with it many myths and legends. All stories agree on one thing: he played the Indian Flute. His music was said to bring fertility to the land and to the People. His trade routes from southern Mexico to the southern regions of Colorado are marked with Petroglyphs of a humped-back flute player. His life was colorfully told around many a Council Fire and his praises sung in many a Kiva. The Kachina Dolls that represent Kokopelli show his body with an enormous erection marking his maleness and fertility. It is said that his seed was sacred and that his line bore children with special talents. Any woman chosen by Kokopelli as a consort was honored among her people for she would bear a child from the race of gods.

Joaquin, my medicine teacher in Mexico, was part Aztec and had many tales of the Toltec, Kokopelli. Joaquin sat and played a Mayan black clay flute as he wove the stories he knew so well into the music. I could feel and hear the Ancestors come to listen to the tales of their old friend Kokopelli as we sat around a fire high in the mountains above San Miguel de Allende one autumn evening. The music was soft and soulful as it echoed down the canyon wall. I envisioned the walls of Mesa Verde full of high cliff dwellings, fires brightly burning, and all the People sitting in wonder as Kokopelli wove the magical flute music into a potion that fed the hearts of young and old alike.

Joaquin's flute took me through time and space and suddenly I was a Raven sitting high above the city watching all the People observing master magician, Kokopelli. Joaquin's words slipped away and I saw his story unfold before my eyes. Kokopelli did not have a humpback, for his hump was sitting at his side and must have been the bundle of sacred objects and Medicine he had brought to trade. His flute seemed to glow in the firelight and he used the reflected light, as well as sound, to mesmerize the observers.

It had been a very dry year and the trust that rain was coming had worn thin. The feathers in Kokopelli's headdress were bright red Macaw feathers, which gave the illusion of his being bathed in the Eternal Flame of passion and creativity. The Fire of fertility that crowned his head also radiated from his body as he swayed in front of the communal fire. When he finished with his flute, he wrapped it like a child in brightly woven material and offered it to the Great Star Nation. His words carried to the farthest reaches of the pueblo. "This flute carries the music of the stars to the Great Earth Mother and calls for the Thunder-beings to make love to her," he cried. "This union will bring a child to the People who will one day lead them back to the stars, through the inner-Earth from which they came."

A cool rush of high mountain air blew past my Raven body and up the canyon to stir the embers of the communal fire into a whirlwind that exploded, filling the night sky with starlike sparks. The gasps of wonder from the mouths of the People echoed through the moonless night. Suddenly the light that the Fire-beings cast, gave enough light for everyone to see the masses of Cloud People who had gathered in the heavens to answer Kokopelli's call. Once again, the People cried out in awe at the magic of this half-god, half-man, Kokopelli. Even the sleeping babies awakened to the spectacle of Kokopelli's magic. Surely the long-awaited rain would feed the Three Sisters and the People would live. Kokopelli called out for everyone to gather up their clay pots so that the moisture could be collected for future use. The Thunderers called out that Rain was about to begin.

The Fire Sticks gave quite a light show before Rolling Thunder broke the silent night. The only other sound was the scurrying feet in yucca-fiber sandals running up and down ladders to grab the pots. One maiden stood entranced near the main plaza marveling at the lightning in the night sky while others around her became frenzied, running to and fro. Kokopelli looked at her beautiful, innocent face filled with wonder and approached her, still holding his flute like a child. She was filled with a sereneness that had piqued his curiosity.

"Why have you not gathered your pots?" he asked. "They are in place high on the mesa," she answered. When he asked the maiden her name, she replied, "I am called Ice Flower of the Winter Clan of White Corn." "Why are your pots already in place, Ice Flower?" he asked. "Because your flute called to me when you came up the canyon and told me you would bring the rain," she answered. Kokopelli was intrigued. He smiled in a knowing way as the maiden returned his smile. "So you are the one," he said.

The People assembled for the Medicine Chief of the Eagle Clan's prayer of gratitude just as the first Rain People began to touch the Earth Mother's breast. Kokopelli took Ice Flower by the hand and led her to the Fire. All eyes were watching the couple as they made their way to the head of the plaza. When the prayer was over, Kokopelli placed the flute, wrapped like a child in Ice Flower's arms as a symbol that this woman would share his music and his seed.

I flew over the couple and heard the gasps of all who were observing the drama. Magic was in the air and the child of this union would use the magic of this Raven Medicine to assist the People in finding their way back to the stars. The legend of the Pueblo People tells that they crawled up from the underworld after creation. Meanwhile the spirits of their Ancestors went back into the underworld until it was time to walk the Earth again. Kokopelli spoke to them of a time before the Creation when each person was a spark of Fire from Great Mystery's Eternal Flame and had fallen to Earth to seed the Mother with fertile thoughts, ideas, and actions. He told them that they would all become like Fireflies in the Great Sky Nation on the day when the Toltec and Pueblo bloodlines came together as one.

The Aztecs say that Ice Flower brought a man-child, who became a great spiritual leader of the Eagle Clan, into the world nine months later. His Medicine was the gentleness of his mother and the Fire of his father. Since Mesa Verde was abandoned hundreds of years ago, we are left with this question: did they leave the Earth and go to live in the Great Star Nation? If so, the fertility and abundance of Kokopelli shines on our world each night.

To fully understand the teachings of Kokopelli we must examine the ideas of Divine Union. When we approach our lives with trust rather than with skepticism, we are allowing our minds to be the fertile ground for enrichment. This growth cycle allows each of us to hear the music of our own unique magic. Every living creature of Earth is magical because each is a unique creation who sprang from Great Mystery. This magic is our personal Medicine, which manifests itself as our gifts, talents, and abilities.

Fertility in life can be called to us through our active seeking when we use the magic inside of ourselves rather than allowing it to gather dust. Kokopelli plays the flute and weaves the magic of his songs to remind us that magic is no more than a change in consciousness. If we want the seed we sow to fall on fertile ground, then we must change our perception and use our talents in a fertile manner.

The Application

If Kokopelli has lured you with his magical flute, it is time to listen to his song. This song is one of fertility. You are being asked to use your talents to create fertility in some area of your life. If things have been slow moving, Kokopelli's song is saying that whatever you intend to plant at this time will be very productive for you.

Planting seeds for the future takes effort on your part, so now is the time to use your skill and resources to make use of the magic. If you have a project to begin or an idea to develop, the timing couldn't be better. Shift away from any old, limiting ideas and move forward. The time is now—the power is you!

≡ Talking Stick ≡

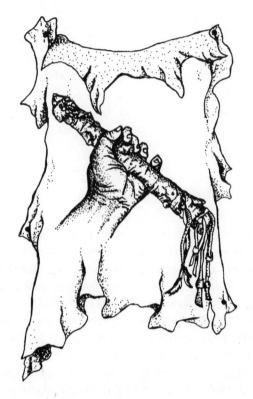

Talking Stick remind me
Of each Sacred Point of View,
Complete within the circle,
Of the Sacred Hoop.

15

Talking Stick

VIEWPOINTS/OPTIONS

The Teaching

The Talking Stick is a tool used in many Native American Traditions when a Council is called. It allows all Council Members to present their Sacred Point of View. The Talking Stick is passed from person to person as they speak and only the person holding the stick is allowed to talk during that time period. The Answering Feather is also held by the person speaking unless the speaker addresses a question to another Council Member. At that time, the Answering Feather is passed to the person asked to answer the query.

This form of parliamentary procedure has been used by Native Americans for many centuries and recognizes the value of each speaker. Every member of the meeting must listen closely to the words being spoken, so when their turn comes, they do not repeat unneeded information or ask impertinent questions. Indian children are taught to listen from age three forward; they are also taught to respect another's viewpoint. This is not to say that they may not disagree, but rather they are bound by their personal honor to allow everyone their Sacred Point of View.

A Talking Stick can be made from any type of Standing Person (tree). People responsible for holding any type of Council meeting are required to make their own Talking Sticks. The

Talking Stick may be used when they teach children, hold Council, make decisions regarding disputes, hold Pow-Wow gatherings, have storytelling circles, or conduct a ceremony where more than one person will speak.

Since each piece of material used in the Talking Stick speaks of the personal Medicine of the stick's owner, each Talking Stick will be different. The qualities of each type of Standing Person bring specific Medicine. For instance, White Pine is the Peace Tree, Birch symbolizes truth, Evergreens represent the continued growth in all things. Other trees such as Cedar denote cleansing. Aspen is the symbol for seeing clearly since there are many eye-shapes on the trunk. Maple can be used for Children's Councils since it represents gentleness and sweetness. Elm is used for wisdom; Mountain Ash (Rowan) for protection; Oak for strength; Cherry wood for expression, high emotion, or love; Fruit Woods for abundance; and Walnut or Pecan for the gathering of energy or beginning new projects.

Each person making a Talking Stick must decide which type of Standing Person will assist their needs and add needed Medicine to the Councils held. The ornamentation of each Talking Stick is important as well. The colors of beads used on the stick all have meaning. In our Seneca Tradition, red is for faith, yellow is for love, blue is for intuition, green is for will, pink is for creativity, white is for magnetism, purple is for healing and gratitude, orange is for feeling kinship with all living things, gray is for friendship and knowledge, and brown is for Earth-Connection and self-determination. All pastel colors are to enhance prophecy. Black is for harmony and listening, and crystal clear is for clarity and focus.

The type of feathers and hide used on a Talking Stick are very important as well. Each Creature-being has its own Medicine and contributes to the Medicine of the Talking Stick as well as the Councils it is used for. The Answering Feather is usually an Eagle feather, which represents high ideals, truth as viewed from the expansive eye of Eagle, and the freedom that comes from speaking total truth to the best of one's ability. The Answering Feather can also be the feather of a Turkey, the Peace Eagle of the South, which brings peaceful attitudes as well as the give and take necessary in successful completions of disputes. In the Tribes that see Owl as Good Medicine, the Owl Feather may also be used to stop deception from entering the Sacred Space of the Council.

The skins, hair, or hides used in making a Talking Stick bring the abilities, talents, gifts, and Medicine (healing qualities) of those Creature-beings to Council in a variety of ways. Buffalo brings abundance; Elk brings physical fitness and stamina. Deer brings gentleness; Rabbit brings the ability to listen with his large ears. The hair from Horse's tail or mane brings perseverance and adds connection to the Earth and to the spirits of the Wind. Horsehair is especially good if the Ancestors that rode the Wind before us are being consulted in Council. If an illness of heart, mind, spirit, or body has affected the group gathered, sometimes Snake skin may be wrapped around the Talking Stick so that healing and transmuting of those poisons can occur.

When I made my first Talking Stick, I went to the top of a very high mountain and called upon the Medicine Allies for assistance. I was sitting under the boughs of a giant Ponderosa Pine and sought the silence and peace of that Chief Tree. This Standing Person was the largest and oldest in the area and therefore had the wisdom of an Elder and the duty of Chief over all other trees in the area. I felt the peacefulness of Mother Earth come up the roots of Ponderosa and fill my body with gentle tingles as the Wind began to sing through the branches and blow the Cloud People across the turquoise expanse of the Big Sky Nation. The song was sweet and filled me with wonder. Then I heard my Medicine Song fill the afternoon, the ancient chant traveling on the Four Winds. The stars of midnight were singing through the arms of the Standing People and telling me that they still shone behind the brightness of Grandfather Sun's light of day.

I wandered out of my physical form and followed the Wind Chief to the Dreamtime, knowing that my body was safe in the keeping of Ponderosa and Mother Earth. I traveled upon a sunbeam to the Wall of Fire on the wall or outskirts of Grandfather Sun's brilliant form. I had no fear as I entered the Fire and saw brilliant flames of all colors speed by. Suddenly all was still, and Great White Buffalo Calf Woman greeted me with gentle smiles and sparkling eyes. She held a Talking Stick out to me and asked me to observe every detail. I looked and remembered. Buffalo Calf Woman began to explain the Medicine of my Talking Stick to me.

"The wood of your stick is to be of the Silver Birch so that truth will mark its use for all of your days," she said. "The tip of the stick is to be mounted with a clear crystal to give it focus and clarity. Therefore the White Buffalo is your main Medicine: the hide of your sacred Medicine Ally will bind your words with the understanding that comes from that Totem. Buffalo Medicine teaches you that the right to abundance is given to all living creatures. Buffalo asks you to walk with a loving heart, truth on your tongue, living your personal truth without doubt, using your talents to assist the whole, and honoring the roles of all others as equal to your own."

My eyes filled with joyful tears as she handed me the Talking Stick and then continued my instruction. "The Turquoise beads are to remind you that you are connected to the Big Sky Nation and that you are protected by those who live in those realms. The Coral is the symbol of the blood that connects all living things. Two-leggeds, Four-leggeds, No-leggeds, Winged-ones, Finned-ones, Creepy-crawlers, and those insects that fly, all have red blood. This is the blood of the Earth Mother that binds the Planetary Family and makes no distinction among them: all are loved and all contribute to the balance of the whole. In using these Stone People's beads on your Talking Stick you see the truth that creates the bridge between Earth and Sky. The Turquoise is from the Earth and the Coral is from the waters of the Mother which is her blood."

Great White Buffalo Calf Woman then pointed to the black markings in the Birch bark. "These markings are black and represent the gift of listening," she whispered. "When even a whisper is spoken across the Wind, someone's Point of View is being sent for a listener to learn from. The Stone People or the Morning Lark can broaden the viewpoint of those who listen. Understand that they are in Council at every moment of their life. Wherever you walk, life is around you, sending the whispers to those who will hear. Use these crystal beads to represent the honoring of the Rainbow Warriors, male and female, who know the value of all viewpoints. The Rainbow is created when Grandfather's light reflects through the crystal and illuminates the colors of all things. Feel the focus of clarity, of hearing, and vision as you take these Medicines to heart."

I felt her love encompass me as I took the Talking Stick and held it high above my head in gratitude, speaking my thanks to Great Mystery. As I held the Talking Stick to my heart, I felt the familiar feeling of moving once again through the Wall of Fire and my reentry into the physical world. I greeted the Earth Mother and Ponderosa and thanked them for sustaining my body while I was in the Dreamtime. I made my Tobacco offerings and walked down the mountain. With new purpose and creativity, I was ready to make my Talking Stick, using the understanding of the personal Medicine it would hold for me.

The Talking Stick is the tool that teaches each of us to honor the Sacred Point of View of every living creature. In Council, if we listen to the wisdom and teachings of others, we can then broaden our understanding and relate in a new manner to others. It has been said that the Great Wheel of Life has many spokes and that each of us will stand on every spoke at one time or another. The lessons we learn on each spoke bring us closer to wholeness and harmony. Disdain for those who have not learned these lessons will not serve in bringing harmony.

The Application

The Talking Stick reminds us of the validity of other viewpoints and teaches us how to listen and apply what we hear. We are being reminded not to interrupt others who are imparting wisdom. We are taught through listening that life has millions of options and answers to any dilemma.

If the Talking Stick has appeared in your spread, you are probably not allowing yourself any options in your present situation or have become too stuck on one idea to see any further than your self-created tunnel. Open up and listen to the opportunities that the Talking Stick says are coming your way. Remember all life-signals and/or options are available to those who will hear. You are being given an opportunity to grow through an alternative route. Use this gift now.

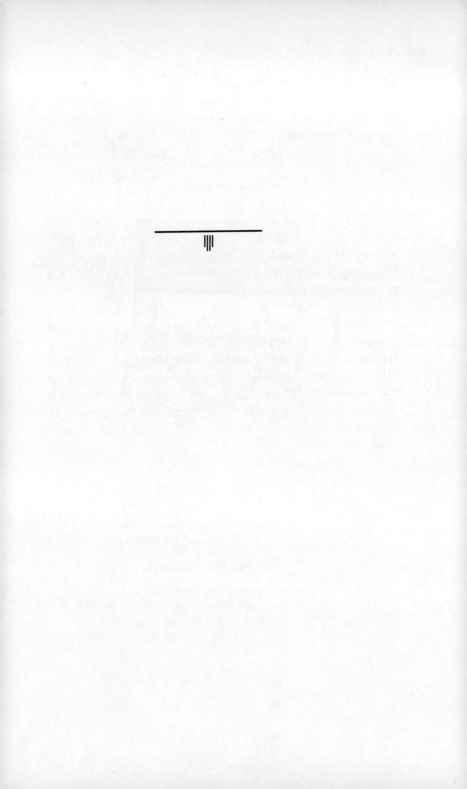

≡ Power Place ≡

Finding Earth Connection
In the place that speaks to me
Sandy beach or mountain,
Forest filled with trees,

High desert or windswept prairie
I will know it well,
It will make my heart sing
Of the river and the dell.

= 16 =

Power Place

EARTH-CONNECTION/EMPOWERMENT

The Teaching

Many books have been written about a mythical or real person going to a place of solace to seek at-one-ment with themselves or Great Mystery. The Bible says that Jesus went to the desert, to a garden, and on another occasion to the sea. Morganna La Fey went to the mound of the Goddess. Buddha went to the Bodhi Tree. Joan of Arc went to a shrine on a hill. The Herican Baba of India sought out a cave in the mountains. Saint Bernadette went to a cave near Lourdes. Hiawatha sought the forests of Turtle Island. Merlin went to a crystal cave in Wales. Quetzalcoatl went to the Tula Tree in Oaxaca, Mexico, and Abraham of the Old Testament went into the wilderness. Each of these people was seeking a place of power.

Power Places are as varied and individual as each person on the planet. The Earth Mother is so beautifully diverse and energetically different that some areas may attract one person where another person would feel no connection. Power Places are not specifically Native American. People all over the world go to special locations where they feel a strong personal connection to the Earth Mother. Every inch of the Earth Mother is sacred and each location is a connecting place for someone.

In Native American Tradition, we believe that the Mother Earth is a living being. When a human being goes to a Power

Place, the attention of the Mother Earth is directed to that spot, and energy begins to flow to that area because our bodies, like hers, are electromagnetic. Every time a human being seeks Earth-Connection, the Earth Mother is there to nurture and give solace to that person. If the person has not honored the Earth Mother or has no conscious feelings for her, the connection can be poor. With practice and patience the alignment comes and the strength of the connection grows.

When Two-leggeds seek vision, they "go on the hill," which is another way of saying one is going on a Vision Quest. The spot they pick may not be a personal Power Place, but it will be a place where they will make their Earth Connection. Every internal thought of the seeker will be recorded by the rocks and earth around that spot. That is one reason many Native Medicine People can read all that has transpired in any location from the beginning. The Medicine People go to the Stone People and listen. This ability is called Rock Medicine and is a common way of learning about the Earth-Records (see card 39).

Our Earth Mother has energy lines that are equal to the energy meridians in the human body. The Stone People are equal to our bones and the soil is equal to our flesh. The waters of our planet are like our blood and weave the tides of our emotions. Power Places are created when energy is drawn to one area. The Thunder-beings reenergize our Earth Mother, since she is magnetic in nature, through the gift of lightning. The Fire Sticks, or lightning, find their way to the areas that have been drained of energy through overuse or human consumption. That is to say that our bodies are fed from the electromagnetic energy of our Mother's surface. That same energy can be renewed through Fire Sticks touching her body.

The energy lines that feed all areas of Mother Earth's surface can be drawn to a specific area simply by calling the energy to the place where it is needed. This can be done through singing, drumming, ceremony, dancing, or any form of ritual energy gathering. When a Two-legged is performing these types of gathering energy, it is to fulfill a need. The Earth Mother willingly supplies energy to sustain the physical bodies of humans and Creature-beings who need her support. Mother Earth sends more energy to the point where it is needed, when her children commune with her through ritual. The ritual may call for rain or a vision, or ask for fertility blessings, or a healing. Wherever we Two-leggeds have come into unity with our Mother, a ceremonial Power Place has been created.

When we acknowledge our gifts with gratitude in any location on the planet, we create a Union with our Mother. That Divine Union is sacred and will be remembered by the Stone People in that location. All other creatures enjoy returning to a place blessed in this manner. We Two-leggeds are Catalyzers who can direct the Four Clan Chiefs of Air, Earth, Water, and Fire. Great Mystery gave us the legacy of using our gifts to redirect the forces of nature to catalyze the elements in order to change planetary conditions. We have the ability to direct our thoughts to influence the path of the energy lines that feed the Earth. In our Tradition, to make Ceremony is to come together in unity and influence the natural order of our world in a positive way.

The Grandmothers who were my Dreamtime Buffalo teachers told me that it is our role as Two-leggeds to seek those places we wish blessed and make them places of power by praying there. When we remember to make Ceremony, blessing every rock and flower on Earth's surface assists in reconnecting us to our Mother. The reconnection process must be done with joy and celebration. When we do Ceremony, we have not forgotten to dance our joy of unity and harmony, thus healing ourselves.

In learning how to find an individual Power Place, it is important to walk the land until we feel a drawing within us to an exact spot. It can feel like a gentle nudge or a bolt of lightning, a whisper on the Wind or a heart-opening. It is different for each person. The keynote is trusting our feelings and then being quiet as we sit on that spot for a while. The energy will build when the connection is made and can be felt as it moves through the body.

When our Earth-Connection is strong, we come to at-one-ment with the Clan Chiefs of Air, Earth, Water, and Fire. We can change the weather, exact healings, and/or commune with the Spirit World when we are totally connected. This is the basic principle that Medicine People have used for centuries to command the elements of nature. Earth-Connection gives the energy needed to use our natural gifts, abilities, and talents; without the Earth-Connection many plans and dreams will vanish for they have no manner in which to become manifest.

We are created in the image of a limitless Creator, the Great Mystery, and therefore we are limitless co-creators. The ability to infinitely create is one of our gifts as Catalyzers. When this gift is discovered and used properly, we become givers and receivers simultaneously, living antennae or bridges that conduct energy between Mother Earth and the Sky Nation like the Thunder-beings. Individual Power Places become the teachers that instruct us in our catalyzing abilities.

The word "power" has been used as a catch-all and has thus eliminated full understanding of the human role of being Catalyzers. The true meaning of power needs clarification. To speak of a Power Place can be unsettling to those who connect the word "power" with control. Control is the abuse or misuse of an ability. Others may connect the word "power" to authority. We may give our authority to others by not speaking or walking our truth, but we cannot give away our power. We may share our gifts, talents, and abilities beyond reason, but no one can force us to destroy them. We may bury our talents, be afraid to use them, or even deny our skills for fear of failure or misuse. In all cases when we come to the Earth Mother in a Power Place for reconnection, we need to clear away these limiting ideas so that we may once again feel her nurturing, which helps us continue the discovery of Self.

As we heal, the Earth Mother feels our joy. We are like cells in and on her body. The power of love, the power of healing, the power of compassion, the power of unity, and the power of knowing are our abilities. These are the gifts our Earth Mother seeks to share with us at this time. Through reconnecting to the celebration of life we are able to let go of our grief and fear. When we Walk in Beauty, we acknowledge every aspect of the Self. The Power Places of our planet are those that have seen the joy of our Earth Mother when her children have grown toward wholeness, celebrating life.

The Application

You are seeking a way to become a Catalyzer of certain life events if you have chosen the Power Place card. Being the Catalyzer in any situation means you are commanding your talents to effect some kind of result. This ability is learned through Earth-Connection. Your body can conduct the energy you need to create the desired outcome if you allow the Earth Mother to feed you the extra voltage.

Find a personal Power Place and call upon the Four Elements through prayers of gratitude. Then you can command your talents for good and effect the empowerment of manifestation. In so doing, your needs will be met. You can make it happen by using your creativity and receiving the energy needed from the Earth Mother. Remember that you are a Catalyzer and are totally responsible for your personal empowerment.

≡ Moon Lodge ≡

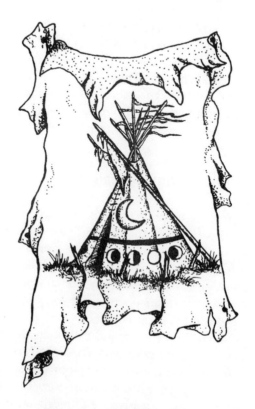

Moon Lodge, place of receiving,
Time of going within,
Observance of body cycles,
Renewing life again.

Retreating in the silence,
Sacred Black Lodge of the West,
Woman-child and Grandmother,
Earth Mother gives you rest.

≡ 17 ≡

Moon Lodge

RETREAT

The Teaching

The Moon Lodge is the place of woman, where women gather during their menstrual time to be at-one with each other and the changes occurring in their bodies. Long ago, during this special time of moon cycles, women were removed from duties of family and allowed to retreat to the Moon Lodge to enjoy the company of their Sisters.

Traditionally, the Moontime is the sacred time of woman when she is honored as a Mother of the Creative Force. During this time she is allowed to release the old energy her body has carried and prepare for reconnection to the Earth Mother's fertility that she will carry in the next Moon or month. Our Ancestors understood the importance of allowing each woman to have her Sacred Space during this time of reconnection, because women were the carriers of abundance and fertility. Women were the mothers who would increase the Tribe by bearing children, bring fertility to the crops through their connection to Mother Earth, and hold the dreams of the Nation in their wombs until those dreams became a reality. During their Moon, they were barren and could not conceive, so it was their time of rest.

Nobody would stop a woman from the necessary retreat during the Moontime. To do so would be a dangerous move on the part of any Tribal Member. To insist that a woman carry on with family duties or chores would break the reconnection period for the woman involved. This could inflict the wrath of the Earth Mother. Thus, if any woman was denied her right to reconnect with Grandmother Moon and/or Mother Earth, fertility and abundance could not be assured for the Tribe or Nation. Much of this connection has been lost in our modern world and it is my opinion that many of the problems modern women experience in connection with their sexual organs could be relieved by honoring the need for retreat and reconnection with their true Mother and Grandmother, the Earth and the Moon.

As Grandmother Moon is the weaver of the tides (the water or blood of our Earth Mother), so a woman's cycles follow the rhythm of that weaving. When women live together in a common space, their bodies begin to regulate their menses and all will eventually have their Moontime concurrently. This natural rhythm is one of the bonds of Sisterhood.

Women honor their sacred path when they acknowledge the intuitive knowing inherent in their receptive nature. In trusting the cycles of their bodies and allowing the feelings to emerge within them, women have been Seers and Oracles for their Tribes for centuries. In our Seneca Tradition, the governing body of the Nation comes through the eight Clans and each Clan has a Clan Mother. These women have the final say in all situations. It has been understood that all growth must come from woman. Like the Clan Mothers, in learning to use the gifts of intuition and wisdom, each woman can access the truth that will guide her on the Sacred Path.

The Medicine Lodges and Moon Lodges of women are sometimes called "Black Lodges." The color black is the color of the West on the Medicine Wheel. West is the place of woman, the place of all of our tomorrows and the home of Bear. As Bear retreats into the cave to digest the information and food gathered during the year, so woman retreats to the Moon Lodge to honor the gifts she has received from the Earth Mother during the past Moon. The blackness of the night sky is dominated by Grandmother's silvery light and is female in nature. This is another reason the women's lodges are called Black Lodges.

It is during their Moontime that the women share their visions, dreams, experiences, and talents. Since the Black Lodges are forbidden to men, just as the Warrior Societies and Clans are forbidden to women, each gender is allowed to reconnect with others within their Brotherhood or Sisterhood who can support them and mutually share the things they have learned that will strengthen the whole. The Black Lodges are the center of Woman's Medicine and the unity of Sisterhood.

In Native Tradition, each stage of a female's growth is cherished and explained to growing girls becoming women. The teaching begins before the girl's first menstrual flow and is marked by the Rites of Passage (see card 21). Every female in the Tribe is shown the honor in being a Mother of the Creative Force. Each is taught about the Moon Cycle when she is ready to be a tide-weaver like her Grandmother Moon. She is taught to respect her body and its needs. Each woman is shown the understanding of what it means to be female and is prepared to take her role among the other women of the Tribe. This includes learning the duties of being a wife and mother, making crafts, developing creativity, using intuition, developing her talents and gifts, understanding Ceremony and ritual, assisting in birthing babies, and using her connections to her personal Totems and Medicine.

During their Moontime, women were not allowed to prepare food, to dance, participate in Ceremony, or to share any life activity with men. Many people today have misinterpreted this custom. This Tradition originated because the women needed to nurture themselves during the barren period. Think of the relief this retreat would provide a modern woman and her family who have to put up with her natural mood swings. The belief among those who misunderstood this practice was that women were dirty during their Moontime, but in truth, it was the highest honoring of woman. It was considered a woman's right to retreat for feeding and nurturing by the Earth Mother, as she had fulfilled her responsibility of nurturing others during the rest of the month.

The unique Moon Lodge teachings of womankind are geared to allow each female to relate to the Mother and Grandmother energies. That is to say the roles of woman are explored in depth. The Mother-Nurturer is one role that a woman will experience during her Earth Walk and will entail pregnancy and the delivery of offspring as well as the deep abiding love and care of the growing youngsters. Children are honored for their particular talents and are guided by their mother to accept, honor, and develop those gifts with joy.

The Grandmother role was very important. When a male child was seven years of age his Grandmother would retreat to the Black Lodge and dream or smoke the young boy's future mate. Discussion with the Grandfather would follow and then the Grandmother would begin the making of the ceremonial buckskins that would be the wedding garb of the future. When the young man came of age and chose a girl he was interested in taking as a wife, he would go to the Grandparents and ask permission before approaching the girl's father. If she was the girl who the Grandmother had dreamed, she was accepted; if not, he was to wait or look further. This function of the Grandmother was one of the most revered in Tribal Law. Each vision or Medicine Dream that came to a Grandmother was highly honored and sacred. Each Grandmother knew the size of her grandson and his mate and sewed the wedding clothes accordingly. This was a true test of the abilities of the Grandparents as Seers.

Women were expected to be chaste as maidens until the courting period preceding an actual marriage and to be faithful as wives. In some Plains Tribes, however, when a young woman was being courted, she was allowed to pick who she would share her Buffalo Robe with before she agreed to marry. In these Tribes, this selection process was considered a woman's right. In understanding that her body was a sacred extension of the Earth Mother, she understood that all acts of pleasure, abundance, and fertility were part of the female nature.

In experiencing coupling for the first time, each woman was respected and loved gently so that no harm would come to the Earth Mother or the Tribe through rough sexual treatment of the woman. Sexuality was understood to be a natural and sacred pleasure. Each woman was prepared through the many lessons given by other women in the Moon Lodge. Sexuality was looked upon as a natural act of fertility. As Earth and Sun created food for the People's survival, so did man and woman create offspring through their shared love. Originally, the woman nearly always had the final say as to which Warrior she chose to share her life or body with. The exception to the rule was if she had been taken prisoner by another Tribe or if her family was so poor they needed connections with strong hunters or wealthier relations who would then be responsible for the welfare of both families.

When the Boat People (Europeans) came to Turtle Island (the Americas), they came to the eastern shore and coined the word "squaw." This word was adopted and used as they moved west. The other Nations of Native America did not know where the word came from and it has been used to name areas of land across the west. In truth, this word is a defamation of woman. It comes from the Algonquin word *Nues-quaw* or "No-squaw," which means "no penis." The Algonquin women screamed these words as they were being raped. To call a Native Woman a squaw is to call her a penis and destroys our honoring of women as well as opens old wounds. If the Moon Lodge teachings and Tribal honoring of women were violated by a Red Man, those violations were punishable by death.

For the old wounds to be healed in a successful, creative way, it is time for women to use the idea of the Moon Lodge and retreat to the sanctity of the Sisterhood. Women must learn to love, understand, and thus heal each other. Every person has male and female sides. Each enters the silence of the heart to discover the beauty of retreat and receiving. The Moon Lodge can be a symbol for men and women alike. Retreating and digesting the feelings that life's experiences have created is very healing.

The Application

The Moon Lodge card speaks of retreat. Take a break. Your influence cannot be felt at this time because you are in need of replenishing your own energy. This is a barren time in a sense because you need to be alone and honor yourself for a change.

Retreat is not an act of weakness; it is an act of strength. Without retreat, the future cannot take hold in the present. Make note that you are preparing for the time of fertile action by taking a rest now. Being alone at this time will allow you to do the things that give you joy without interference. Remember that miracles can happen when you repose and allow yourself to come to your new starting place in a gentle way.

≡ Whirling Rainbow ≡

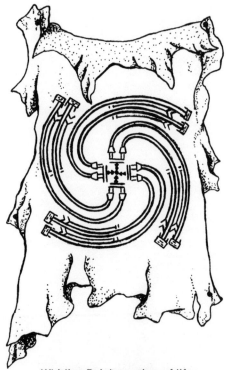

Whirling Rainbow, giver of life
  Through your cleansing rains.
Uniting all colors, the Children of Earth
  Will walk in peace again.

Whirling Rainbow prophesy
  Your Warriors now arise,
Sisters and Brothers in harmony,
  Your light in their eyes.

Whirling Rainbow,
  Touch our hearts,
We will surely fly.
  Never lonely or apart,
Our whirling colors in the sky.

≡ 18 ≡

Whirling Rainbow

UNITY/WHOLENESS ACHIEVED

The Teaching

To the Navaho and the Hopi, the Swirling or Whirling Rainbow Woman is the bringer of friendly rains that nurture the Three Sisters—Corn, Squash, and Beans—during the summer so that the People will be fed. Many times an image of the Whirling Rainbow is created in Sand Painting, an ancient Sacred Healing Art performed by the Medicine Clans of those Nations. The Whirling Rainbow Woman comes from all Four Directions and curves like a swastika covering all directions. The outside of the Sacred Circle is protected by another Whirling Rainbow Woman bending her body in the space below creating a cup-shape to catch the rain and protect the circle. Without the Rain, the Three Sisters will die and the People will not be fed.

The Whirling Rainbow is the promise of peace among all Nations and all people. The Rainbow Race stresses equality and opposes the idea of a superior race that would control or conquer other races. The Rainbow Race brings peace through the understanding that all races are one. The unity of all colors, all creeds working together for the good of the whole, is the idea that is embodied in the Whirling Rainbow. When all pathways to wholeness are respected by all cultures, the prophecy of the Whirling Rainbow will be completed.

When I lived in Mexico and worked with the Grandmothers, the Dreamtime Buffalo Society, or Sisterhood, had many prophecies derived from Seers and Dreamers that had come down through the ages. The prophecy of the Whirling Rainbow was very specific. When the Time of the White Buffalo approaches, the third generation of the White Eyes' children will grow their hair and speak of love as the healer of the Children of Earth. These children will seek new ways of understanding themselves and others. They will wear feathers and beads and paint their faces. They will seek the Elders of the Red Race and drink of their wisdom. These white-eyed children will be a sign that the Ancestors are returning in white bodies, but they are Red on the inside. They will learn to walk the Earth Mother in balance again and reform the ideas of the white chiefs. These children will be tested as they were when they were Red ancestors by unnatural substances like firewater to see if they can remain on The Sacred Path.

The generation of Flower Children have moved through this part of the prophecy and some have remained on The Sacred Path. Others were lost for a while and are now returning to the natural way of being. Some were disillusioned and have forgotten the high ideals that gave them life when their hearts were young, but others still are waking up and quickening into the remembering.

Grandmother Cisi would look at me with her obsidian eyes piercing my soul when she spoke of the Whirling Rainbow Prophecy, and I would feel my heart skip a beat and then fill with promise and love. She would tell me about the return of the Buffalo to Turtle Island and how the herds would once again be numerous. After the time when the Buffalo returned, the generation following the Flower Children would see the dawning of the Fifth World of Peace. Grandmother Cisi called the beginning of this Fifth World the wobbly pony that on being born would try to use its legs. She said that the wobble would be felt by the Earth Mother and changes would occur in the soil and waters. Inside the Children of Earth, the wobble would create rolling emotions and feelings that would bring the quickening and the remembering. Colorful dreams would be brought into the Sleeptime and Dreamtime dreams of these newborn Warriors of the Rainbow and they would begin to learn how to Walk in Balance. The changes in our Earth Mother would create fear in her children, which would later lead to the understanding and unity of One Planet-One People.

Grandmother Berta would giggle when we came to this part of the prophecy because my eyes would be round as saucers and I could not sit still. Grandmother Berta would urge Grandmother Cisi to stop for the day and leave me hanging on the edge of the cliff just to tease me. Cisi would finally begin again and slap my knee to make me pay attention to the rhythm of the prophecy because my mind would be spinning with probabilities and my own projections. I wanted to ask so many questions about how, when, where, and why. I wanted to know details, details, details. I was twenty-two and very impatient, but I kept my silence so she would continue.

The Whirling Rainbow will appear in the form of a Sun Dog to those who are ready to see. The Sun Dog is a full Rainbow Circle around the sun that has bright white lights at the Four Directions. The Sun Dog is a rare natural phenomenon that was named by Native Americans. The name is now used by scientists all over the world. Many Sun Dogs will be seen around the Time of the White Buffalo, which will be the Sky Language sign that the Secret and Sacred Teachings are to be shared with all races. Enough of the Children of Earth will be awakened to carry the responsibility of the teachings and the healing process will begin in full swing.

Grandmother Berta would smile with a faraway look in her eyes, knowing that she would be on the Blue Road of Spirit when the time of the White Buffalo came. Grandmother Cisi would also be in the Other Side Camp, but both promised they would be assisting me in bringing out the things they had taught me when the time was right.

Both Grandmothers spoke of the change in feelings the Children of Earth would have during the wobble or healing process as the Whirling Rainbows permeated their dreams. They said, "Many will remember their purpose for being on this Earth Walk and will learn to develop their gifts to assist the whole of humanity. Truth will shatter the bonds of separation and goodness will prevail. Some details of Earth changes will come into the dreams of those who are being warned to move where they will be safe. Others will be told that their talents will be needed in areas where the changes occur. Everyone will have to trust their personal vision and follow their hearts in order to assist the whole. Each person will be able to use their gifts with joy and share equally in the bounty created by all those working together. The other teachings of the prophecy of the Whirling Rainbow will be released at a later time when more have awakened to the potential they carry."

In our Seneca Tradition, Grandmother Twylah has taught us many uses for the Whirling Rainbow of Peace. When we are having difficulty in any situation, we visualize the Rainbow of Peace encircling the situation, the people involved, and the disharmony. Then we twinkle our eyes with joy, sending our inner-peace to the situation. In using this technique and following it with ceremony, we place our intention inside the Whirling Rainbow of Peace.

Our intention follows the Iroquois Peace Confederacy Tradition that uses the Twelve Cycles of Truth to bring peace. The Twelve Cycles of Truth are: learning the truth, honoring the truth, organizing the truth, observing the truth, presenting the truth, loving the truth, serving the truth, living the truth, working the truth, walking the truth, and being grateful for the truth. When we invite total truth into our Sacred Space, we shatter the bonds of separation and illusion that create discord. The Whirling Rainbow of Peace destroys the lies that have made the Children of Earth mistrust one another and replaces the illusion of separation with the truth of unity.

When the Whirling Rainbow Woman of the Navaho and Hopi brings the cleansing and regenerative rains to the Earth Mother, her children are also cleansed and healed. When the Rainbow of Peace of the Seneca encircles each person's Sacred Space, all will walk in truth respecting the Sacred Space of others and the harmony of living on Earth will be restored. These Knowing Systems are the teachings of the Warriors of the Rainbow who are Sisters and Brothers uniting the Fifth World and working for peace.

The Application

If the Whirling Rainbow has appeared, you are being asked to remove any type of discord from your life in order to grow. Don't feed the negativity. Look at any lessons being presented at this time, learn from them, then focus your attention on creating new beauty and abundance in your life. Do not allow yourself to be caught in the quicksand of petty tyrants. A true, worthy opponent will present lessons to make you grow beyond any high drama and into a sense of unity with the Self. Other petty tyrants are not worthy of your attention or your energy. You need not take on the issues of others when the discord is due to their lack of unity within themselves.

Encircle any discord with the Whirling Rainbow of Peace and consider the unity you have with Great Mystery when you keep your eye on the goal and your feet on the Sacred Path of Beauty. Remember that any challenges to unity are equal to your ability to overcome them.

≡ Painted Face ≡

Painted Face expresses
   the inside of me
Not my nose or my eyes
   the parts that others see.
My feelings and my Medicine
   are painted in design,
Colors of Great Mystery
   who created me in kind.

≡ 19 ≡

Painted Face

SELF-EXPRESSION

The Teaching

Many movies have been produced in years past showing Native Americans fighting cowboys. In these battle scenes, the Warriors of the Red Nation have faces painted by Hollywood makeup artists. A Warrior would never paint his face in a ridiculous manner when going to battle as portrayed in these early movies. These artful, yet incorrect, face paints never portrayed the two real forms of Indian self-expression. Warpaint and Ceremonial Paint were two different types of personal Medicine. Since Native American Tradition places a great deal of emphasis on the development of uniqueness and personal talents, it was of paramount importance that each person be allowed the right of personal expression. One way this was achieved was through the Painted Face.

The Painted Face of the warpath was intended to frighten the enemy and to add to the expression of that Warrior's bravery. The Painted Face of feasts or Ceremony was to show the beauty of the individual spirit to all others of the Tribe. The extended family represented by a Tribe was a safe place to reveal the way in which each individual Walked in Beauty. There was no need to use the Painted Face as a mask in ceremonial situations for no enemies were present. Masks were used in many dances or rituals when it was necessary to portray someone other than one's Self. The Painted Face was never used to cover one's identity but rather to express it in a more personal manner.

Warpaint was used on a Brave and his Pony to show them as being a team. This is one reason why the Pinto and Appaloosa, used by Plains Tribes were often called "Paints." The warpaint representing the Medicine that protected the Brave was also the Medicine that protected his Horse. Sometimes the way to express personal Battle Medicine came through a Medicine Dream. The more frightening the War Paint, the easier it was to create fear in the enemy. Using the element of surprise when jumping an enemy, a Warrior would howl a war cry displaying his contorted Painted Face. This show of courage could instill fear and temporary paralysis in the opponent, an advantage in battle.

After Horse was brought to Turtle Island, the Red Man and his Pony became inseparable. This hard-working team would hunt Buffalo so that the People's needs would be met. Horse took over the job that had formerly been reserved for Dog by carrying the goods of the Tribe from camp to camp. Horse became the extension of a Warrior's spirit and his new best friend. When these two friends were together on the warpath, each Brave painted his body and that of his Pony with the colors found in the Earth.

The clays that were used for paint carried the names of the areas where they had been found so others could find them by returning to those locations. These clays were then baked on the side of cooking fires, then pulverized into a powder and stored until needed. Whether the paints were used for a ceremony, a feast, or for going to war, the preparation was the same. Bear grease or Buffalo tallow was mixed with the colored powders to a certain thickness then applied to the body. These colors of the Earth are not as bright as paints used today because they are totally natural. Sometimes the flowering parts of herbs and natural grasses could be added to intensify the brightness of the clay but on the whole the colors were, generally Earth tones.

The Traditional colors of red, black, white, and yellow, which represent the colors of the Four Directions and their Medicines, were the basic palette. The use of blue and green was not as common because it was more difficult to find clays of these colors in certain regions. Blue represents Father Sky, and green, Mother Earth.

If a Tribal Member had a special Medicine Vision that marked a change in that person's life path, he or she could be known from that time forward by a new name. If this occurred, it was certain that the new identity would change the Medicine of the person and therefore change the Painted Face. These changes were celebrated by everyone. The discovery of a new talent, the completion of a test of bravery, the move from childhood to adulthood, or a Coup was one of the many blessings of physical life honored by the People. Each person used his or her individual intuition and creativity to create the Painted Face and that, in itself, was an exercise in personal growth that aided the Tribe as a whole.

The designs I am most familiar with are ones passed on to me through my Medicine Teachers. These cover a broad expanse of Traditions but are by no means the only ones used. One universal symbol was the use of yellow lines above the eyes. This denoted a Seer with proven talent to interpret dreams, receive Medicine Visions, or journey with successful results, which aided the Tribe.

A face painted totally black denotes mourning the loss of a loved one. Blackened eye sockets tells the observer that this Painted Face acknowledges the West, is a fair judge, sees the truth, is strong like Bear, and would be a good adviser, one not swayed by the opinions of others. A red line down the nose can mean two things. The first meaning is that the person trusts the path they follow. The nose leads us in every direction we turn. Therefore the nose, when painted red, is also the sign of a leader, because that leader has the trust and faith of the People.

In other cases, red is used as a line down the middle of the forehead and again at the chin; this signifies that the wearer is a protector of women and children. When yellow is used in any design, the color means that the wearer is connected to East and Eagle and has served the People through sharing new ideas and inspiration. Yellow paint also means that the wearer honors the lives of all things that Grandfather Sun shines upon. White in any design means that wisdom has come to the life of that person through a major event and altered that person's perception. Blue and white can mean that the Painted Face had a sign from the heavens regarding some wisdom sought. Green and/or brown designs can mean the connection to the Earth Mother that has produced a new-found talent or ability.

A lightning bolt means the wearer is connected to the Thunder-beings and that usable energy is a part of his or her Medicine. If the Fire Stick is painted in white, the person has been struck by lightning and is now designated as a Medicine Person of the Tribe. If the lightning bolt is blue, it means the spirits of Thunder and Lightning have spoken to the person in visions or dreams. A red lightning bolt can denote a Rain Medicine Person who can call the Rain-beings to quench the thirst of Mother Earth.

White horizontal lines under the eyes can speak of the wisdom of seeing the truth and being grateful for the power of observation. Seven white circles, fully colored, with one in the center of the forehead and three on each cheek traveling down to the jaw is a Chocktaw symbol of a Moon Medicine Person. A Moon Medicine Person can read omens and signs in the night sky and makes these portents known.

Every symbol of a person's Medicine will be painted in the color of the direction that brought the realization of that gift. For instance, East is yellow, South is red, West is black, North is white, Above is blue, Below is green or brown, and Within is usually green. In the Sioux Tradition, Black Elk saw red in the East and yellow in the South as did Lame Deer, but most other Traditions see those colors reversed. The Navaho have a totally different wheel with colors, which applies to their Creation Story.

If a healer has Snake Medicine, we would see a wavy line painted on their face in the color of the direction they were walking when the Snake came to them. Any symbol that is painted in red can represent a family gift or Tradition that has been passed down through that bloodline. A red wavy line could denote a child of a Snake Medicine Person and that Snake protects his or her life path through the Medicine of their Ancestors.

Every person carries a legacy of needed talents that will support the growth and expansion of a Tribe. When the Painted Face is shown to the Tribe's extended family during feasting or ceremony, those gifts are noted by the Elders and can be called on in times of need. The Painted Face had no room for boasting because if one claimed a talent, it was communal property in a sense and could be used to benefit the whole. To "lose face" was to be shamed by claiming talents one did not have. When the needed talent was called on by a Tribal Council and could not be produced by the false claimant, the other claimed gifts would be in question. The Painted Face of the deceiver would be wiped clean and no one would ever believe that person again.

Remember that the gifts exposed by the Painted Face were talents that each person brought to the whole Tribe as a Give-Away. It is Good Medicine when we assist others by sharing our abilities. As others prosper along with us, we gain a sense of self-worth that is not ego-based.

The Application

The Painted Face speaks of self-expression. It tells you to use your creativity in order to express your feelings, your talents, or your desires. Expressing who and what you are at any given moment is healing as well as productive. As you change and grow you may feel the need to alter the way in which others perceive you. Changing your appearance, attitudes, and activities to match the new you may be called for at this time.

The keynote is that this card asks you to open up and allow others to see your Medicine. In that way, you are offering a gift to others who may have need of your talents. Don't deny how you feel, what you think, or what you can offer the world. In truth and with grace it is now time to allow the Medicine of the Self to emerge. You will never lose face by presenting the true Self minus the self-importance.

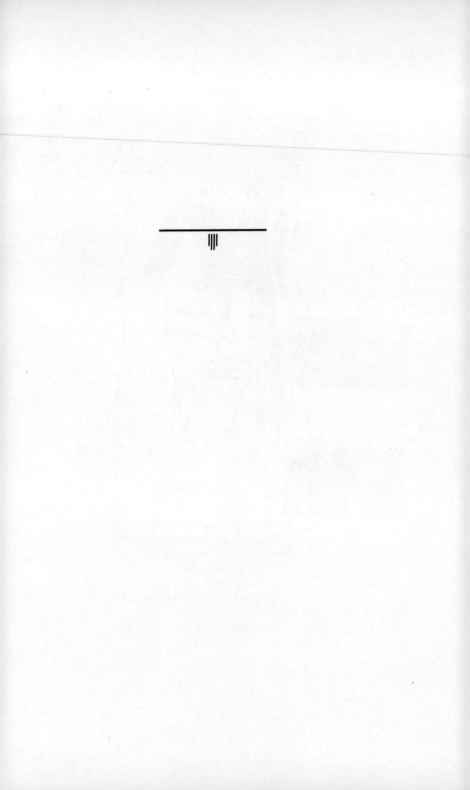

≡ Counting Coup ≡

To know that I have honored
  My words with my deeds,
Sweet victory is shared by all,
  In filling other's needs.
Humankind rejoices!
  The prize of Counting Coup,
Harmony and balance,
  A peaceful world anew.

≡ 20 ≡

Counting Coup

VICTORY

The Teaching

The act of Counting Coup signifies a victory over an enemy or an accepted challenge. The Warrior Clans of Native America used many methods of stealth, guile, surprise, planning, and physical strength to claim prizes from their opponents. The Traditional prizes taken on raids were Horses, Eagle feathers, Medicine Bundles, Medicine Shields, tomahawks, bows, and other weapons. Scalps were not honorable prizes of Counting Coup before the Boat People came to Turtle Island.

Trappers and traders sold scalps to European curiosity seekers saying that the "savages" in the new world cut each other's scalp off, when in fact the practice of scalping was started by those who sought money from the wealthy in Europe. As the scalping horror spread and Native women and children were being killed and scalped or scalped alive, the Warrior Clans began to retaliate. The men of any race or Tribe were of the Warrior Clan in the eyes of Native Americans and were charged with the honor of protecting women and children. It was the highest form of shame for a Warrior to have the women and children under his protection hurt in any way.

Anger and hatred began to grow on all sides, Tribe against Tribe and Indian against white. The act of Counting Coup had been soiled and the honor normally between Warriors and soldiers had been cast aside. In the original meaning, Counting Coup had been an act of victory. A Warrior would steal something from the Brave he had bested to show how strong his Medicine was against his rivals. This practice varied among Tribes. Members of the Warrior Clan among the Plains Indians often had a Coup Staff or Stick, much like a shepherd's crook that was placed inside his lodge and carried the reminders of his personal victories. The Coup Staff had various prizes tied to it. These objects could include Horse hair (if he had stolen the mount of another Warrior), Eagle feathers, a piece of material, beads, or a Medicine Pouch, which had been tied to the mane of an opponent's Horse. Later with the practice of scalping, a scalp could also be seen hanging from a Coup Stick.

In marking a victory, there were certain things that a Brave was then allowed to do that would tell others of his Counting Coup. He could use the designs in his face paint which added honor to his status and told those who knew how to read its meaning that he had one or more acts of bravery added to his name. These symbols could also be added to his Horse's war-paint when he rode into battle again. The more Coups Counted, the stronger the Medicine of that Warrior.

Four to six major types of Coups were Counted among the Sioux, the Crow, the Blackfoot, the Apache, the Cherokee, the Cheyenne, the Kiowa, the Flathead, the Ute, the Arapahoe, the Pawnee, the Shoshone, and others. The first in importance was to strike an enemy with bow and arrow, tomahawk, or later a rifle's bullet. Another important Coup was "riding an enemy down." To ride an enemy down was to knock the Warrior off his Horse and finish him off with hand-to-hand combat. To steal an enemy's Horse was another important Coup. Stealing Horses was to steal the means of retaliation, and therefore, steal Warrior-power, or strength. The fourth Counting of Coup was to steal the opponent's weapon. The fifth was to steal some of the enemy's Medicine, which could be his Shield, his Eagle feathers, his Medicine Pouch, a beaded medallion, a Buffalo-bone chestplate, or scalplock. A scalp-lock is one tiny piece of hair that is braided with some kind of Medicine representing that person's Allies, connections, or strengths. A scalplock can have a strip of hide, a feather, a tooth, beads, and/or other small objects tied to it. To cut the braided scalplock from a Warrior's hair was to strip him of his War Medicine. The final recognized form of Counting Coup was to destroy a Warrior's Lodge or Tipi, take his woman, or personal possessions. This form of Counting Coup was not as honorable and was used only as a last resort, to humiliate rather than to conquer another Warrior's Medicine.

Among the Plains Indians, if a death occurred, the raiding party would smear black paint on their faces when returning to camp. The women would start their mourning trills and cries at the first sight of the Black Faces. The grieving family would be relieved from the duties of daily life and work for four days. The four days of mourning honored the Winds of the Four Directions, which would take the loved one to the Sky Lodge after having "dropped his robe" (dying). If the raid was not victorious, the entire Tribe observed the death with mourning. If the Warriors had Counted Coup, the grieving family was taken care of and waited upon, but the Coup celebration would continue for the other Tribal members.

At the Coup feast, the leader of the war party or raiding band would give those who had witnessed the individual victories of their friends the honor of telling the events. A Warrior was honored by his friends and was not allowed to tell the story himself. This practice added another dimension to the celebration since a friend's pride in another Brother's accomplishments came into play. This insured the participation of those who had not accomplished an act of Coup personally and made them a part of the celebration as well. It also ruled out any embellishments on the part of those actually involved. To speak in an exaggerated manner was considered prideful and to lie was to lose face. A true witness was bound by honor to speak honestly of a Brother's courage or lack of it. If someone had shamed the Warrior Clan, it was spoken of in the Council of that Clan and never in front of the entire Tribe. A loss of courage was a blemish on all of the Brothers of the Warrior Clan and since they acted as an elite group or unit, "shame-faces" were not allowed to continue as members.

"To add a Coup Feather to one's Bonnet" is an expression that comes from the idea of personal achievement or accomplishment that will aid or assist the whole. In the concept of Counting Coup, jealousy and envy have no place. There is no victory when anyone is belittled through the boasting of another. There is no honor in self-importance.

Actions speak louder than words when victory is sought. A Coup Feather is never awarded to someone who intended to do something but did not follow through. Walking One's Talk is the essence of true victory. As reflected by our Ancestors, the victory of the Coup Feather is based upon the high ideals of Eagle. Those ideals are followed by action. Just as Eagle marks and kills its prey, so must we mark and attack the weaknesses that keep us from fulfilling our words. As Counting Coup is a personal victory that affects the whole, so is the war we wage on the old patterns that keep us from knowing world peace. These enemies can be ignorance, inner-conflict, envy, jealousy, willful pride, laziness, fear, bitterness, hatred, greed, bigotry, gossip, resentment, and broken promises.

Our modern Medicine Shields are made from truth, our weapons are living that truth, and our prize is our future, bringing the healing of Earth Mother's children. Every Two-legged has been asked to accomplish these Coups through the discovery and healing of the Self.

The Application

The war cry has been shouted and victory is assured if you have received the Counting Coup card. You are being put on notice that a personal victory is in the works. You may have overcome a long-time challenge or conquered an opponent, so now it is time to share your victory with others. Whether the victory is one of a spiritual nature or of winning a lottery ticket makes no difference. You are to honor yourself at this time and be grateful for this blessing.

Counting Coup represents the success of forward movement and the acknowledgment of right action. You have been true to yourself and are being rewarded for staying on The Sacred Path. Congratulations! Victory is sweet but sweeter still when the spoils are shared with those you care for. Share the joy of your Coup with those who want to see you winning. Remember: Warriors who had Counted Coup always took care of the widowed, aged, and feeble. The material victories shared bring further honor, providing another Coup Feather for those willing to Give-Away.

≡ Rites of Passage ≡

The changes of many winters
   mark the cycles of the Wheel,
The lines across my ancient face
   show all that I can feel,
The nature of my passage
   remains a mystery,
For in my heart of hearts,
   I hold my destiny.
When I was but an infant
   in the beginning of time,
I marveled at the wonder of
   discoveries I did find.
Now that I am ancient,
   I have learned once again,
That the weight of every winter,
   brings discovery like a friend.

≡ 21 ≡

Rites of Passage

CHANGE

The Teaching

The Rites of Passage in Native American Tradition refer to the changes from birth to childhood to adulthood or passing from life to the Spirit World. The exceptions to this rule are special Rites of Passage that occur in certain Medicine Societies when a member is being initiated into the mysteries of new levels of awareness. These new levels of understanding and spiritual knowledge are opened only to those who have earned the right through the way they live their lives. To have earned the right to pass through the Golden Door that leads to all other levels of imagination and awareness involves many years of proven good conduct, demonstration of spiritual gifts, as well as the willingness of Elders to pass down that kind of Medicine.

The Rites of Passage that every Native American goes through as a part of the growing process are quite different. The particular Rites of Passage used in ancient times for Native boys, usually involved the ownership and care of the boy's first Horse. This was the first step to manhood and began a rather long process of learning what it meant to be a Warrior. The second step involved going with tried and true hunters to observe and learn how to track and eventually to become a provider. In this case, the young man was taken as a moccasin carrier. Moccasins were in need of changing rather often if it was snowy or wet and the young man was responsible for making each party's member's dry moccasins available for quick changes.

As the young man learned more and more of the proper conduct for a Warrior, he was given more responsibility until finally he was chosen to be responsible for a hunting party or raiding party of his own. If one Horse or man was lost when he was in charge, it was a disgrace to his judgment and the honor of his family's name. Becoming the successful leader of a hunting or raiding party marked the end of adolescence and the beginning of manhood.

Young women, on the other hand, had several Rites of Passage ceremonies as they came into womanhood. The first was among the women of the Moon Lodge and marked the first menstrual flow or Moontime. In my Choctaw Tradition, the girl's mother or eldest female relative would go to the creek and cut a piece of moss from the bank and return to the Moon Lodge. The moss was then placed so that a couple of drops of Moontime blood would touch it and then it was replanted along the creek bed. This ceremony was to establish a link to the Earth Mother and to rejoice in the fertility of the young girl coming of age. This young woman was then acknowledged by her Sisters as a Mother of the Creative Force and a Mother-Nurturer of the dreams of the Tribe. She was honored as an equal in the Women's Council and this coming of age was celebrated by a feast given by her family. This feast was a public ceremony that involved the parents of the woman-child. In this ceremony, the Tribe gathered for the feast given by the girl's parents and everyone came in their finest ceremonial buckskins with Painted Faces. This would be the first time that the young maiden painted her face with a red moon, which marked her first Moontime and therefore, womanhood.

In the Rites of Passage Ceremony that preceded the feast, the maternal Grandparents would ceremonially tie the parents together at the waist with a braided buckskin rope. The rope, about eighteen feet, was then extended to the young woman and tied around her waist. The young woman would then dance around her parents, stopping at the Four Directions to call out her gratefulness to each direction for her parents' guidance and love during her childhood. The parents acted as the hub on a wheel and turned toward each direction with their daughter as she danced around them. The circle was made four times and with each round, the daughter called to each direction with a prayer of gratitude for some past kindness her parents had shown her.

At the end of the young woman's dance, the parents would publicly acknowledge her right to make her own decisions. The parents would then speak of their daughter's virtues and talents and of their continued love for her. The assurance was made at this time that the parents would be available for further guidance but would not interfere with her life as she was now responsible for all of her future decisions. The daughter then cut the buckskin rope in a ceremonial manner marking the final cutting of the umbilical cord, and joyous cries would go up from all observers. Then the feasting would begin and could last for up to two days depending upon the ability of the family to provide for the observers.

In Sioux Tradition, another Rite of Passage for a young woman marks her reaching a marriageable age. This ritual is called Hunka by the Dakotas and involves the announcement of "open season" on the young girl for any young man who wishes to court the young woman in question. In the Hunka ceremony, the girl is carried from her lodge to a Ceremonial Lodge by members of the Warrior Clan, who are her father's age, and set down in the presence of an honored Elder male who will discuss with her the responsibilities of being an honored woman of the Tribe. She will receive a new dress, which is the symbol of her new role in the Tribe, and will be expected to follow Tribal Law, spoken and unspoken, regarding the conduct of women.

In all Traditions, each woman as a Mother of the Creative Force, is called upon to nurture children, the feeble, the ill of health, the Elders, the Warrior at her side as well as to nurture the dreams of the People. Native women are held in high regard because they follow the Path of Beauty. The Sacred Path is one of loyalty, compassion for others, hospitality, sharing, sense of family, use and development of personal talents, discretion, inner-strength, marital fidelity, and selflessness balanced with a good appreciation of Self.

Another Rite of Passage is the last Rite made for Tribal Members when they pass into the Blue Road of Spirit. Some call it Dropping Their Robe, others call it going to the Other Side Camp and other Tribes call it going to the Sky Lodge. The Plains Tribes used to place their loved ones on the death scaffold, which some call the Sky Lodge. The Pueblos bury their dead so they may return to the Underworld and nurture the Earth Mother with their bodies. The prehistoric Red Ochre People covered the bodies of their dead with red ochre and placed them in Mother Earth's womb in a fetal position to be reborn in another time. Some seafaring Tribes in the Northwest would bury their dead under a cairnlike mound of shells to assist the dead in listening, via the shells, for the time to reawaken and be born again in the physical. Other Tribes had burial mounds that contained all of the deceased's Sacred Medicine Objects, which would carry the spirit, with his or her talents, into the Other Side Camp to assist those still in the physical. In every Native American Tradition, death is seen as a new cycle of learning.

This final Rite of Passage insured a safe and speedy transition into the Spirit World. The popular movies have called this transition "the happy hunting ground." This is a slang term used by the White Eyes to denote the joy that Native Americans feel upon returning to the Ancestors after having successfully completed their Earth Walk. Every type of Rite of Passage marks a major change in the way Native Americans view their life path. Each Rite of Passage brings new privilege to experience the beauty of each phase of life. From the newborn in the Cradleboard to the oldest Elder, each life-cycle adds to the wisdom and experience of the Tribe as a whole.

Beginning with the Birth Rite, which welcomes the new infant into the Tribal Family, and ending with the Death Rite, which sees the graduation of that spirit into a new life, each Rite of Passage is celebrated as a part of the Sacred Hoop or Medicine Wheel of life-cycles.

The Application

A Rite of Passage marks a time of some momentous change in life. If you have drawn this card, you are being asked to make note of the growth and change that is occurring because it will shape your future. The changes may be small or gradual, but you are changing. The changes may be drastic and earth shaking, leaving a sense of confusion, but each one is benefiting your growth in some manner.

The Rite of Passage card can also speak of need for a change if you have lost the magic and spontaneity of life. Only you can make the decision to change the doldrums to excitement. If this decision is made, be ready to fly with Eagle and experience the new freedoms those changes can bring.

In all cases, change is the key. Remember, if the moment you are experiencing is not beautiful, recreate it and you will have initiated your own Rite of Passage.

≡ Heyokah ≡

Aho Heyokah!
　　Make me laugh so I'll be human again.
Allow me to see my crooked path
　　And the Trickster as my friend.

Aho Heyokah!
　　How contrary you can be,
Yet you make me learn.

Aho Heyokah!
　　The joke's on me,
But next time it's your turn!

≡ 22 ≡

Heyokah

HUMOR/OPPOSITES

The Teaching

The Heyokah is a contrary clown who holds total wisdom and teaches the People through laughter and opposites. This Sacred Trickster is one who makes you wonder if what they are saying or doing is actually correct, thereby making you think and figure it out for yourself. When people are made to think on their own, the wobbly beliefs that have been a rubber crutch for them in the past are tested. If the rubber crutch gives way and they end up on the ground on their rump, a lesson was learned. If they stop and think, test out a teaching for themselves and it stands in good stead, the wobbly belief becomes a Knowing System for their lives.

This Divine Trickster is called Heyokah by the Plains Tribes and Koshari by the Hopi and Pueblo Indians. Many Tribes have Trickster Teachers who dress in costume for Ceremony and wear regular clothing in daily life. Their jokes do not stop just because it is not a feast day. All Heyokahs operate through opposites. The Heyokah's purported wisdom, imparted to a seeker, could be the exact opposite of the answers the person would find for the Self. The laughter surrounding the results could be a lesson for the entire community.

The Heyokah is known for creating lessons at the expense of another's seriousness. Laughter is the ultimate lesson that breaks the bonds that destroy balance in people. If the Heyo-kah is successful, all is taken in good fun, and the bonds of old habits, no longer helpful, are broken. The Medicine Ally of the Heyokah is Coyote. The Heyokah is a master at Coyote Medicine and can use the joking part of Coyote's nature to trick others into enlightened states of understanding. Occasionally the Coyote Medicine will backfire and zap the Heyo-kah in a blind spot. If this happens, the true Heyokah will take it in stride and laugh at the backfire, learning from the lesson along with others.

Native People understood the value of being good sports. In earlier times it was not considered "losing face" to have the Heyokah play a trick on someone. In fact it was an honor to be singled out for a trick that contained a valuable spiritual lesson. Each Tribal Member was a valuable part of the whole, and many times the joke had consequences for more than one person. Everyone seeing the actual prank or talking of it later could relate those events to personal situations and grow from the lesson. All are forced to reflect on how they would react if they were the person the joke was played on. The Heyokah is able to master the art of balancing the sacredness with irreverence.

The true art of knowing how and when to use Heyokah tactics comes through the ability to laugh at one's Self while being compassionate in using the Trickster elements of teaching in a way that is not cruel or self-imposing. An experienced Heyokah will know how sensitive a student is and would never use a trick on that student to create more pain. In this situation, the Heyokah would make a joke and become the laughing stock of the situation so that the student could reflect on it through another's experience. This art of self-sabotage is planned and in no way makes the balanced Heyokah feel lesser or abused. The joy of the wise Elder within the Heyokah knows well that the results have created growth in another. The lesson is complete and even the self-sabotage was staged and yet, served its purpose.

The Sacred Medicine Path of the Heyokah can involve diminishing fear through laughter. Many people are frightened by the mystery of the Void. They have to be tricked out of their fear so that they can see that their self-created "boogeyman" was the only obstacle to Divine Connection. The Heyokah excels in situations where stubbornness stops growth. If a Heyokah knows that someone is stubborn and has to do it his way, the Trickster will tell him to do the exact opposite. Many days later we might find the Heyokah alone in the lodge giggling at the wondrous Medicine Story moving through the camp. The stubborn person had done exactly what Heyokah said not to do and had a mystical experience that was life changing. Only the Heyokah knew that due to Stubborn's refusal to be guided, the trick had worked and spiritual growth ensued.

Since the Magical Coyote is the Divine Trickster's Ally, all of the antics of Coyote are suspect. When a hunter tracks a Coyote, the trail will double back on itself many times and can fool even the most experienced tracker to the point of total frustration. Anyone trying to guess a Heyokah's next move can likewise become befuddled. Coyote teaches Two-leggeds to find joy in their own foolishness. When the Heyokah calls upon Coyote to assist him in keeping prying eyes off his trail, Coyote will assist in a multitude of ways.

I learned my first Coyote lesson in Mexico when Joaquin, my Medicine Teacher, wanted me to see how ridiculous my seriousness had become. We spent one whole day gathering dried Cow dung, Rabbit pellets, Coyote, Dog, and Owl waste and carefully placing each in an old tin bucket. The next day we spent mixing all of it together, crushing each part into powder and slowly adding water to make a paste. After this was completed, I was told to mark a circle in the earth with string and a stick making sure that the circle was perfectly round. Then Joaquin told me to fill the tiny groove in the soil with all of the paste I had made from all of the feces. I was very careful to make a perfect circle and not to let any of the circle be crooked. Joaquin praised my work and how careful I had been during the two-day process. He then told me to enter the circle and sit in the center until I understood the value of the lesson.

I sat there for at least three hours, thinking that maybe this was a way to contact the Power Animals. Finally Coyote came into my consciousness, took one look at me, and rolled on the ground in side-splitting laughter. Coyote was laughing so hard he could not speak. I was fascinated, while still sitting in my circle of poop, serious as ever. In between his guffaws, Coyote spit out the words that taught me my lesson. "For the past three days you've been examining other people's shit!" he screamed. "Now you've surrounded yourself with it and you are so serious you can't even see how ridiculous you look."

I started to laugh at myself as I imagined how Joaquin must be rolling in hysterics at the joke he had played on me. I wondered how he could have kept a straight face for two days. It finally came to me that I had spent the previous days worrying about the problems of others. All of these worries had left me, in effect, sitting in a circle of others people's mental garbage.

The lesson hit me hard, and I laughed until I was aching with no breath and tears ran down my face. It has taken me many years to master the lesson and I still get sucked in the drama of others at times. Joaquin was an excellent Teacher and even now he will come to me, in spirit, and break my seriousness with more Heyokah antics.

The primary lessons of the Heyokah trick us into revelations rather than giving us all the answers. Heyokah is needed when we refuse to allow ourselves alternatives. The view will always expand if we use the Divine Medicine of laughter. Nothing is beyond repair. We may need to use comedy to crack a smile so we can reclaim our Sacred Space.

Heyokah Medicine can be called upon through Coyote. Remember that the Divine Trickster is the perfect integration of all things wise and foolish, sacred and irreverent. When we ask for those lessons, we need to be prepared for adventure. We need to be willing to laugh and to have others laugh with us. We will have achieved the ultimate union of opposites when we learn to celebrate more than we mourn. The time has come to laugh and reclaim our divine right to find pleasure in the sacredness of being human.

The Application

If the Trickster has appeared on your horizon, you are in for a barrel of laughs. You may be doing exactly the opposite of what you need to be doing and are about to get busted for it. Stop leaking your creative energy on other people's problems or high drama. Stop being so serious and crack a smile, or Coyote will dog your dreams. Remember that some days you are the fireplug and some days you are the Dog. That goes for everyone, so don't let getting pooped on get you down. Learning through laughter or opposites can be fun.

The keynote to the Heyokah card is to lighten up and start balancing the sacredness with irreverence. If you are just being stubborn, it may be time to create a contrary lesson that will force you to crack up, crack a smile, or trick you into going into the crack in the universe to find out what's really important!

≡ Smoke Signals ≡

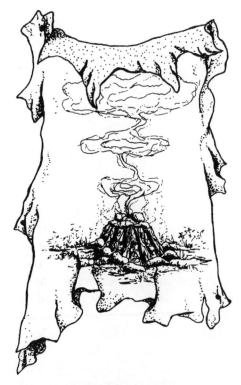

Sacred language of the sky
   Please speak to me.
You who live where Eagle flies,
   Spirit I can see,
In the form of Cloud People,
   Coming from the Fire.
Sacred smoke you call me
   To be my desires.
Let me travel skyward
   With a heart so true,
That may fly like Eagle
   And be close to you.

≡ 23 ≡

Smoke Signals

INTENT

___

The Teaching

The Red Race has understood and utilized many unspoken languages for centuries. We have been taught to read the signs in the faces of the Cloud People; the changes in the weather; the movement of the herds; the habits of our Brothers and Sisters, the Creature-beings; the cries and howls of the wild; the messages in our Medicine Dreams; and the language of the heart.

Smoke Signals are another universal unspoken language of Native Americans. This Sky Language is achieved through lighting a fire of mixed green and dry wood and using a wet blanket to smother and then release clouds of smoke. In times of battle, each Tribe used different signals to mark a path of action or to change their secret plans. This constant activity kept the enemy bewildered and confused.

Smoke Signals are the bridge between the Earth and Sky. The smoke from the Pipe is the essence of our prayers in visual form, traveling to Great Mystery. In this manner, All Our Relations are put on notice that the prayers of the People are traveling to the Great Star Nation to be heard. The Smoke Signals used as communication between scouts sitting long distances apart are no different than the Smoke Signals sent through the Pipe to Great Mystery. Both are unspoken languages that signal the sender's intent.

Few people know that the first revolution in the United States began with two unspoken languages. These were the knotted cord carried by runners to various locations and Smoke Signals. In 1680 the brave, yet peaceful, Pueblo Indians had been made a slave race by the invading Spaniards. The Rio Grande Valley of New Mexico was formerly known as Aztlan. It was the homeland of the Aztecs long before Cortez and Coronado began their quests for gold. Each Pueblo had a different set of laws and a different language; however, all had lived in peace with each other and in harmony with the Earth Mother for centuries.

After many years of cruel domination, a Pueblo Medicine Man named Popi united each Pueblo and helped to orchestrate the revolt that crushed the hold of the Spanish. This brilliant plan signaled the return to power by those who lived with the land rather than taking from it. Runners were sent to the first Pueblo with cords knotted in a certain manner but were caught and killed by the Spanish. The Smoke Signals that told of revolution were issued forth three days later. The runners' attempt was pure subterfuge and it worked. The Spaniards had tortured two young runners who had carried knotted ropes and were told that the revolt would take place on the fourth day after the runners were shot. The actual revolt began on the third day and was begun by Smoke Signals.

The possibility of victory for the peaceful Pueblo people struck a chord in the hearts of the raiding Apaches who had plagued the Pueblos for many years. The Apaches joined the fight in some areas and the Spanish were ousted from the mountains and valleys of Aztlan. The intent of the Red Race was to reclaim their right to their own Knowing Systems and to use their own Medicine. The Masks, Kachina Dolls, Rattles, Drums, Eagle feathers, and other sacred objects had been burned by the orders of the Catholic Padres in an effort to force Christianity upon the Pueblos. The Smoke Signals sent the intent of the People to the Sky Nation as a resounding cry for freedom and they were victorious. The unity of one heart and one mind among the different Tribes who could not speak each other's languages was accomplished through the unspoken tongues of Smoke Signals and knotted ropes.

Smoke Signals are the language of the Sky Nation that relay the intention of the sender to those spirits who understand the heart's whispers. The answers to the Smoke Signal's questions can be read in the faces of the Cloud People. When Smoke Signals are sent to Great Mystery via the Fire or Pipe, a seeker is asking for an inner-knowing about some question. Smoke-forms are one way in which spirit can be visually seen by humankind and the manifestation of these Medicine Helpers can bring serenity to the heart of a seeker. If, on a Vision Quest, a person lights a Fire to send the heart's intent to the Sky Nation, the answers may come to that person in forms created by the Cloud People.

On a night years ago, I was floating in a natural hot spring looking up into the fullness of Grandmother Moon high above me in the starry night. I had built a Fire twenty feet in front of me where the ravine was flat and treeless. I had gone to this special place alone to seek some answers for my hungry heart. The tears of frustration rolled from my eyes and sent silver circles into the effervescent waters of the pool. I sought the answers of how to return to the city and deal with the lack of substance I found in those who were trying to be "somebody" instead of being who and what they were.

Then, I saw an ancient Medicine Man walk to my Fire and lift an old red trade blanket. He walked toward me and dipped the blanket into the pool, wrung it out, and moved back toward the Fire. As he turned toward the Fire and began to sing, I recognized Grandfather Taquitz, who is one of the Ancestors who guides my path. Grandfather Taquitz beseeched the spirits of the Four Directions. The energy began to build as he sang the chant in which he called to the Great Star Nation to hear my prayers and speak to my heart.

Each time I spoke an internal prayer, Grandfather Taquitz would move the trade blanket over the Fire and then raise it, allowing the Smoke Signal that represented my prayer to rise in the indigo night. At first, a stray Cloud Person or two drifted by and then others came to see which Two-legged and which Ancestor spirit had called them. The Chief Cloud Person was to the right of Grandmother Moon and began changing form as the Smoke touched his face, producing the faces of Buffalo, Wolf, Eagle, and Bear. My Allies had come to greet me and give me answers! I was overjoyed and nearly missed the exit of Grandfather Taquitz, who held a gleam in his eyes and a knowing smile traced across his mouth.

I floated in the warm waters of my Earth Mother's womb and heard the messages of my Medicine Helpers with my heart. Buffalo told me that Two-leggeds who hurt one another were those deluded by the fear of scarcity. These humans had lost their trust in Great Mystery and the Field of Plenty. Their need to be connected to something or someone they believed to be important was based upon the fear that their talents were not equal to those of others. Wolf spoke and told me that the Pathfinders of my world would never need to boast about who they were or where they were headed. Those who broke new ground for others to follow were too busy to be hurt by another person who claimed, out of envy, to be who they were not. Eagle spoke to me and said that true freedom was only to be found by those that found illumination through the truth that lived inside their hearts. Bear then appeared and spoke of the strength I needed to find inside of myself in order to Walk My Talk in the city, away from the womb of my Earth Mother. Bear said that the tomorrows are met when each person seeks strength in the truth of today.

Knowing that my intent had reached the Sky Nation through Grandfather Taquitz's Smoke Signals and songs gave me new inspiration and purpose. I was ready to hold my truth high and to use my intent to touch the hearts of my fellow Two-leggeds. I no longer needed to be hurt by lies or to take on the pain of those that "talked their walk" instead of being the beauty that Great Mystery had created them to be.

The Application

The Smoke Signals being sent your way call for clear intent. If your purpose or direction in life has been muddled, now is the time to "walk your talk." The signals you send to others may be bringing unwanted attention your way. Observe what it is that you are putting out and straighten up so that you will attract the kind of experiences and people you want inside your Sacred Space.

Another message is a reminder from the Spirit World. If you lack direction or have unclear intent as to what your needs are, the Allies cannot assist you with those requests. Clear intent brings rewards on all levels and will speed your growth process. Pay attention and take advantage of the power of your intentions. You've won half the battle when your clear intent removes the barriers to decisive action.

≡ Council Fire ≡

Elders gathered
   The fire of wisdom's light.
Words . . .
   Decisions . . .
      Conclusions . . . all through the night.

≡ 24 ≡

Council Fire

DECISIONS

The Teaching

It is an ancient Native American custom to call a Council Fire when decisions need to be made that affect the whole Tribe or Nation. To sit on any Council as a representative of the People, a person would have to have proven through example that he or she was worthy of the honor. Many years of being truthful, brave, compassionate, sharing, a good listener, a fair judge, a discreet counselor, and honored Tribal member went into the making of the Council of Chiefs. These same qualities were necessary for any member of the Council of Women, War Councils, Treaty Councils, Clan Councils, or Medicine Councils. In every decision regarding the life-paths that could change the destiny of the People, a Council had to be called so that every Sacred Point of View could be heard and every possibility explored.

As late as the 1800s, travelers on the water ways of Turtle Island would see great fires built in the clearings in the forests. There the Elders huddled in their blankets sitting in a circle making decisions long into the night. These Council Fires remind Native People that our destiny is determined by those whom we trust, who have walked the Earth, and gathered much knowledge in their lives. When they speak of the Elders it is with great reverence because the Elders have proven the value of their wisdom through guiding each Nation with self-less courage and wisdom.

Before any Council begins, the Pipe is shared and All Our Relations are asked to add their Medicine to empower those gathered. Great Mystery and Mother Earth are asked to add their wisdom to the Council Fire. The powers of the Four Directions are beseeched to add illumination, trust and innocence, inner-knowing and introspection, wisdom and gratitude to the gifts the Elders bring. Then the Creature-being relations, who are Winged-ones, Four-leggeds, No-leggeds, Creepy-crawlers, and Finned-ones are asked to be present. Then the Stone People, the Standing People, the Cloud People, Grandfather Sun, and Grandmother Moon are invited to be a part of the Council Fire. The Great Star Nation and all Sisters and Brothers from other galaxies are invited to assist in decision making, along with the Four Clan Chiefs of Air, Earth, Water, and Fire. All of this Good Medicine is put into the Pipe; then the smoke from the Pipe brings the spirits of All Our Relations into the Council as advisers.

Any personal burden is left outside the circle. Any talent for discovering solutions is brought into the circle. Any disagreement between Council Members is handled by Burying the Hatchet before the Pipe is smoked. Parliamentary procedure is observed by using the Talking Stick and the Answering Feather (see card 15). All viewpoints are heard when the subject being addressed needs opinions or solutions. After every member has stated his or her viewpoint, a common decision is reached by vote. Benjamin Franklin and Thomas Jefferson, who visited the Iroquois Peace Confederacy and sat in Council with the Clan Mothers of the Six Nations, were inspired by our form of democracy and incorporated their findings into the United States Constitution, using our wisdom for the Bill of Rights.

Every Council is ended with a prayer of gratitude and a meal or feast, depending upon the purpose of the meeting.

When the course followed by an entire Nation depends upon the decisions made at a Council Fire, great importance is given to those decisions. All conclusions drawn and laws made will rule everyone in the Tribe. Any Tribal Member choosing to refuse a Council decision will have to answer to the Council. To lose face by refusing any new rule or law can mean expulsion from the Tribe or some form of amends making if the offense is small.

Most Councils of Nations are made up of Chiefs, Clan Mothers, Elders, Historians, Medicine People, Counselors, and Seers. The exceptions are the Councils of younger people, or Councils of Societies, which combine the wisdom of the Elders with the new ideas held by youth. In the case of a combined Council of youth and Elders, the viewpoints of the new generations are looked upon as equal to those of the older generations. The guidance is provided by the Elders and the new ideas and creativity are the gift of youthful expression. Our Holy People are Seers who can discern what the future will hold for generations to come. Having seen the vision of these aspects of future, the Elders can approach the ideas supplied by the youth of our Nations with wisdom and discernment.

The decision making process that guides the path of Native Americans is multifaceted. All Sacred Viewpoints of those affected by the decisions are treated with respect. If someone has received a Vision or Medicine Dream regarding the wisdom of the final decision, that information is reviewed. The manner in which a situation was handled in the past is taken into consideration. The way in which a probable decision will affect the lives of the People is carefully weighed. The desired outcome is always to keep the Peace. If the decision involves two parties at odds with one another, Tribal Law is consulted to bring a fair judgment.

When someone calls a Council, that person must have the courage to accept the decisions of that Council with grace.

For example, if a man is not being fair with a neighbor and receives a judgment against him for poor behavior, he must follow the Council's decision on how to right the situation. To admit wrongdoing and to make amends builds character and makes a Tribe or Nation stronger. There is no losing face when a person is willing to make amends. Honor is found in the willingness to change. This act of courage, which is the willingness to right a wrong, allows everyone to see how the offender is once again walking the Sacred Path.

One comes to realize a sense of unity when observing the way our Ancestors had of making democratic Council decisions. When the good of the whole is placed before the good of the few, all are assured of a future filled with abundance. These teachings stress that until all the People are doing well, in truth none of the People do well. This idea encompasses all races and creeds because Grandfather Sun shines on us all. We then respect the value of the individual and acknowledge the need to nurture the Self first so that the talents each individual brings into the world can feed all of the People. If these guidelines are followed, the Children of Earth will break the bonds of inequality and dictatorship.

The Application

If you have been waffling over what to do next, the Council Fire card is insisting that you make a decision. There can be no forward movement if you fail to decide which trail will lead out of the swamp and into the forests. It takes courage to make changes in your life and all changes must begin with a decision. Do it and don't look back. Life awaits you in all of its beauty.

If the decision of another has left you in a precarious position, make new decisions of your own. There is no need to make your decisions based upon another's. Consider all possibilities and how your decision affects others, then be courageous enough to act. Find your truth and stick to it.

≡ Pow-Wow ≡

Gathering of tipis
New friends and old
Trading of stories
Told and retold

A blanket for a basket
A horse as a prize
Footraces and dances
Night 'til sunrise

Exchanging the goodness
That each member brings
Allowing the heartstrings
Of our Nation to sing.

≡ 25 ≡

Pow-Wow

SHARING/QUICKENING

The Teaching

Each year when the richness of summer moved across the Earth Mother and Old Man Winter was just a memory, most Bands and Tribes of each Nation gathered for what has become known as a Pow-Wow. This time of gathering was a "quickening" for the People. As the growth of a child in the womb feeds its mother's heart with joy, these gatherings produced a quickening of talents that fed the People.

Pow-Wows brought old friends together again and many a night was filled with the stories of what had occurred since the last gathering. The sharing of new methods of tracking, fishing, and hunting filled the men's circles and the women shared new techniques for beading, tanning hides, making foods and remedies. The Medicine Circles discussed new uses for plants, the needs of the People, Visions, and Medicine Dreams. The Warrior Clans told of acts of bravery and Counting Coup. The Black Lodges shared women's teachings and shared dreams of the People that needed nurturing by women. The children shared new games and traded stories they had learned from their Grandparents. Everyone was filled once again, renewed by the sense of unity.

Since many Tribes still do not allow marriage among the same Clan, it was during the Pow-Wows of long ago that young people found life-mates. Eligible mates might not be the right age in one's own band and so many couples pledged life-long love at the summer gatherings.

The Making Of Relatives Ceremony usually took place at the Pow-Wow and has been called Blood-Brother Ceremony by some. This honoring or commingling of blood ceremony forms a lasting bond between two people, making each responsible to the other for life. The Medicine Allies of both participants are called through ceremony to be present. The Powers of the Seven Directions are honored and beseeched to witness the union. Then each participant cuts the hand of the other. The two small cuts on the bottom outside portion of the palm, below the pinky finger represent two family lines. Then the hands are joined and held together while the two new relatives dance, sing a song, and circle a fire four times. In some Traditions, these two, now joined, jump the fire together.

Since all women are already Sisters through their Moon-time cycles, the ceremony is called Blood Brother or Making Of Relatives. A man and a woman can become Brother and Sister or two men can become Brothers, but it is unnecessary for two women to come together in this fashion because they are already together as potential Mothers of the Creative Force. The union of the Sisterhoods was strengthened every year during Pow-Wow with the sharing of new ideas and talents that were reviewed in the Women's Councils.

Other activities of the Pow-Wow included games that high-lighted the prowess of young Warriors. These could be races on horseback, in canoes, or on foot as well as hunting competitions that provided the food for feasts on special occasions. Everyone wanted to bring honor by representing their Tribe, band, or Clan, and the games were very competitive. The beautiful thing about the Pow-Wow was that it was just as great an honor to be bested, finding joy in the winner's abilities, as it was to win. To be a spoilsport was to lose face among all Tribal Members.

Swapping and trading were important parts of any gathering and to make a fair trade that pleased both parties was considered an art. Many hides, beads, knives, bows, arrows, herbs, blankets, Horses, pots, and Buffalo Robes changed hands during the Pow-Wow. Etiquette was of utmost importance. It was considered rude to look directly at someone else's lodge or possessions. If it was known how much you liked something, the trade could go by the wayside. You could be asked to give too much for the object that you admired, and you would then lose face with family members. Each person had to feel that he or she was getting a fair deal.

Pow-Wow nights were filled with dances depicting the acts of bravery each Warrior Clan and Hunting Clan had achieved during the preceding year. Some nights were filled with the Medicine Stories of the Twisted Hairs, or Storytellers, who were teacher/historians for the Nation. Other nights were feast nights, if the hunting had been good. Sometimes one family would sponsor a feast to mark a special occasion such as a son pledging to Sun Dance, a daughter's first Moontime, a Counting of Coup on an enemy, a betrothal or Making of Relatives. Every reason to celebrate life was shared with the whole Nation during Pow-Wow.

During this summer gathering, plans were made for the Sun Dance and those Warriors who had pledged the previous year met with their sponsors to prepare through purification and fasting. The purpose of each year's Sun Dance was discussed in the Council of Elders and then the Council of Chiefs. Every year, the foremost needs of all the People were the object of the prayers surrounding the Sun Dance. At the end of summer when the Pow-Wow was ending, the Sun Dance was performed. Other Ceremonies were shared during Pow-Wow, but the highlight was the Sun Dance because it showed Great Mystery that the People were faithful and willing to give back to the Earth Mother for the sustenance they had received during the previous year (see card 6).

Today Pow-Wows and Mountain Man Rendezvous are springing up across our Nation to gather the People together again. These are gatherings of energy, talents, and people of like mind as in ancient times. Swapping, storytelling, and the selling, trading, or bartering of food and goods are central to the Pow-Wow. The Earth Mother sings her joy when these gatherings produce unity rather than separation. Each pilgrim that goes to a Pow-Wow comes home with new and different ideas about how to reconnect to the Earth Mother. This new alliance with others is the quickening that brings the Children of Earth together.

Since Pow-Wows also gathered the best in all of the Tribes to mark the strength of a Nation in days long gone, so does the idea of the Pow-Wow teach us how to gather the best of our energies and talents today. Coming together to share our new discoveries and information will strengthen our ability to heal ourselves and live in harmony with our planet. Many Clans and Medicine Societies are beginning to share information as we embark upon the dawning of the Fifth World of Peace. There is no place for secrecy or jealousy in this new world we are creating together. The Warriors of the Rainbow represent all Traditions, colors, and paths joining as one. The quickening is upon us and we will be able to use this sharing of energy and talents to insure a stronger Planetary Tribe.

The soldier of the Fourth World has no place among the Warriors of the Fifth World of Peace. A soldier stands at the outer edge of his or her Sacred Space and fights others and their different ideas. The Warriors of the Rainbow stand in the same outer edge of their Sacred Space, facing inward, confronting the elements within themselves that keep them from honoring all paths equally and as one. The gathering of the Rainbow Warriors is the quickening that signals the rebirth of the Earth Tribe. The Talking Drums are calling all of the Children of Earth to the Pow-Wow that will mark the sharing of those of like hearts.

The Application

If the Talking Drums have signaled a Pow-Wow, you are being put on notice to gather together with others of like mind and exchange ideas. The quickening of some aspect of your life will be aided if you use a support system and see what type of support you can call upon from others.

The Pow-Wow card is marking a time of calling in your markers. You may need assistance or just a friend to be a sounding board. Your focus will become clearer, and you may receive the boost you need just from an encouraging word or two.

The quickening is inside of you and speaks of the time just preceding birth. Whatever you are giving birth to at this time can be assisted by gathering your friends around you for the needed support.

≡ Warbonnet ≡

Warbonnet of the Warrior Clan
  Honors you have earned.
Eagle Feathers
  Lofty thoughts
    Courage you have learned.

Teach us of the forward thrust
  Advancing to the right
Parlay now,
  Council Fire,
    Wisdom true and bright.

≡ 26 ≡

Warbonnet

ADVANCE

The Teaching

The Warbonnet was the symbol of a Chief, a Warrior whose counsel was sought because his wisdom was recognized by others; he had come to terms with his Personal Medicine. He had earned the right to wear the Warbonnet because he knew how to advance himself through acts of bravery, advance his Clan through Counting Coup, and advance his Tribe or Nation through providing for all its members. The Warbonneted Chiefs of Native America won the Coup Feathers in their bonnets through serving the needs of the People.

The feathers of the Warbonnet are not acquired from killing Eagles. Young Braves set traps with live Rabbits. The rock crevice below the nest where the Rabbit was tied had one or two young Braves silently waiting. When Eagle came for its dinner, the Braves would have to be very quick in snatching a tail feather or wing feather. If they were not so quick, the Eagle could maul their hands with razor sharp talons or beak. This way of getting an Eagle Feather was one of a young man's tests of courage on the pathway to becoming a Warrior and was one form of advancing his position in the Tribe.

Full Eagle wings, tails, or skulls were gifts from the Eagle Nation. When the Eagles were ready to "drop their robes" (die), they would call to a Warrior or Medicine Person in a dream or vision to let the Two-leggeds know where they would leave their bodies. In this way, a Medicine Person or Chief would have extra feathers to bestow on those who had earned the right to wear them.

The Eagle wing is divided into several categories of feathers. The spike-tip of the wing is considered the Destiny Feather. Through reading the markings on the Destiny Feather, a Medicine Person could tell what the Warrior's future would hold. The Destiny Feather could tell if the Warrior's life would be full of joy or sorrow, whether this Earth Walk would be a long one, or if the seeker was soon to join the Ancestors by Dropping the Robe. If the Destiny Feather had a broken quill, death was to be sudden and in youth. If the Destiny Feather had any markings, as with the Spotted Eagle Feather, the faces or shapes that appeared told the story of that person's future life events or their Allied Totems.

The small feathers on the cutting edge of the wing were called Hopes and Dreams Feathers. These feathers marked the path of the desired destiny of the owner. Often a pattern or set of events could be seen in the way the feathers grew from the skin. A trained Seer could divine the meaning for the wing's owner and accurately foretell the events and challenges that life would provide. The personal goals of the wing's owner were also shown in the markings of the feathers. If those goals were inclusive of the advancement of the Tribe or Nation, the selflessness of the seeker was sure to be blessed by the Grandfathers and Grandmothers in spirit. The selfish person's wing might show many challenges or trials that would, if approached in a humble manner, aid in changing the person's character for the better.

The four feathers in back of the spike-tip are Healing Feathers given to the Medicine People of the Tribe. These Healing Feathers were used to clean the Sacred Space around the body of a sick person. Since the Eagle feather is used to gather negative energy or bad Medicine with quick, firm strokes near the sick person's body, the spirit of the Eagle can be felt by the patient. Eagle represents spiritual illumination and if the illness was psychological, a person might feel a great deal better just by being feathered. The trained Medicine Person can see the energy needing to be removed and can use the Healing Spike Feather to remove the bad energy from the body.

The round-tipped feathers on the underside of the wing nearest the Eagle's body are Warrior Feathers as were the tail feathers. These Warrior Feathers were added to the Warbonnet. The Warrior Feathers are still used in a sacred manner and are passed down through families who carry the bloodline of the Chiefs in each Tribe. As Medicine People train the future generation to take their place, many Warrior Feathers as well as Healing Feathers are passed to those who honor the teachings and take responsibility for the roles they will inherit. These feathers are a part of the trust given to the future generation that embodies the advance of the Tribe or Nation. The passing of this Medicine is a reminder that the Tradition and Teachings will be preserved so that our way of life will be protected.

The Plume Feathers are from the Eagle's breast. One plume is tied into the scalplock of those who return from Vision Quest or complete the Rites of Passage. These special plumes are also used as ornamentation and protection on the Cradleboards of babies. They may represent the Eagle Medicine that may be carried in a Medicine Bundle. Since the plumes are much smaller than a full feather, for the sake of convenience, they could be placed in the Bundle that would be taken to the Sun Dance or on Vision Quest. The purpose of placing these plumes in the Medicine Bundle is to call upon guidance from Eagle's Medicine during these rituals.

If a Warrior Feather had a Coup mark on it, it was a sign that the feather had been taken from another in battle. This was to note the change of ownership and that the spirit of the feather now owed allegiance to the Warrior that Counted Coup on another brave. About five or six rows of the feather hairs are cut from the quill by the new owner and some feathers have several cuts denoting how many times the feather has changed hands.

If the quill of any feather is broken, the spirit of that feather has been released and is in the Without Fires Camp, also called the Other Side Camp. The world of spirit on the Blue Road is the place where all spirits live. Spirits are part of the Air Chief's Clan and ride on the wind. As each spirit desires to send a message to those on the Good Red Road of physical life, he or she will come on the Wind and take the form of a Cloud Person so that Two-leggeds can read the spirit Smoke Signals. Warriors learned to read the signs so that their Medicine would be strong and victory would be assured. It was through the signs of the Medicine Allies that the Warrior Clan knew when to wait and when to advance.

Every Chief who had acquired enough feathers for a Warbonnet had demonstrated certain qualities as a role model for the People, male and female alike. Warbonneted Chiefs were the strength of the People. They listened to the hearts of those they protected and never spoke in anger. Each Eagle feather represented a lesson learned in patience, bravery, Tribal etiquette, hunting, Medicine, leadership, Ceremony, Counting Coup, and the Father-protector role. The lessons gained by these Chiefs included spiritual illumination tempered by courage and the quick action necessary for proper leadership. The Warbonneted Chief showed leadership in times of battle, but he also exemplified the spiritual lessons that each feather in his Warbonnet represented. The message was loud and clear: each Warbonneted Chief was the holder of powerful gifts and abilities. Each Chief used the gifts Great Mystery had given him for the advancement of his people and by so doing was worthy of his position of leadership.

The Application

If the Warbonnet has appeared in your cards today, it is time to advance. Don't waste energy on going backward or staying in the doldrums. You are now able to move to the next step on the Sacred Path. Like a Warbonneted Chief, you have earned the right to learn the next set of life's mysteries. Take your Medicine Bundle and all of the strengths it represents and charge forward.

The advance can be on any level. Your spiritual, physical, mental, and emotional healings are understood through life's experiences. You can now approach your destiny with every feather you have earned marking your past victories and see the destiny you have chosen emerging before you. Your Medicine is strong and will allow the advancement you need at this time.

≡ Cradleboard ≡

Cradleboard of Creation
　　Protect this child from harm.
Child of all tomorrows
　　Sleep safely in my arms.
Until the time
　　　You will wake
　　　　Then you will be
　　　　　Able to respond in kind
　　　　　　to humanity.

≡ 27 ≡

Cradleboard

ABILITY TO RESPOND

The Teaching

The Cradleboard is a carrier for infants that has been used in almost every Tribal Tradition in Native America. The Cradleboard frame is made of wood so that the body of the child can be supported. The inside is cushioned with Sage leaves then covered with Rabbit fur. Diapers for the infant were originally made from Rabbit fur and filled with Mullen or Sage leaves to absorb moisture. The outer covering of the Cradleboard is made of soft Deer hide and is laced in front so that the child is secure and yet accessible for changing or feeding. The bonnet, or hood, shades the baby's eyes from strong light and protects the child from rain while traveling or breaking camp. In every instance, the Cradleboard holds the responsibility of protecting the child's body from harm. If the Cradleboard should fall from the travois, or carrier, behind the Pony, the child will not be harmed since the sturdy wood frame and bonnet create a sort of armor.

Since the Traditional understanding of responsibility in the Native way of thinking is the "ability to respond," we find that the Cradleboard has all of the needed characteristics. Native Americans, particularly on the plains, were nomadic people that adjusted and responded to living life in a natural way. It was natural to move with the herds and the seasons.

Children too small to walk needed to be carried, so the Cradleboard became a necessary helper for young mothers who had to tend to other duties of camp life. A child could be placed in a Cradleboard and literally hung on the outside of a Tipi to sleep, while its mother made pemmican by crushing chokecherries into rolled meat, tended a cooking fire, tanned hides, or beaded moccasins. When moving from camp to camp, the Cradleboard could be strapped among Buffalo Robes and other belongings on top of a travois. Most often the Cradleboard was strapped to the mother's back, papoose-style, while she moved about camp.

While the Cradleboard has always had the duty and responsibility of protecting the children, the symbol of the Cradleboard is much more. As Native Americans, we have been taught that our purpose in life is growth, understanding, and living in harmony. We know that all things are placed upon the Wheel of Life and will continue as we take responsibility for the three fates; Past, Present, and Future. The ability to respond to the Past is to honor the Traditions of our Ancestors, their wisdom, the Sacred Medicine Objects that have guarded and guided our path. We must joyfully pass these Knowing Systems to our children.

The ability to respond to the Present is to seek beauty in every moment of the day, using our gifts, talents, and abilities for the greatest good of all. As we walk gently on the Earth Mother, honoring the Sacred Space of all life-forms, keeping a twinkle in our eyes and joy in our hearts, we learn gratitude for every blessing of life.

The ability to respond to *Future* lies in understanding *Present*. We understand that the survival and the well-being of the next seven generations depend upon every thought we think and every action we take in the now. For this reason, we are constantly reminded of our roles as Keepers of the Cradleboard for the future generations.

Every person walking the Good Red Road of physical life today is a keeper of tomorrow's Cradleboard. The children who will live in our world long after we are gone look to us to preserve the Earth Mother and the Knowing Systems that will allow them to become successful Guardians of all our resources. If the rain forests are gone, if there is no clean water, if the air is fetid or no longer breathable, if the Earth Mother can no longer grow food, we will have failed in our responsibility to carry the Cradleboard in our hearts. If the knowledge of how to recognize healing plants, how to grow Corn, how to live in harmony with All Our Relations has not been passed down to those who will follow us, we will have destroyed the rich heritage of the Elders that walked the Red Road before us.

When I was with the two Kiowa Grandmothers in Mexico, much of the prophecy of the Cradleboard of Creation was passed to me. I want to share these prophecies because they will help us look to the future with hope rather than doom and gloom. Our Earth Mother has never destroyed all of the Children of Earth in any of the four preceding worlds and will not do so in this one. I was told that the girth of Earth has expanded at the end of each world creating new land masses and eliminating others. Each time those of her true children who were able to read the omens were shown safe places to live. Some went into subterranean tunnels below the surface. The race that went below the surface is called the Subterrainiums by the Seneca Wolf Clan.

The Cradleboard prophecy speaks of the coming alive of thousands of Rainbow Warriors of both sexes who will suddenly see manifested the dream of the Fifth World of Peace. We are now in this process during this age the Grandmothers called the Time of the White Buffalo. It is during this time that the teachings are to be released to those with ears to hear and eyes to see. The prophecy says that these Warriors of the Rainbow will remember their legacy and use it for the good of all the Children of Earth. Chief Two Trees of the Cherokee says that these people may be white on the outside but are red on the inside. I feel this is due to the fact that the Warriors of the Rainbow are Guardians of our Mother Earth, and they are our Red Ancestors returning to assist All Our Relations.

The prophecy of the Cradleboard of Creation also says that Fire will come from the sky and hit the Earth Mother in the Water Nursery of Creation, or oceans. This cometlike object will fertilize the ovum of Earth and recreate purity in all four Earth Clans. The Chiefs of Air, Earth, Water, and Fire will be whole once again. The condensation from this interaction of Fire and Water will give us back our ozone. These prophecies will be fulfilled sometime between now and the year 2015.

Many persons who have disconnected from the Earth Mother and do not know how to grow food will need to learn. Many who have no knowledge of healing plants will need to rely on others who do. The ability to respond to the ensuing changes is carried in the understanding of the Cradleboard and each person's duty to share and be of service. It is time now to start the teaching process that will allow us to relearn Mother Earth's abundant lessons so that future generations will have the Knowing Systems needed for harmonious life.

Many ancient plants and animals will reappear in our new world as they have need to interact with us again. Some plants will be used for healing and others for food. We will understand the Language of the Creature-beings again and allow their instinct and wisdom to teach us how to take care of our needs. The Cradleboard will become a symbol of our first life-support system and we will become a world community. Communication in unity will prevail over one thousand years of peace when the Earth Mother will become a second sun or star in our solar system. We will not burn, living on her surface for we will have immortal bodies of Fire. The races from the stars will come to assist the Children of Earth in recultivating ecological balance and some will go with them to learn these new, yet ancient, Knowing Systems. Those who cannot accept the new Cradleboard of Creation will be removed to the body-double of the Earth Mother, which will house the memory of the devastation of her scarred and abused body. Many wonders will appear in the Time of the White Buffalo as governments will no longer control the actions of Earth's Children and the people-to-people connections will be made strong again.

As we carry the Cradleboard on our backs, it will carry the child of future dreams who is becoming manifest through our love. We are all responsible for all of the tomorrows to come. The Cradleboard is our reminder. We can protect *Future* by responding to the now.

The Application

Cradleboard says that the papoose you are carrying is your future. If you wish to influence it, you must respond now. Whatever your situation, the ability to respond is called for at this time. The Warrior side of your nature has the courage you need. Don't sit and wait for someone else to do something. Use your creativity, speak your truth, and respond.

You are being reminded that it is your responsibility to find your own answers and act upon them. Whether it is a past, present, or future challenge makes no difference. You can respond in a way that will promote your growth. Look at how you can use your personal Medicine to respond to the situation and how that action will make you grow. You have the ability, so now you must recognize it in the Self and use it.

≡ Medicine Bundle ≡

Symbols of connections,
With Allies of the Earth,
Medicine to heal us
And give us rebirth.

Talents to honor,
Abilities to praise,
Strength and compassion
Guide our Medicine ways.

≡ 28 ≡

Medicine Bundle

ALLIES/SUPPORT

The Teaching

The Medicine Bundle is a collection of items that has come to you in a variety of ways and that represents the Totems of your Power Animals or Allies among nature. In a Medicine Bundle you might find a seed pod, a Tobacco tie, a ball of dried sap from a Pine tree, a scalplock, an Elk tooth, Horse hair, a quartz crystal, an Otter tail, a Stone Person, a special string of beads, and/or any other item that represents Medicine to the Bundle's owner.

In ancient times many of the items were of special significance among the Tribes and Nations of Native America. For instance, the Crow believed that an Elk tooth was Medicine that would bring abundance in a material manner to the owner. A piece of blue cloth meant good luck, Bear hair and claws would keep a Warrior's Horse in prime shape, and a Swallow wing would give the power to evade enemies.

Medicine Bundles were used for many different things. There were Bundles for personal Medicine, Tribal Bundles, Warrior Bundles, Sun Dance Bundles, Giving Birth Bundles, Hunting Bundles, Dreaming Bundles, and Vision Bundles. Some Bundles would be created by a Medicine Man or Woman for special needs, or people could create their own. Some were passed down before death to a family member or worthy Tribal

Member. This passing of the Medicine was to ensure the proper use and Guardianship of the Medicine Bundle.

Each Medicine Bundle came with its own set of rules. For instance, if the owner had a Warrior Bundle that gave him great strength in battle, his Allies connected to that Bundle may have forbidden him to eat female Deer meat and never to paint his face with blue. The gentleness that is a part of the Doe could inhibit his actions in Counting Coup. Blue face paint could draw him toward the Road of Spirit and might bring an early death. Every Bundle has a specific purpose, and most have regulations that will strengthen the Medicine of the Bundle's Allies. Thoughtless actions can create havoc in the harmony achieved between the Medicine Helpers and the person seeking assistance if there is no respect for the Bundle's natural sense of order. The same rules apply to a smaller Bundle worn on the person, which is called a Medicine Pouch.

Some Warriors purchased special copies of a Bundle from another Tribal Member whom they respected. If these Braves had no vision of what their own Medicine was, they were left with no protection. The Allies of nature had been called upon but for one reason or another, some Warriors could not receive their Medicine Dreams. I feel that the problem may have been that they were not in touch with their female receptive energy due to the rigors of having to prove their right to be Warrior Clan. In any case, to be an unprotected Warrior meant sure death at an early age.

To lie about having received messages from your Power Totem or a vision of your path was to invite disaster, and yet for a Tribe to have a Brave without a Medicine was worse. The predicament was solved by wise Medicine Men, Chiefs, or great Warriors. These men would accept Horses or other valuable items for a copy of their Medicine Bundle. The Bundle's maker never put every object that represented his total protection into the copy. The reason for this was that to Give-Away all of your Medicine would leave your spirit at risk. No one should ever know all of the items in a Personal Medicine

Bundle. If someone was trying to use bad medicine to attack a powerful leader in a Tribe, they could harm that person by knowing their Medicine and using sorcery. The penalty for stealing another's Medicine Bundle was death. Unless invited, it was forbidden to touch *any* personal possession belonging to another Tribal Member—man, woman, or child.

Tribal Bundles, called the Grandmothers, were the oldest and most sacred. Next came the Sundance Bundles and then the Warrior Bundles. This order of sacredness reflected the Medicine and strength each Bundle had provided the Tribe over long periods of time. Every winter that passed successfully gave further strength to the Bundles.

Individual Sun Dance Bundles were made up by each Brave's sponsor, who was already acknowledged through acts of courage. The sponsor placed Totem objects into the Sun Dance Bundles that had been passed through many lines of Ancestor Warriors. No Bundles, however, were more sacred than the Tribal Bundles. These Grandmother Bundles ranked highest in the most ancient, tried and tested Medicines and represented the combined spirits of all Tribal Members—past, present, and future generations. The Grandmothers were so named because they are Tribal Bundles that carry the nurturing Medicine needed by all their children. Like every grandmother in humankind, these Grandmother Bundles seek only the best for their grandchildren.

The Tribal Bundles have been passed down through a line of Guardians. At one time these Bundles had to have their own Tipi and were set up in the camp as a protection for that Tribe. These Grandmother Bundles were protected usually by Warrior Chiefs who had honored themselves and carried strong Medicine. The Tribal Bundles were considered living beings and were never left alone and unprotected. Today the Grandmother Bundles have been secreted away and many are protected by Grandmother Elders as well as by some Medicine Men. These are among the most sacred objects of our people and still hold the spirit of all of the Native American Nations.

218 MEDICINE BUNDLE

The Personal Medicine Bundles can be carried or worn on the person. These Bundles are called on when needed for strength and/or courage during daily activities. Some Medicine Pouches are worn around the neck and are smaller versions of the Medicine Bundle. These Medicine Pouches are a reminder for the wearer of the talents, abilities, and Power Animals who will aid them in walking tall and in balance. They are also used for protection.

The Bundles carried by women are not spoken of very much in written history due to the secrets of the Medicine being reserved for the Sisterhoods. The Warrior Clan knew that the women were naturally more adept at receiving due to their female nature, and thus, the women were always honored for their inner-knowing and the Woman Medicine they carried. These female Medicine Bundles could be used to promote fertility, to aid the male Warrior who walked at the woman's side, to seek new healing techniques with herbs, to aid in delivery of a child, to bring abundance to the lodge, or to maintain a happy family. The women have always been separate in their use of Medicine and have honored their own societies. They have never had to go through the rigors of physical tests of strength to achieve vision. They are Mothers of the Creative Force of the Universe and naturally receive the messages of their Medicine Helpers to keep and maintain the strength of their Personal and Sisterhood Bundles.

Each object that comes to you to be a part of your personal Medicine can be placed in a piece of hide and wrapped like you would cover a gift, folding all four corners of the hide to the center and then tying the Bundle four times with cords of buckskin. Medicine Bundles vary in size from something that fits in the palm of your hand all the way up to the size of a newborn baby. Some Medicine Bundles are rolled and some are folded into the pieces of hide. You may want to put some of the smaller objects into a Medicine Pouch and wear it at your waist or around your neck.

If you want to make a Medicine Bundle for a special friend, you would need to look at what kind of Medicine you want to share. Then call on the Four Clan Chiefs to send you a dream or vision of what to include. This could be a Bundle for a young wife who fears her first pregnancy, a young man going into the armed forces, a newly-wed couple, someone buying land who would need a Guardian Spirit for the protection of that land, or a friend who is ill. Every kind of Bundle is a gift of Self and is only to be shared with those who will honor the sacred responsibility of the Bundle's Medicine.

If you are an Elder, you may want to pass your Medicine to a younger person who you know will accept the responsibility with honor and courage. The Bundle may also be passed to another if you do not intend to Drop Your Robe (die). If a person should Drop The Robe before passing the medicine Bundle to someone else, that Bundle and all of the Sacred Medicine belonging to the deceased person should be burned so that the spirit will have no Medicine strings attached to this Wheel of Life and may be free to move on to the Blue Road of Spirit.

Accepting Medicine that has been passed from an Elder or another person with great strengths is not to be taken lightly. It is a great responsibility to respect the life and deeds of another person, carrying yourself in a manner that would allow the original holder of that Medicine to take pride in your actions. If you dishonored the life of that Elder or the Medicine, you could receive your share of hard knocks from the Allies. The Allies understand that all acts of physical life are sacred in their proper time. The Allies teach us how and when to experience every act along the Sacred Path with beauty.

The Application

If the Medicine Bundle has come into your hands today, you are being asked to honor the wisdom of your Ancestors and the Allies. If you are not sure what the messages are, look at the strengths that are now being given to you and count them as your personal Medicine. This assistance is supporting your present path and should be recognized as blessings from your Medicine Helpers. Through them, you may find the courage to support the Self.

The focus of this card tells you that you are not alone. The Path may be difficult at this time, but you are being supported during your climb. If The Path is progressing easily, you are in alignment with the Allies and are experiencing their assistance. Be grateful.

In all instances you are being asked to note who is helping and see if you can return the favor by supporting others. The assistance of the Medicine Helpers does not falter when you stumble on your path. By example, you should also remain true to others you have assisted. Betrayal after trust is deadly. To have Allies, you must also learn how to be one.

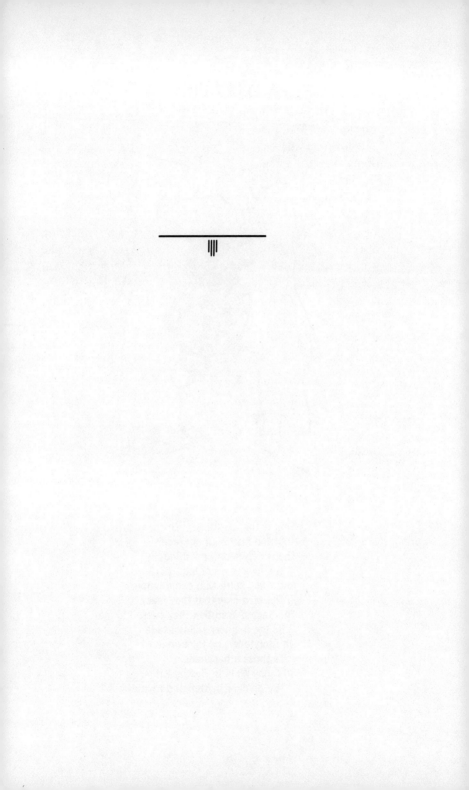

≡ Storyteller ≡

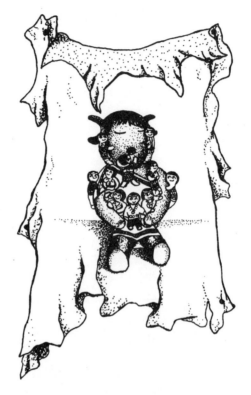

Sing to me, oh Ancient Ones,
   Of the history of our race.
That I may see in my mind,
   The love in every face.
And every spirit that came before,
   The Medicine that they made,
The Sacred Tradition they passed to me
   So the memory will not fade.
Oh Storyteller, be my bridge
   To those other times.
So I may Walk In Beauty with
   The ancient rhythm and rhyme.

≡ 29 ≡

Storyteller

EXPANSION

The Teaching

The Storytellers of Native America are the Guardians of our history and our Sacred Traditions. They ensure the future expansion our children will bring to the Earth by keeping our ancient knowledge alive. Storytellers traveled among the Bands and Tribes of various Nations carrying news of events that affected the whole. The Storyteller would recount the events of other camps at the communal fire after dinner. The Storyteller would tell of brave deeds, Coups that had been counted on an enemy, a Medicine Dream that prophesied coming events, Medicine Stories that kept Tradition alive, or the latest news of births and deaths.

The Plains Indians sometimes called their Storytellers Twisted Hairs. These Storytellers wore a small knotted and twisted bun that fell in the center of their forehead and marked them as historians and teachers of the Tribe. A male Twisted Hair was not expected to go into battle but rather to observe and recall the fight blow by blow. A female Twisted Hair was the historian of women's lore and Medicine Stories that assisted young women in maintaining pride in their Tribal roles.

The Storytellers of all Tribes and Nations are the bridge to other times and ancient teachings. The children of future generations learn from the Storytellers and apply lessons of the

Medicine Stories to their own lives. Although the grandparents or parents would tell Medicine Stories to their children as they tucked them under the Buffalo Robes each night, it was not the same as when a Storyteller of the Nation arrived for a visit.

Medicine Stories are told and retold year after year to keep the teachings of the People alive. Every story has many meanings and relates to life in a multitude of ways. Each time a story is retold, the level of understanding grows and expands along with the maturity of the listener. The same events inside a story may be repeated many times in different ways to allow listeners to discern how the story applies to them.

The Red People's way of thinking is very different from that of other races. We do not tell others what the true message is in our Medicine Stories but rather allow people to use their individual gifts of intuition and observation to discern what the true meaning is for them. In this way, the teaching of the Red Race insists that everyone be allowed to learn at their own speed, in their own way, and to apply or not apply the teachings to their lives.

The Storytellers were trained to allow freedom of thought among those who sought their wisdom. In this manner, children were taught that they had a perfectly good intellect and were equal members of the Tribe. Every child who came to the Storyteller was placed on an eye-to-eye level with the Twisted Hair, as an equal. If children were acting silly or being disruptive, they were simply ignored as if they did not exist. This lack of acknowledgment and attention put a stop to the bad behavior. The Storyteller could act as if that child was unheard and invisible for days. This was a much stronger form of discipline than spanking a child because the child lost face with the other children as well.

Memory is a special part of our Native American Tradition. Since our histories are passed down orally, the remembering is an art. Every herb, plant, or flower used in healing must be remembered for future generations. Every dance, Ceremony, ritual, initiation, and teaching must be committed to memory. All Tribal Laws and prophecies must remain intact for future generations. The Coups and losses have to be remembered for future strategies. It is obvious that one person could not remember all of these things or be an expert on every subject. This is why the various Clans had historians who held the oral history of an area of expertise in their memory. These fragments of Tribal Teachings were passed down to the next generation, and each person held one fragment that was a part of the whole way of life.

A Tribe's Storyteller held a position in the Council of Elders. As a historian, the Storyteller was called upon to recall past events with total accuracy so that the events could be used to pattern a present solution. The Twisted Hairs taught how to live life in a balanced manner through the actions of the characters in the Medicine Stories. A Medicine Story that was told in a timely manner could end arguments, change the course of a life, bring courage in hard times, or encourage the youngsters to take on new responsibilities.

Without directly criticizing the actions of another, the Storyteller could recall a Medicine Story that could point out a trail of folly or fear. The listeners would then be able to discern for themselves. All Native Wise Ones teach through stories rather than by pointing the finger at others. In our Teachings, we are always reminded that when we point our finger at someone else, there are three fingers pointing back at us. On the other hand, the Storyteller can gently remind us of our wrong thinking and allow us to correct the erroneous behavior without shaming us in front of others. This teaching art is one way of allowing each person to decide what the story means for them.

Raised Hand was a Twisted Hair who came every summer to share his knowledge with the children of the Ogalalas who had gathered for the Pow-Wow before the Sun Dance. The Horse had been used among the Sioux for two generations and so Raised Hand came to the Pow-Wow on his paint called Red Arrow. The children ran to the edge of the camp when they saw Raised Hand approach with his noble companion. Raised Hand had two Eagle Feathers tied to his scalplock and the Twisted Hair knot hanging in the middle of his forehead.

"The Twisted Hair has arrived!" screamed the children as they ran to greet him. Eyes filled with wonder, the children watched Raised Hand move into the camp. He was sitting proud and erect on Red Arrow looking straight ahead with his jet-black eyes glued to the center of camp. Raised Hand was the oldest Twisted Hair in the Sioux Nation. No one knew how many winters he carried on his back. Even the Chief who came to greet him remembered Raised Hand as an Elder when he was a little boy.

Dismounting in the center of camp, Raised Hand was greeted with great respect and warm *Hau-Kolas* (hello friend). The Council of Chiefs was called, and Raised Hand went to smoke the Pipe with the leaders of the Ogalala. After the Pipe was smoked, food was brought and news was shared among those inside the Medicine Lodge.

When evening came and the last light of Grandfather Sun's rays of love touched the swirling Buffalo Grass of the prairie, the feast began. Everyone always enjoyed a reason to celebrate. The return of Raised Hand to this band of Ogalalas was very special. The expectations ran high and all eyes were focused upon the Storyteller as he began sharing the news of births and deaths, the Coups that had been counted, and the decisions of the various Councils in other bands over the last winter. When this oration was complete, Raised Hand told a Medicine Story.

"Many winters ago," he began, "when the Buffalo were plentiful and the only enemies of the Sioux were the Crow, I was nursing at my mother's breast. I was small, but I watched the camp and heard the Drums of my Ancestors speak to the People. I understood what the Drums were saying and the stories they told. For such a small one, the stories were comforting when my mother was occupied tanning hides or making pemmican."

"So it was that ten winters passed, and I had become a young boy with responsibilities. At that time, my name was Hears the Drums because the Medicine Woman that assisted in my birth had noticed my fascination with the drumbeat. Crooked Leg, my father, had been stampeded by a Buffalo when saving the life of a careless youth on his first hunt. I was now partially responsible for hunting small game for my family. After returning one day with a Squirrel and a Rabbit, I brought them to my mother and was greeted by the Storyteller, Yellow Face. Yellow Face was a Twisted Hair who had served our people since before my grandfather was a boy."

"Yellow Face asked me what I had learned on my hunt and if I had heard the Creature-beings speaking to me. I was startled because I had never told anyone that I followed my own heartbeat, like the Drum's music, to the place where the animals told me who was ready to be my family's meal."

"Until Grandfather Sun died in the West, I sat and told Yellow Face about the wondrous stories I had heard from my friends, the Creature-beings. I told him how I raised my hand and commanded my heart to drum *Hau-Kola* to the Sisters and Brothers of the prairie. The "hello friend" that my heart drummed brought the creatures to me, and they gladly shared their Medicine Stories. So it came to pass that I was chosen to train as a Twisted Hair with the Storyteller, Yellow Face. My name was changed to Raised Hand because I greeted all creatures with the open hand, raised in friendship.

The Application

The Storyteller card speaks of expansion on all levels. You are now growing and encompassing many new ideas if you have received this card. See which area of expansion needs your attention and feed your personal Fire of Creation. Create more and enjoy the expansion, knowing you earned it.

Note that the expansion will continue if you are willing to share how you achieved your success with others. Many lives are influenced by another's story. In the good fortune of your present situation you may be instrumental in encouraging others.

In all cases, expansion occurs when people are allowed to grow at their own rate and with their own understanding. The wisdom of the Storyteller is a part of the art of remembering. Note that you are now remembering your personal Medicine and how to *be* your potential.

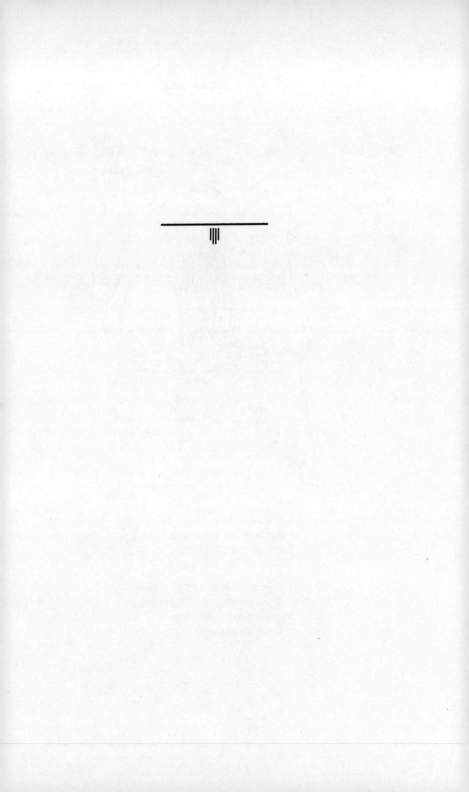

≡ Fire Medicine ≡

Sacred Fire within us,
  Place of eternal flame,
Burn away the barriers,
  In Great Mystery's name.

Teach us warmth and goodness,
  The love of Grandfather Sun,
Melting every difference,
  Until we are truly one.

≡ 30 ≡

Fire Medicine

PASSION/SPONTANEITY

The Teaching

Fire is one of the Four Clan Chiefs of the Earth Mother's world. Air, Earth, Water, and Fire are the elements that regulate the weather, the composition of matter, energy, space, and time. The six forms of Fire as we know them are the Fire in Grandfather Sun, the Fire in Mother Earth's core, the Fire that comes from lightning, the Fire in lava that forms the Stone People, the Fire that burns wood, and the Fire within each of us that is the Eternal Flame of Great Mystery and is our life-force and spontaneity.

The warmth of Fire is a basic part of the human, Two-legged's makeup. We have been taught that Grandfather Sun was the warmth of the First World that became manifest after Creation and that he represented the love of Great Mystery for all of Earth's Children. During the First World the only Fire that the Children of Earth recognized came from Grandfather Sun and the fiery volcanoes that erupted as Mother Earth continued to cool. Two-leggeds did not know how to capture or use Fire until the Second World, which brought the Great Ice Mountains and the bitter cold that changed the climate of the Earth Mother. It then became necessary for the Two-leggeds of all five races to band together in families and Clans seeking warmth and shelter. In the First World, before the cold winds of change brought the Ice-beings, the Children of Earth depended upon unity, loving each other, and the warmth of Grandfather Sun for love and nourishment.

Grandfather Sun lives inside us as well as in the Sky Nation and is located in our Vibral Core, or middle-body, just above our navel. When we radiate our love to those around us, we allow the Grandfather Sun who lives within us to shine. The proper use of this love energy is one form of Fire Medicine. On the Trail of Tears when starvation and cold were the constant companions of our people, many times the children were saved from death's clutches through the use of Fire Medicine. The healthier adults would call upon Grandfather Sun within them to add heat and life-force to their bodies and actually become blankets for the children during a snowy night. Having nestled around the children's bodies to give them warmth, many adults would Drop Their Robes by morning knowing only that they had saved the future generation through the use of Fire Medicine.

Fire Medicine is our passion for living, our desire to love and be loved, our need for human companionship and warmth, our physical strength, the compassion we have for others, our creativity and spontaneity as well as the Fire that fuels our Medicine Dreams. Our physical passion comes from the Fire within our Earth Mother. This form of Fire Medicine can fuel our bodies with stamina, allow us to express our sexuality, spark our creativity or spontaneous actions. When we bring our Mother Earth's love up through our feet and into our Vibral Core to meet Grandfather Sun's inner fire we have accomplished a type of inner creation: the Divine Union of male and female.

When we disconnect from our Earth Mother, this union of the two Fires will not be able to feed our bodies the Fire Medicine we need and we may become ill. I have seen this happen to people in the cities who must guard themselves through shutting off any external stimulus in order to survive the noise pollution or unwanted attentions of those whom they do not wish to know. When the external stimulus is shut off, so is the connection to the Earth Mother. The boundaries of people's Sacred Space become very small and their natural roots, which draw energy from the Earth Mother's internal Fire, cannot feed their bodies with her nurturing. This type of contraction breeds mistrust and the feeling of separateness that eventually spread from the mind to the body creating a disjointed sense of Self. Dis-ease will set in and can only be healed through the warmth of reconnection to Mother Earth, her Creature-beings, and All Our Relations. Later when trust has returned, it will be time to continue the healing through reconnecting with other Two-legged humans on a new level.

When we suppress our natural humanness and ignore our body's need for warmth or Fire Medicine, the body will become cold in places. Soon the body will forget to send life-force to the areas that need warmth, love, and attention. In this modern world where people are afraid to embrace a friend, to touch someone's arm when they are speaking, or to allow themselves to be nurtured by the Earth Mother, many have lost the Fire Medicine that produces a sense of unity.

Another aspect of the warmth of Fire Medicine is sexuality. Native People have always considered coupling a sacred act. When two people are attracted to each other sexually, a sacred union is in the making. During the Fourth World of Separation, the Children of Earth forgot to honor the sacredness of sexuality, which originally was considered a holy extension of Mother Earth and Father Sky's union that brought fertility and abundance. We Two-leggeds are most like Wolves and mate for life when there is no fear or separation inside our hearts. The modern-day custom of rapid marriages and divorces is allowing us to heal all aspects of ourselves that have become separate and cold. We are being forced to see the reflection of ourselves we cannot love in the actions of those around us or in a mate. In a sense, this custom is a discovery process that will eventually lead us back to the ideas of natural, sacred union that has its roots in the unconditional love of Mother Earth and Grandfather Sun's love for us.

Through the ages, many Medicine People have used Fire to assist them in remaining connected to the Earth when they Journey through the Dreamtime. A twig Fire could be built and continually fed by an assistant during the Journey. The body's natural impulse is to use a campfire to draw warmth into the body while the Spirit is walking the Dreamtime. In this way, a Medicine Person can remain out-of-body for longer periods of time without concern that the body would be physically harmed. Just as we must be open to receiving the information from Medicine Helpers and Allies, we must be open in order to use Fire Medicine for Journey Work. When all parts of the body are nourished through Mother Earth and Grandfather Sun's Fires, the body will feel comfortable enough for the spirit to leave.

The sensory perceptions become finely tuned when there is no internal need and no external sense of danger. The internal Fire nurtures and protects just as Mother Earth nurtures and Father Sky and Grandfather Sun give protection. In this balanced state we can once again achieve our native state of being, which is perfect internal balance. The Fire of our spirit is then empowered and can break the illusion of time and space and can leave or return at will. This is why our Elders can decide for themselves when "it is a good day to die." Having journeyed many times, they are able to release the body and Drop Their Robes when they feel the pull of the Spirit World.

Fire Medicine is the reminder that all things come from and contain Great Mystery, which is Original Source. The Fire of Creation lives within us and in All of Our Relations. When we balance the Sacred Fire inside ourselves, in every form it takes, we can then perceive and become anything in Creation through melding with the Sacred Fire in all things. This talent is spontaneous creation. Passion for living is the fuel for this inner Fire and is found through appreciation of every blessing physical life offers.

The Application

If Fire Medicine has appeared in your cards today, you are being asked to acknowledge the Fire within. Your spontaneity for living depends upon your connection to Fire. You can support your passion for living through acknowledging all of the Good Medicine present in your life. Your ability to create adventure and excitement comes from your willingness to give yourself pleasure and joy. All that is needed to continue the passion is to decide you are worthy and proceed.

If you have any judgments about passion on the physical level, it may be time to clear them. All acts of life are sacred when treated in a respectful manner. Any old fears of intimacy or commitment can act as limitations to relationships. If this applies to you, clear the fear. As the fear leaves, so will the coldness of past hurts, and you will be ready for more rewarding future relationships.

In all cases, Fire Medicine insists that we use the Fire within to fuel our lives with energy. This energy comes from Mother Earth's passionate physicality and Grandfather Sun's spontaneous love. When we are in balance, this Divine Union sparks our natural desire for experiencing life. If the spontaneity is already happening to you, continue.

≡ Medicine Bowl ≡

Medicine Bowl of healing cures,
  Of visions, dreams, and what endures
    Beyond the Void of time and space
      You bring the healing of every race.

For Seers and healers the water you hold
  Brings ancient wisdom now retold.
For seekers and for those in need,
  Your healing unguent brings reprieve.

≡ 31 ≡

Medicine Bowl

HEALING

The Teaching

The Medicine Bowl is a Traditional tool used by the Seers, Dreamers, and Medicine People of Native America. A Medicine Bowl that has been handed down through many generations of Medicine People can be several hundred years old and will carry the strengths or weaknesses of its former Guardians. So sacred is this tool for healing, it would never be brought out of hiding for Tribal Ceremony. Its counterpart, the Ceremonial Bowl, would take its place in the public's eye. This assures the holder and Tribe that no harm would come to any sacred healing tool or object through its exposure to disrespectful observers. The Ceremonial Medicine Bowls may be very ornate representations of the working models.

Almost all Medicine Bowls are carved from wood or made from the shell of Turtle. A few are made from basalt, fired clay, or lava rock, but this is rare. A Medicine Bowl can be used by a person in the healing arts for grinding herbs or mixing cures. Medicine Women also use the Medicine Bowl for the first bathing of newborns. Seers use a Medicine Bowl in a much different way. Often the bottom of a Seer's bowl will be blackened with charcoal and rubbed with beeswax until no color remains from the wood. The Seer using a blackened bowl will fill the bowl with water and use the reflection of firelight to create an image of the Void where Future lives. In so doing, the Seer is able to see the destiny of a Tribe.

The Black Lodges of women are known for their Seers. The women Seers of any Tribe are highly valued for their clarity and focus. The Seer may "smoke a person," "dream a person," or use the Medicine Bowl to go into the Void on the person's behalf. To smoke a person, the Pipe may be used to see beyond the reality of the apparent illusion. In this instance, the smoke from Tobacco mixed with red Willow bark, sweet Clover, Osha root, and Mullen leaves may allow the Seer to travel with the smoke to another dimension and see what is needed.

The use of the blackened Medicine Bowl sometimes requires the assistance of the Seer's Sisters of the Black Lodge, depending upon the reason for the use of the bowl. In the Kiowa Tradition, the women would fast that day and then have a special Purification Lodge Ceremony for the success of the Seer and the healing of the person needing assistance. Then the women would enter the Black Lodge, sit around the edge of the Lodge, and hold a circle of protection and energy for the Seer while she sought the wisdom of the Void. This is accomplished in silent vigil with only the flute or drumbeat being used to lead the Seer out into the Void and safely home to the Lodge. Afterwards the Seer was bathed by her Sisters and massaged to assist the circulation returning to her body. Then the Seer was bundled in blankets and left alone until she was ready to share her vision.

In our Seneca Tradition, it is never announced which of the members of the Nation are the Medicine People. A true Medicine Person never says, "I am a Medicine Woman or Man." Others may say it of a person, but it is forbidden to say it of yourself. The tests of initiation include long years of study and practice.

There are five requirements for a Seneca Medicine Person. First, the Medicine Person must be a Counselor. The Counselor must have knowledge of how to assist others in using their personal talents, their personal Medicine, and finding a productive life-path. The Counselor must know how to assist a person in using their gifts in relation to the Medicine Wheel of the Tribe. The Counselor must be able to impart Traditional solutions through Tribal Law and wisdom.

Second, the Medicine Person must be a Historian of Earth Records. This includes the Creation and the first Four Worlds as well as the prophecy of the future Fifth, Sixth, and Seventh Worlds.

Third, the Medicine Person must be an Herbalist/Healer. This includes knowledge of the use of healing herbs and natural healing cures that come from the Earth Mother. The Herbalist also knows the Medicine of the Creature-beings and the manner in which they assist Two-leggeds in finding spiritual or mental cures. This requirement also includes the ability to recognize and diagnose illnesses of the body, mind, and spirit.

Fourth, the Medicine Person must have as a personal talent or ability, the Gift of Prophecy. This means the Medicine Person must be a Seer, a Dreamer, or in some way be able to connect to the Spirit World at will, as the need may arise at any moment. This is not to say that Medicine People will not take all the time they need but rather that their training must ensure that they are able to access the needed information on cue. Clarity and focus are honed to precision until this gift is fully developed within the Seer.

The final requirement of a true Medicine Person is the teaching of all aspects of the wisdom and knowledge to others. It is fairly obvious that such understanding would cover many years and would grow with time. The expertise of a Medicine Person must be shared for the Medicine to live and assist future generations.

The teachings of the blackened Medicine Bowl come from my training with two Kiowa Grandmothers in Mexico. In using the Medicine Bowl to seek answers, I was taught to put a question into the bowl mentally. Then I added a small Stone Person, a pinch of soil, a few drops of water, a kernel of Corn, a pinch of Tobacco, a piece of Sage and a piece of Medicine from the Creature-being I was calling to assist me. These objects were mixed together by rotating the bowl in my hands. Then the bowl was placed in the North of a small twig fire for a few moments while I sat in the South and spoke my prayers and sang my personal Medicine Song. When I had completed my prayers of gratitude for the answer I would receive, I brought the bowl to the South and blew Tobacco smoke into the bowl and sat in silence as the answer came to me.

The Medicine Bowl is where ideas are nurtured, the future is held, and growth is accomplished. Many women call their wombs their Medicine Bowl. We never know what our children will look like or what abilities they will hold until birth. So it is with the Medicine Bowl, the visions or answers are not predictable until viewed. We must be open to what *Future* brings. Some of the lost Medicine of our Ancestors is returning through the use of the Medicine Bowl. These sacred healing bowls remember their former uses and willingly share the memories for those trained to hear, feel, or see.

The Application

If you chose the Medicine Bowl card today, healing is on the horizon. This can be a spiritual, mental, emotional, or physical healing. Pay attention to the events in your life and acknowledge with gratitude the healings that manifest themselves. The steps toward wholeness are often marked with small healing releases and can often be overlooked. Become aware of shifts in attitude or a new sense of well-being, and you will understand the healing as it manifests. In this way you are assisting your future, beyond the Void, to heal you in the present.

In all cases, the Medicine Bowl speaks of Good Medicine. It is being offered. Your present task is to find it and use it to heal the Self or to assist another.

≡ Drum ≡

Drum that marks the heartbeat
    Of our Mother Earth,
Constantly reminding us
    Who gave us birth.
The rhythm of connection
    Pulse of flame and Fire,
The perfect reflection
    Of our heart's desire.

≋ 32 ≋

Drum

RHYTHM/INTERNAL TIMING

The Teaching

The Drum came to the Children of Earth during the Second World, which was the first Ice Age. It was at that time that Clans and families gathered around the new discovery of Fire and shared its warmth in unity. During the long winters inside the caves it was necessary to pass the time working on tools to be used during the spring as well as dancing, making music, and performing ceremonies. A leg bone, left after a meal, served as a drumstick to beat out a rhythm. Hides were stretched over hollow logs of different widths and depths to make Drums of varying tones.

It was during this Ice World that all five races of the Children of Earth connected with the heartbeat of the Earth Mother. They learned that the Mother was active in their Ceremonies and that amidst the drumbeats there was a common, almost imperceptible rhythm seeming to emanate from the Earth. Whether in a cave or in the open of the forest, Earth's heartbeat would attune their heartbeats one to another. The Drum gave a low resonate sound that built the energy to a heightened state of frenzy as the stories of victorious hunts were acted out before the Fire.

Tribal Peoples all over the planet still rely upon the Drum to connect the energy of each person participating in ritual or Ceremony. In so doing, there is a collective energy present that can be used for healing, prayer, gratitude, requests for information, or Journeying. The Drum can be used as a map or blueprint for those seeking altered states of consciousness or parallel universes. The Drum will connect the heart of the person doing the Journeying to the heartbeat of the Earth Mother and provide a safe way to return to the body. The possibility of reaching other realities and getting lost or losing touch with sanity is highly improbable when the Drum is used as a guide.

The Shaman's use of chants, animal sounds, the drumbeat, or flute to make a roadmap to the outer realms of the under-world is as ancient as the art of Journeying. Often great stress is put upon the body when the spirit is freed of its physical shell and seeks the other realities and parallel universes. After being out-of-body for several hours the limbs are stiff and very cold. The control of the breath brings the heartbeat down to a very slow rhythm and the body no longer places its attention on maintaining its normal, active state. A type of suspended animation occurs that allows life-force to collect in the areas needed as a reserve. This condition is a nonactive embryonic state. This same consciously directed state of slowing down the metabolism is natural among Dolphins and Whales.

The Drum is audibly heard and internally felt by Two-leggeds. This gives the human race a new sense of the first sound any human ever heard. That sound was in the womb and was a double heartbeat. The child's own heart and the heart of its mother resonates through the water of the amniotic sac and mirrors the human connection to the Earth Mother. The Drum can be used to assist the reconnection process outside the womb.

When a sense of nurturing connection to the Earth Mother is strong in a person, the trust factor is present and that person has a better chance of successful Journeying. Native Americans have always lived in harmony with the Earth Mother as have Tribal Peoples of the other four races. The sense of belonging to the Earth and being of the Earth, in a natural way, has enabled the Medicine People to see other worlds with ease. The stress factor is not present in the bodies of those using the Earth Mother's heartbeat for sustenance while their spirit Journeys through parallel universes. Many Seers or Dreamers will hold a Stone Person to maintain the Earth Connection while Journeying. In Mexico the Grandmothers Cisi and Berta taught me how to flow with the Drum and control my heartbeat so that I could travel to a new time and space.

The day was dry and dusty. Grandfather Sun sent clear, undulating waves of heat up the dry arroyos to change my view of the horizon. I passed all of the Geraniums growing out of coffee cans and the various succulents and flowers growing from old juice cans nailed to the walls surrounding the patio. I softly scratched on the peeling blue paint door and entered the cool shadows of the Grandmothers' humble living room.

This was the day we were to discuss rhythm. Grandmother Cisi hauled out a Rattlesnake skin from a pink plastic laundry basket filled with bits and pieces of her jumbled collectibles and made me sit down on the earthen floor. We began by discussing the rhythm of Snake and how Snake tracks made S-like trails across the sand. The movement of Snake had a rhythm that connected every part of its body to every other part. Snake would scurry across the desert in a manner that gracefully used every part of its body in unison thus creating a continuous rhythm of its own. This unified rhythm is healing because all parts are able to work together like a finely tuned machine. Illness results when missed beats cause the rhythmic unity of the body to falter, Grandmother Cisi explained.

When Snake sits under the shade of a rock, the lull of the rhythm is balanced by the memory of the activity that preceded it. Snake can then rely upon the heartbeat of the Earth

Mother it feels within the Stone Person to maintain its Earth Connection. Grandmother Berta brought out the Drum and began to beat out the Snake rhythm that matched Snake's scurrying across the desert floor. Then she changed to the Deer beat, then the Buffalo beat, showing me the difference in each Creature's natural active and resting rhythm. Each time, I could feel and hear the heartbeat of the Creature-beings as distinct patterns.

The Talking Drum spoke to my heart, and I could understand the Medicine. Each Tom-Tom gave a different message because it spoke of the activity of a different animal either charging, walking, or resting. The habits of Creature-beings were like a signal of what to expect next. If one Tribe made their Drum to speak in the manner of a charging Buffalo, the message could mean the herds were moving in the listening Tribe's direction. Although this type of communication is more common in Africa, the practice was used between different bands of the same Tribe or Nation in Native America. I smiled at my discovery, then turned my attention back to the Drum-beat in the room.

Grandmother Cisi then had Grandmother Berta beat out the human heartbeat as it rested. I sat with my eyes closed and felt my own heart slow to the pattern the Drum sounded. My body swayed slightly, and I felt myself align with a new unified body pattern. In a sense, I was finding the center of my personal Sacred Space. I was not pushing my body to be or do certain things any longer. I was allowing it to find its own rhythm. At twenty-two it was a wondrous discovery to see that I had a rhythm of my own, my body had its rhythm, and that the two could actually work together.

All life has rhythm whether in the physical or Spirit Worlds. The Drum allows us to access the patterns of life-force inside and outside of ourselves so that we may come to the understanding that all exists simultaneously. This simultaneous unified beat is the heartbeat of our Mother Earth. When we cross the border into parallel universes we find the unified heartbeat is that of Great Mystery. If we have ever experienced those rhythms, we may then share them through the Drum to show others the rhythms of all of Creation.

The Application

If the Talking Drum has spoken to you, you are being asked to find your own internal timing. You may be pushing too hard or missing a beat. In any case, being out of sync calls for realignment with the body's needs. Rhythm is a personal thing. To honor your own rhythm is to come back into harmony with the Self. From this point, personal comfort allows you to harmonize with other rhythms of life.

The Drum also speaks of allowing yourself to be supported by Mother Earth's heartbeat. That is to say, your mind may be outdistancing what your body can handle and the body cannot pull needed energy from the Earth because it is trying to keep up with your thoughts. If this applies, you are missing a beat. Slow down and rediscover the heartbeat of your true Mother. Then the synchronicity of your movements will be effortless.

In all cases, rhythm is the key. Become aware of all rhythms and see how yours fits in. If it feels right, you become the music and the dance you are dancing becomes a celebration of life.

≡ Dreamtime ≡

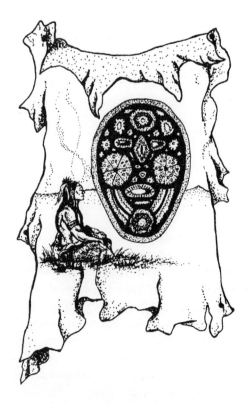

Dreamtime teaches other realms,
That exist within the whole,
Body-double wanders here,
Solutions for the soul.

Touching other Sacred Space,
Across the Milky Way,
Traveling to distant stars,
Connecting night to day.

≡ 33 ≡

Dreamtime

UNLIMITED VISION

The Teaching

In recent times, a lot of misinformation has been disseminated about the Dreamtime. I decided that it was very important to share the teachings I have received in order to provide a Knowing System that will assist those Journeying out-of-body.

In Choctaw Tradition, there are four kinds of dreams. These sleeptime dreams are the ones that come when you are sleeping. The first type of dream is a "property" dream and presages events that will bring the dreamer material possessions. This is also called a "wealth" dream and is brought by the Allies to show the sleeping dreamer the actual physical situations that will bring abundance to the Tipi. In this type of dream, the abundance a person will receive in their life can be foretold.

The second type of dream is a "no account" dream. In this type of dream, nothing more than ambiguous or foggy remnants of unconnected thoughts are remembered upon waking. Due to the lack of information presented, these dreams don't have any real value and are lowest on the Totem Pole in importance. These dreams may also be called "gives-away nothing" dreams. The reason for this is that no secrets are given away.

The third type of dream is a "wish" dream and may contain the dreamer's hopes for his or her future, which do not always manifest physically, because they are not backed by trust. If this type of dream is dreamed by another person and has you in it and you are told about it, the dream can have some Medicine value. Of course, it still may not come true due to the fact that you have free will. In modern terms, this "wish" dream could be the pipe dream of someone who is always dreaming of grandeur but never works toward those goals.

The fourth type of dream is a "Medicine Dream" and brings vision of the person's future in correct and impeccable form. This type of sleeptime dream is a rare gift and is the type most sought after by those seeking the Void. It has always been Tribal custom to keep these dreams to yourself until someone else was told by a waking vision that you had received a Medicine Dream. At that point, if the Medicine Dream was something that would aid the whole Tribe or Nation, the dreamer could decide whether or not to "open the vision" through the telling of it. If the other person's waking vision was shared, and if the Elders saw the value of the original sleeptime dream, it could determine future Tribal plans. Following and trusting the Medicine Dreams is still of utmost importance. To deny a message of this proportion is to destroy the validity of the Medicine.

In ancient times, if a Medicine Dream was not heeded, the Medicine Helpers could decline to assist further. If a person abandoned their own Medicine, the embittered years that followed might be filled with "should-have-beens." Consequently very few hesitations came up when the dreamer was asked to act out any messages the dream imparted.

These are the dreams that come from the *sleeptime, but they are not the waking dreams that come from the Dreamtime*. Joaquin was very specific when he started initiating me into Dreamtime Journeying. These waking dreams are out-of-body Journeys that come when you are totally aware of your body in the physical world but are also aware of being inside the dream. The Dreamtime is a parallel universe. All things that occur in that parallel time and space directly affect our physical reality.

The parallel Dreamtime reality is where your soul or spirit is operating on a continual basis to send you information that will allow you to be aware of all things that are happening in physical life. Why? Usually in the Dreamtime your spirit, or body-double, has picked up some piece of information you need to know. Since the Dreamtime is a parallel reality, it may look like an exact duplicate of your present surroundings. The main difference is that there are no limitations. For example, since you are not using your physical body in the Dreamtime, you can fly, walk through walls, or dive into the solid earth.

The waking dreams of the Dreamtime can overlay into the sleeptime reality if the need to know is strong enough. Many Dreamers in the modern world are so busy with daily life that the visions of the Dreamtime must impinge on their sleeptime in order to get their attention. I believe that this is the major reason that so much confusion has cropped up in recent years regarding the difference between the two. Dreamers are not being acknowledged in today's world as they were in the past. To be a Dreamer was a highly honored position in a Tribe or Nation. The place of the Dreamer was similar to a prophet or healer by today's standards.

The Dreamers could use a variety of tools that would allow them to pass through the barriers of time and space and "see" both realities. Some Dreamers would use the drumbeat to take them out-of-body and others would "smoke the person" needing healing. Both techniques aid the Dreamer in going into the past or future realities to seek the answers needed to effectively heal a patient. Ending a crisis of indecision for a person standing at the split in the trail could return that patient to the Sacred Path.

The Dreamtime reality is as ancient as our universe and holds all possible doors to every level of awareness. Many of the "carry-over souls," who have been Dreamers before, are awakening and tapping into their abilities to be Dreamtime travelers again. A "carry-over soul" is one who has carried talents and abilities from other lives into the present. Usually those talents were well developed and therefore the residuals are fairly well defined during childhood.

Some of these talents lay hidden because they are unused. Redevelopment of those abilities can be achieved through contacting the four animal Allies who are most strongly connected to the Dreamtime. The Dragonfly is the doorkeeper who allows the gates to the other dimensions to be opened through the breaking of the physical illusion. The Lizard is the daytime dream guide. The Swan is the guardian of surrendering to the Dreamtime pull or magnetism. And last is the Dolphin who teaches us how to enter those realms through the use of breath.

The Application

If the Dreamtime has called to you, you are being asked to see with unlimited vision. Wipe the dust from your eyes and pay attention to the messages you are receiving from the parallel universe. Our world is pregnant with possibilities. All time is now. You are a co-creator in the Two Worlds and will be given unlimited sight and knowing if you ask for it. This vision may come in a sleeptime dream or through out-of-body Journeying. It will give you the insight that you need at this time.

Unlimited vision allows any seeker to pierce the veil of unconsciousness and come to an inner-knowing. In all cases, this card marks a time of seeing truth on all levels of Creation. You are now being given the ability to go beyond the accepted reality. The cocoon is open, trust yourself, your Allies, and your Medicine. You may now take flight.

≡ Burden Basket ≡

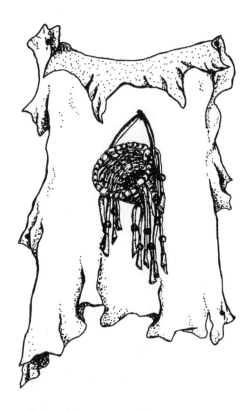

Burden Basket carries my grief,
  And gives me strength to go on.
Burden Basket reminds me not to take
  My burdens to other's homes.
Burden Basket sings to me,
  When the winter is long,
Reminding me of summer's heat,
  Bringing warmth to ancient bones.

≣ 34 ≣

Burden Basket

SELF-RELIANCE

The Teaching

In our Native American Tradition, there is little use for the Burden Basket in these modern times. The Traditional Burden Basket has been replaced by cardboard boxes stacked in the back of a reservation pickup truck. In looking at the original usage for the Burden Basket we must travel to the times when our people still wandered freely across the Earth Mother without the restriction of fences.

Before the Trail of Tears forced the proud Red Race onto reservations, wood could be gathered by women for their cooking fires or the Grandmother Fires used to heat the inside of the lodges. These heating fires received their name because the wood was small enough for even a Grandmother to carry and was placed in a Burden Basket leaving the hands free to gather and carry tubers, chokecherries, or herbs for cooking. A Grandmother Fire was like a twig fire and burned hot with very little smoke, which might fill the lodge and eventually the lungs of the inhabitants. A Grandmother Fire heats a lodge even in winter and provides the needed warmth and light for nighttime activities such as the evening meal or beading new moccasins.

Native women were never asked to bear a burden heavier than their Burden Baskets could handle. When the Burden Basket was not in use, it was hung outside the home for another reason. Native American etiquette is very different from other cultures and demanded that custom be honored by all Tribal members.

It is obvious that the flap of a Tipi, Karnee, or Wigwam cannot be knocked on like a door. To receive permission to enter the Sacred Space of any Native American home whether Hogan, Tipi, Longhouse, Cliff Dwelling, or Earth Hut, it was necessary to scratch lightly upon the door. Since every dwelling was the Sacred Space of the family, if there was no answer, entry was not permitted at that time. The family could be eating a meal, having a Family Council, or just wanting some privacy. The decision was always honored. No feelings were hurt because the idea of Sacred Space was understood. If permission to enter was granted, the Burden Basket was the reminder to the guest to leave his or her personal complaints or problems in the Burden Basket before entering another person's Sacred Space. The custom was honored, or the visitor was barred from entering that dwelling ever again.

Assistance in relief of a burden was sometimes given in the home of Elders. This practice was an exception to the rule of leaving all burdens outside the door. To seek counsel, one would go to the Elder, relative, or Medicine Person and bring a gift of Tobacco, a trading blanket, a Buffalo Robe or another appropriate gift depending upon the magnitude of the favor being requested. The meeting was not usually held in the presence of others and the person seeking counsel had to wait three days for the decision. On the fourth day the answer would be given. During the three-day waiting period the wise person whose counsel was sought would smoke the answer or dream the solution. Although these wise ones were not required to say more than yes or no, they usually used the opportunity to give a teaching through Storytelling to the seeker.

If Great Mystery had determined that the seeker's burden was to be carried further in order for a life-lesson to be learned, this was accepted gracefully, to allow the lesson to build character. Unlike many seekers in today's world who seek and then refuse advice, the instructions of a wise person in Native America were sacred and holy. In Tribal Law, the burden of finding answers rested on individuals and their ability to be connected to the Ancestors and their Medicine Helpers. If a seeker sought counsel, the wisdom given was honored to the letter.

Burden Baskets served the People in many ways. As utilitarian carriers for wood, herbs, tubers, Acorns, rushes and berries, the baskets assisted the women in keeping the lodge or camp in good order. As the Guardians of the home, the Burden Baskets were a reminder to respect the happiness and privacy of each family's Sacred Space. When the Burden Basket was hung outside of any lodge, it reminded each visitor of the strength of character needed to set aside personal problems. To enter another's home with a black cloud of worry or neediness was considered very poor manners. To be in the present moment and to be willing to be a welcome guest requires strength of character. If everyone considered the Sacred Space of others before speaking or acting, balance would be easily maintained in all communal living situations. As a symbol of the internal strength necessary to keep our own counsel and bear our own burdens without inflicting them upon others, these Burden Baskets still teach each of us to trust the value of knowing our own answers through our connection to Great Mystery and the Medicine Helpers.

Self-reliance is the keynote in all of the Burden Basket teachings. Physical strength is best supported by using leverage and the body's appendages to balance the number of baskets we can carry. To have compassion for the burdens of others, and yet not take those burdens on as our own, requires a strong heart. Strength of character is called for in order to keep from adding to the problems of others through gossip or complaints. Great sensitivity is necessary for impeccable timing in knowing when and how to speak to others. Personal balance brings the self-reliance we need to be in present time. Inner-strength is created through trusting our personal knowing and only seeking counsel when we have exhausted all other paths. When the Children of Earth learn self-reliance and interdependence, our common Burden Basket will one day be tossed in the Fire of Creation. The smoke rising from that Fire will signal the answer to all the prayers of the Fifth World of Peace.

The Application

If you are carrying a Burden Basket today, this card is telling you to pull from your inner-strength and become self-reliant. You can conquer the world when you let go of the burdens by trusting your ability to find your own answers. Problems cease being burdens when solutions are found.

The Burden Basket also teaches us not to drop our woes at the door of another. Relying on ourselves and our connection to Great Mystery teaches us to stretch into our potential. If confusion sets in and counsel is sought, use the advice. Don't waste the precious time of others if you do not intend to respect the wisdom offered. Know also that it's not your job to solve the problems of others. Don't rob others of their right to self-reliance.

In all cases, we only carry the burdens we wish to carry. If it makes us feel good or important to have so much to handle, we might need to look at our ideas of self-importance. The reminder is that we are all self-reliant and must use our talents to find our own solutions. The best answer is one shared equally by all travelers on The Sacred Path.

≡ Shawl ≡

Earth Mother welcomes her children home
When they have lost their way.
The trail was lonely and so long,
She whispers for them to stay,
Within the protection of the Shawl,
Where love abides again.
Their hearts may open to recall,
All Relations as their friends.

35

Shawl

RETURNING HOME

The Teaching

Many people across the world have heard the saying "Home is where the heart is." Traveling bands of Native Americans have known that each time they broke camp and moved to another location, home moved with them. Home was not necessarily the movable dwellings or belongings of Tribal People but rather their connection to the Earth Mother and to each other. The home of any gypsy, nomad, or wanderer lives inside the hearts of those loved ones who represent security and nurturing no matter where that traveler may be.

The sense of loss was devastating when Native Americans were forced to walk the Trail of Tears and leave the areas where they had been the Guardians of the land for centuries. The Living Teachings which bound them together were the Spirit of the People. Each Tribe knew that a new home could be created in another place because as long as the Teachings lived, the Spirit of the People would live.

After the Trail of Tears, many new Traditions began to emerge from the ashes of the broken spirit of the People. The Peyote Ceremony, the Taking of the Shawl, and many other Teachings marked the hard road back to finding the heart, the spirit, and the home of Native America. The Ghost Dance became a Tradition just prior to the Trail of Tears and was originally intended to call back the Buffalo, clean the Waters, bring back the prairie grasses, and rid the White Eyes from Sacred Ground.

The Taking of the Shawl is a little known Paiute Teaching that came into being when some members of the Red Race could no longer live in the white world. Those Native Americans who chose to return home and embrace the Teachings of their Elders took on the Shawl. The Shawl was a symbol of coming home to the arms of the Earth Mother and being wrapped in her nurturing love. To accomplish the Taking of the Shawl, one would have to return to the Traditional Teachers of their Tribe and ask permission to live among the People who honored the ways of the Ancestors.

Those who had Taken the Shawl moved from the clapboard houses provided by the Board of Indian Affairs and took up residence in the Traditional Paiute homes called Karnees. Although it was much warmer in clapboard houses, those who had Taken the Shawl were very happy to live in Karnees. Their hearts had once again found a home in the Traditional Teachings of the Good Red Road and the material things no longer mattered.

Many Native Americans who left reservations during the years following the Trail of Tears lost touch with the Traditional Teachings when they moved to cities in order to find work. Many generations have married into other races, and some have lost touch with the Earth Mother. In the ensuing years, as the Traditional Teachings have come to the attention of the public, the return of Native Americans to the ways of their Ancestors has increased. Many of the mixed blood children of the Red Race, sometimes called Mateé, have chosen the Good Red Road as well. It is now the Time of the White Buffalo and people of many races are Taking the Shawl.

The Grandmothers of the Sisterhood of the Dreamtime

Buffalo taught me that the Time of the White Buffalo would mean many things. Their prophecy said that the return of the Buffalo to Turtle Island would mark the return of many Red Ancestors who would not necessarily come back to the Good Red Road in Red bodies. Many people would feel confused at having no Indian blood and yet be Red on the inside and white on the outside. Grandmother Cisi told me that Great Mystery was going to play Heyokah with everyone who refused to honor the paths of others. Grandmother Berta told me that some Native People would deny other Native Teachers who shared their Traditions with all races. Then Grandmother Cisi laughed and laughed at the raucous battle of egos she had seen in her Medicine Bowl that would be caused by the fighting between all of "those people" claiming to be the only true Native Teachers. The Grandmothers promised me that this jealousy and envy would eventually serve as a growth tool for all concerned and would iron itself out as the Fifth World of Peace continued.

The difference between "The People" and "those people" is that "The People" have stayed on The Sacred Path because the behavior of "those people" has reminded them of why they need to Walk in Beauty. This Teaching applies to every race. The People are those who have Taken the Shawl and live in harmony, honoring the Sacred Space of all life-forms.

In Taking the Shawl, we are taught that the Earth Mother loves all her children and welcomes everyone home no matter how naughty they have been. We are not here to heal the Mother Earth, she is quite capable of doing that herself. We are here to heal ourselves so we may discover our roles in Creation. During the former four worlds, the Earth Mother has purged herself of many civilizations that did not honor her right to life. Mother Earth has the potential and the ability to cleanse herself again if the need arises. This is not to say that Two-leggeds should not be mindful of assisting in cleaning up any damage that has been done; on the contrary, that is a part of our human role as Children of Earth.

Each person who Takes the Shawl comes into alignment. We are being taught to acknowledge the beauty in each unique expression of Creation whether it be human, Creature-being, Plant Person, Stone Person, or our worst enemy. The Shawl may be too heavy for some people to carry on their shoulders if it means that harmony must be lived daily, without exceptions.

For centuries, every time there was a need, new ideas and Traditions have appeared among Native Americans. In the more than 380 Tribes in North America, there are hundreds of Traditions that could not possibly be named in this work. For anyone to say that one Tribe had the corner on Tradition would be foolish. For anyone to say that they had been trained in the only Traditional Native methods would be very limiting. Taking on the Shawl also means that one is willing to exchange information and allow all Traditional Teachings to live so that the goodness of each can be shared by many. It is time to let go of the "I" and Take the Shawl that covers the eternal "We."

The Application

If the Shawl has fallen across your shoulders, you are being invited to return home. If you have forgotten yourself recently, it is now time to remember your essence and potential. If you have walked a crooked trail by falsely judging others, it is now time to come home to the loving heart and see the value in all paths and chosen lessons.

You may be coming home to the magic that you once believed in or to a new sense of well-being, but in every case you are returning to a temporarily forgotten state of being. In every life there is a need to return to the simplicity of happiness. If you have forgotten how to find the simple truths that once supported your inner joy, it is time to return home.

Wearing the Shawl is coming home to the arms of the Earth Mother and being loved. The responsibility of Taking the Shawl is being loving to others who have forgotten the Sacred Path or the way home.

≡ Thunder-beings ≡

Thunder-beings that give us
  The Fire from the sky,
Energy for Mother Earth,
  Divine Creation flies,
Through the air to touch us
  Electrifying change,
Bringing love's true essence,
  Into our hearts again.

≡ 36 ≡

Thunder-beings

USABLE ENERGY

The Teaching

The Thunder-beings make up the love call of the Sky Nation. The Fire Sticks, or lightning bolts, are a rare gift from the Sky Father to the Earth Mother. The Thunderers who accompany a storm carry the mating call that announces the Divine Union of Earth and Sky. The Thunder-beings are the host of lovers who give energy to the Earth Mother. The Thunder Chief proclaims the beauty of the love between Father Sky and Mother Earth. The Fire Sticks create a bridge between the two lovers and are a physical expression of their love for one another. The Cloud People gather where the dance of union is to be held and house the Thunder Chief and Fire Sticks within their bodies awaiting the joyous time.

Through this intricate mating dance, our Earth Mother is reenergized so that life may continue through the nurturing Rains who feed her body. Since our Mother Earth is magnetic in nature, she has need of the electric energies supplied by the Thunder-beings. The Rain People recycle the moisture of Sky World and give back to the Earth Mother so that her body may feed all things green and growing.

As the cloak of Father Sky covers the Earth Mother in a mantle of blue each day, we Two-leggeds see the beauty of his love for her when the Cloud People form and the thoughts of their combined ideas take physical shape. In our Seneca tongue, *Hail-lo-way-ain* is the Language of Love. This Language of Love is at work between Father Sky and Mother Earth.

When Mother Earth needs the love and warmth of Grandfather Sun to support the needs of all of her children, we see thunderstorms, lightning, and rain as their bodies dance the Sacred Dance of Divine Union. The Thunder Chief calls out in *Hail-lo-way-ain*, the ancient Language of Love, for the Earth Mother to prepare herself for her bridegroom. The Fire Medicine that comes between them is lightning (Fire Sticks), which is directed along the lines of energy that form a grid system over her body.

If a Fire Stick touches Mother Earth in one area, the electricity may travel great distances to reenergize those places that need the male energy that Father Sky supplies. The individual needs of all parts of her body are assisted by the Thunder-beings since they are Father Sky's Medicine Allies, or Helpers.

This act of love between Mother Earth and Father Sky can be tender and gentle or torrid and passionate. This lovemaking is experienced as weather changes and climatic shifts by the Children of Earth. Floods and fires, hailstorms and tornadoes, hurricanes and typhoons are the freedom of nature. In every case, the end result is the fulfillment of our Earth Mother's needs and must be looked at from the viewpoint of the greatest good for all living creatures. Great Mystery has a hand in all acts of the Uniworld and each act supports the need for growth and change.

My own life was saved in March 1986 by the Thunder-beings. I was driving across Utah, heading back to California after my Grandfather passed to the Other Side Camp. I was accompanied by a very disturbed young man who had sought my counsel and healing. On that day, we had agreed to travel in total silence and I had allowed him to drive my car. We were going to take a shortcut through a pass that was not usually open until summer. Fourteen miles up the pass we began to see snow. We were going to go see if the Medicine Man, Rolling Thunder, could help my companion. I had been frightened by his erratic behavior at the beginning of our journey two days earlier, and I needed some assistance.

I broke the silence when he refused to look at the sign that blocked the pass, warning of snow and poor road conditions. The light was disappearing fast. When I spoke of my concern, referring to the map that said the pass was over 10,000 feet high with no more than a gravel road over the top, the young man snapped. He gunned the accelerator and propelled the car over a three-foot deep snowbank that covered the entire road. We slid on ice and the car ended hanging precariously over the edge of the icy road.

The Cloud People had gathered and Grandfather Sun was far below the horizon about to disappear for the day. I was paralyzed with fear for a moment or two. I had never met Rolling Thunder, but Grandmother Twylah had spoken of him as a wise and good Medicine Person. I Entered the Silence and called upon his Medicine. At that exact moment, a plea from my heart reached the Cloud People and a clap from the Thunder-beings gave me courage. In that moment, I realized that the young man wanted to die and he would take me with him if he had to.

I distinctly heard the voice of my Grandfather's spirit telling me to take charge. "I don't know how," I replied. His voice told me to grab the camping hatchet in the backseat and follow his instructions. I did. I scuffled across the car seat, angrily ordering the man out. Then I told him to start cutting Sagebrush and instructed him to put it under the wheels for traction. While he was occupied, I called to the Thunder-beings for assistance and then called once again on the Medicine of Rolling Thunder, the Medicine Man in Carlin, Nevada. I got into the car and felt the Thunder-beings calm my heart and send me the message that help was on its way. I gunned the motor and was able to slide the car onto the one patch of gravel in the center of the road. In less than ten minutes, a car appeared.

The old green Impala was filled with a family of tow-headed children and their parents. The father helped the young man accompanying me push my car while I raced the engine and finally the car bounded over the avalanche of ice and old winter snow. We thanked the family and then asked why they passed the sign saying the road was closed. The man replied that some man at a service station down at the last town had told him it was open.

We all agreed to turn around and go back down together. We turned on our headlights and began the slow descent. After the fifth turn in the road, I looked back because I could no longer see the lights from the Impala. I stopped and waited. Finally, ignoring the screams of my companion, I turned the car around and went back to look for the family. The young man was so full of anger and hatred that it stunned me. It was dark and raining, and he was hungry. My companion didn't see why we should go back. The Impala had disappeared. No car, no skid marks, no wrecks, nobody over the side of the mountain. They had simply vanished. I know that this story is one mystery that I will never be able to explain. I do know that I am protected. I never met Rolling Thunder, but I honor his Medicine. The Thunder-beings are now my Allies too. They have proven to me that they love and serve the faithful.

The rolling Thunder-beings, the Fire Sticks, and the Cloud and Rain People taught me that I could be strong in the face of death. They cleansed my fear of being controlled by another person. They also assisted me in cleansing my guilt of not being able to help that young man when he committed suicide one month later. The Thunder-beings can bring us the courage to do those things and to master our sense of loss by seeing the expansive plan.

The lovemaking of Mother Earth and Father Sky bring renewal to the whole of Creation. Our personal renewal, which Nature reflects, can be brought about by cleansing our fears, cultivating new growth, releasing old habits, or allowing ourselves to be loved and protected. The Thunder-beings bring us the raw energy we need to change and renew our lives. We humans are Catalyzers who have electromagnetic, giving and receiving, bodies. We are the bridge that connects Earth and Sky when we are in harmony. Like Mother Earth and Father Sky we are male and female in nature. The command of usable energy comes when male and female are in balance within us.

The Application

The Thunder-beings card is telling you that you are a Catalyzer and may now command the usable energy at hand. You are being funded with the energy needed to complete any task you have in mind. If you have been trying without results or just couldn't get enough steam going, this card signals relief. You can drop the frustration and get on with it. The energy is now yours. Call it to you and use it.

Usable energy comes in many forms. See which kind of energy applies to your present situation and then command it. Your body is the lightning rod and will conduct all the energy you need. Shout your intention to the Sky Nation. The Thunder-beings remind you to replenish yourself equally to the amount of energy you expend.

≡ Great Mystery ≡

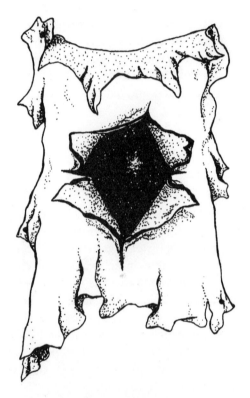

Original Source of Creation,
  The Void of All That Is,
Thank you for the breath of life,
  Thank you for my gifts.
Eternal Mystery, touch my heart,
  In beauty may I walk.
Sacred Mystery, be my guide,
  So I may Walk my Talk.
Infinite Source, remain with me,
  So I may always know,
The warmth of your Eternal Flame,
  Deep within my soul.

≡ 37 ≡

Great Mystery

ORIGINAL SOURCE

The Teaching

The Original Source of Creation is called Great Mystery by Native Americans. Great Mystery, called *Swenio* in our Seneca tongue, cannot be limited and is the Creator of Great Spirit. Many Native people also call upon the Great Spirit when praying; however, these are two different things in our Seneca Tradition. The Great Mystery lives in everything, is everything, and encompasses everything in Creation. Being the Original Source of Creation, Great Mystery created all things in beauty, harmony, and interdependence. Each facet of Creation was, is, and will always be. The forms may change, but the energy of Creation is self-regenerative and eternal. Inside of this infinite Creation that is Great Mystery, there is a Vibral Core, or primal energy source, that is the Great Spirit, or creative principle. The two are different. Both Great Mystery and Great Spirit are individually complete, unique, and independent of each other.

Great Mystery created Great Spirit to direct the creative flow of the Uniworlds, which include all universes, all levels of consciousness, all understanding, and all life. The key for seekers who wish to know the answers of the Void is that Great Mystery does not need to be solved! As we explore and discover the Mystery further, we learn that more is created and allowed to evolve. Trying to figure out all the answers to the Great Mystery is foolish and impossible because we are a part of that infinite, progressive Creation.

These concepts were alien to the Boat People who came from Europe to the shores of Turtle Island. When these White Eyes began to understand the languages of Native Americans and tried to conceptualize Indian understandings regarding Great Mystery, the limits of their religions blocked their paths of knowing. The white idea of God was rather primitive in that most Europeans believed that God was more or less human with many extra abilities. The Red Race was more expansive and all encompassing in their views of the Original Source of Creation. Native Americans had been taught through more than a hundred thousand years of oral history that all of Creation and each individual life-form was an expression of and contained Great Mystery. A part of Great Mystery lives in everything and knows no boundaries or limits. Every life-form has free will to co-create with the Original Source in beauty and truth or in ugliness or despair.

The Eastern Tribes of Native America tried to communicate the understanding of Great Mystery without success to the French trappers who were among the first to learn sign language and some Native tongues. The concept of all life coming from the Thought World, which is the Spirit World, then being manifested in physical forms on the Earth Mother was not fully understood. Since these concepts were limited by the Christian backgrounds of the settlers, the Original Source was interpreted by the Boat People as one Great Spirit equal to the white idea of God. The joke among Native People is that according to the white understanding, "In the beginning was the word . . . and it was misunderstood."

This misunderstanding of Great Mystery was handed on to the descendants of the Red Race when they were forced to learn the English language in boarding schools. The unfortunate use of Great Spirit as the term for all of Great Mystery has created a limited use of Native wisdom even among Native Americans.

Every life-form has one common mission as well as their individual ones. Each life-form is created to learn to be an equal contributor to the beauty of the whole. The purpose of the common mission is to discover who you are, why you are here, what talents you can use to assist the whole, and how you are going to go about it. This mission of discovery is the Sacred Path of Beauty that allows every living creature to express uniqueness in a way that exemplifies harmony and truth.

The human race is the only one of All Our Relations that has lost the inner-knowing about its purpose. The Two-leggeds have been given much assistance by Great Mystery since they must answer the questions of the common mission before understanding the value of their individual missions. This assistance has come in the form of teachers who are All Our Relations.

The common misunderstanding that frightened the missionaries who came to "save" Native America was that the Red Race was a pagan race. I suppose since American Indians did not acknowledge Jesus, the common consensus was that the Red Race was primitive, savage, and pagan in orientation. From the Native point of view, Great Mystery is ALL. The aspects of Creation that are manifested by Great Mystery are sacred parts of the whole that are here to serve and be honored in that service. Native Americans do not worship idols, but use Sacred Medicine Objects of their Totems as reminders of the Relations assisting their evolution on this Earth Walk.

The Red Race sees Great Mystery as the life-force in all of Creation and not as an angry or jealous god. Great Spirit is seen as an unlimited creative force within Great Mystery that feeds all of Creation, all the time. Nothing in Seneca Wisdom limits Great Mystery or Great Spirit to gender, form, texture, color, or intent. All creations are a part of Great Mystery's whole, just as every cell in the human body has a different function and yet together those cells make up a carbon combustion unit that houses a spirit with a unique identity. All human ideas are birthed from the spirit inside the human body, are fed to the brain, and then acted upon through the will of the total being. All ideas in Creation come from Great Mystery, are gathered by Great Spirit, and then are used to feed the rest of Creation. To limit the power of Creation in ourselves or others is a human concept. If we acknowledge the limitlessness of Great Mystery, we must acknowledge that this life-force is also a part of our makeup because we are created by that same Original Source.

The Application

The Great Mystery card tells us the Original Source is the Creator of all life and that we are created in that likeness. We are free-willed co-creators who become the source of all we choose to experience in life. The buck stops here. We are totally responsible for all our joys and all our pain.

In receiving this card, you are being reminded to give gratitude for all of your lessons; it changes any pain to gain. Focus on your creative capacity and you can change anything. It may be time to drop any blame, shame, or regret and take charge of your life. The victim role doesn't suit Two-leggeds. We are created in the image of an infinite Creator and are therefore limitless co-creators.

In all cases, Great Mystery will continue to confound and astound us every time we try to figure it all out. Stop your mind's chatter and listen to the Source. Original Source shows us that the Mystery lives within us and contains all the answers we need to find along The Sacred Path. The Sacred Path of

Beauty is experiencing the mystery of life without having to control the outcome from our tunnel-vision command post. Go with the flow and watch the glory of limitless co-creation. After all, Great Mystery is the Divine plan and everything is on schedule.

≡ Field of Plenty ≡

Field of Plenty,
  Abundance for all,
    No hunger . . .
      No more pain.

Great Mystery holds
  Earth's Children dear,
    And feeds them with
      Eternal Flame.

Children of Earth, trust again!
  Be grateful and give praise!
    The Field of Plenty will remain
      To sustain us all our days.

≡ 38 ≡

Field of Plenty

IDEAS/NEEDS MANIFESTED

The Teaching

The Field of Plenty is an Iroquois Teaching that has to do with the understanding of Creation. When Great Mystery created our world, everything that would ever exist was created as ideas in the Thought or Spirit World. This nonphysical plane of awareness is eternal and can be drawn upon anytime there is a need. The thought-forms that provide all that is ever needed on the Good Red Road of physical life exist in eternal readiness inside the Field of Plenty. To call these ideas into manifestation, one need only come to Great Mystery with a grateful heart, which will bring the needed ideas into physical reality.

In our Seneca Tradition, the Field of Plenty is seen as a spiral that has its smallest revolution out in space and its largest revolution near the Earth. This shape could be likened to an upside-down tornado. When our Ancestors assisted the Pilgrims in planting Corn and raising crops so they would not starve, we taught them the understanding of the Field of Plenty by bringing the cornucopia baskets full of vegetables. The Iroquois women wove these baskets as a physical reminder that Great Mystery provides through the Field of Plenty. The Pilgrims were taught that giving prayers of gratitude was not just a Christian concept. The Red Race understood thanksgiving on a daily basis. The Field of Plenty is always full of abundance. The gratitude we show as Children of Earth allows the ideas within the Field of Plenty to manifest on the Good Red Road so we may enjoy these fruits in a physical manner.

When the cornucopia was brought to the Pilgrims, the Iroquois People sought to assist these Boat People in destroying their fear of scarcity. The Native understanding is that there is always enough for everyone when abundance is shared and when gratitude is given back to the Original Source. The trick was to explain the concept of the Field of Plenty with few mutually understood words or signs. The misunderstanding that sprang from this lack of common language robbed those who came to Turtle Island of a beautiful teaching. Our "land of the free, home of the brave" has fallen into taking much more than is given back in gratitude by its citizens. Turtle Island has provided for the needs of millions who came from lands that were ruled by the greedy. In our present state of abundance, many of our inhabitants have forgotten that Thanksgiving is a daily way of living, not a holiday that comes once a year.

Since the Vibral Alignment, or Harmonic Convergence, in August of 1987, our Elders have seen the Field of Plenty actually touch the Earth Mother and come to rest like a blanket over her body. In so doing, the Field of Plenty is now able to provide instant manifestation for all Earth's Children who call for their needs with gratitude prior to receiving those blessings. The Field of Plenty houses all thought-forms that supply abundant creativity to the Children of Earth. These new ideas are available to every Two-legged and can be made manifest through acknowledging the ideas, then acting on them. When there is a need, it is sent by the Field of Plenty, in idea form, to the consciousness of all life-forms. These ideas begin to manifest as they enter the physical realm and are acted upon by humans. Every need in our world can be met when we act upon any good idea that comes into our minds.

If there is a mass need for a new invention, the ideas that would allow an inventor to create that invention are made available to many people at the same time. The inventor who acts upon those ideas and completes the project is responding to the new ideas and assisting the manifestation process. Every time an artist, dancer, writer, scientist, musician, architect, or any creative person acts upon an idea and creates something that can be shared by everyone, that person is developing his or her personal gifts as well as bringing abundance into physical reality. Every time a teacher, mechanic, homemaker, or counselor assists another person, the same abundance is made manifest. Every talent and every role in physical life plays a part that assists the whole in manifesting abundant life.

When the Native Americans are in need of some tool or the services of a skilled person, they give thanks to the Field of Plenty for the manifestation of the needed item before it actually appears. The Field of Plenty always has a way of putting the needed item into the hands of the person who needs it. The keys to manifesting what is needed are gratitude and trust, balanced with action.

There is no need for scarcity in the Fifth World. Abundance for all the Children of Earth is manifesting. Thought always precedes form. If ideas of sharing and equality precede that reality in the hearts of Two-leggeds, the manifestation of physical needs being met will follow. This is Great Mystery's promise in creating the Field of Plenty.

The Application

The cornucopia is full of an abundance of ideas, talents, clothing, experiences, food, companions, and feelings that will serve the needs of the Children of Earth. If the Field of Plenty card has appeared, you are being assured that what you need at this time is manifesting. Your needs will be met. Give thanks now, before your needs are met. Show Great Mystery the trust you have in your process, dropping any doubt, becoming childlike again.

Do not limit the manner in which the physical manifestation occurs. Original Source operates in mysterious ways, placing the perfect people, places, and things on our paths to be answers to our true needs. We are asked to recall the differences between true needs and material crutches, which are mere illusions of happiness. In all instances, the Field of Plenty reminds us of our Divine right to have our prayers answered and our needs met.

≡ Stone People ≡

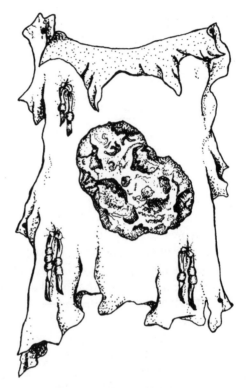

Record holders of the Earth,
Will you please explain
The history that gave us birth,
The truth you do contain?

Like your cousins of the seas,
The shells that let us hear,
Sacred whispers are the key,
To the history we hold dear.

Stone People we will hear you.
Teach us the ancient ways,
So we may build a future
Based on prayer and praise.

≋ 39 ≋

Stone People

RECORDS/KNOWING REVEALED

The Teaching

The Stone People are the record holders for the Earth Mother. These great Teachers can give the seeker much knowledge regarding the history of our planet and her children. The Stones' mission of service is holding energy. This is to say, the body of Mother Earth is made of rock that breaks and moves with weather, breaking down into smaller Stones that later become soil. Rocks carry records and transport electromagnetic energy on Mother's surface. The Stone People collect the energy and hold it for later use. The mineral kingdom is dense matter that has a magnetic quality that allows the Stones to record all that occurs on the planet.

Many healing uses are being discovered for various members of the Stone Clan. Native Americans have always used clear quartz crystals for focus and clarity. Medicine People in the northern part of Turtle Island have carved and carried many fetishes made of crystal for centuries. The magnification of knowledge and the ability to clearly see through the physical illusion has been greatly assisted by using the clear quartz crystals.

Many colored Stones have been used throughout the centuries for healing purposes. These are usually specific minerals that can tell a healer of their gifts and talents in assisting a healing process. Other Stones have been used for facepaint pigments by boiling them with Deer tallow and Elk fat until the color is released and settles to the bottom of the pot. The dirt is cleaned off the top and then the grease paint is cut into sticks to be used by the whole Tribe.

Another use for the Stone People was found when food was scarce during a long period of separation from hunters of the Tribe. Pebble soup was discovered by a young girl who had lost her way while picking berries with her grandmother while her Tribe was raided. Everyone had been killed and the remaining food only lasted a week or two. Winter was creeping upon them lighted by the late autumn moon when the little girl had a dream. A Stone Person was calling her to walk down by the creek. In her dream, the little girl followed the voice and found the Stone Person sitting on the bank. The Stone Person showed the little girl which herbs, mosses, and plants were edible and which Stones had minerals that would be released in a soup if boiled along with the Plant People.

When the little girl woke up, she saw how weak from hunger her grandmother was and felt that familiar ache in her own belly. She ran to the creek and found the Stone Person from her dream and collected the plants and Stones for the pebble soup all day. The pebble soup was the nourishment that kept the two women alive for a month before they were discovered by the hunters from another band of their Nation.

The Stone People who are Teachers for the Children of Earth come in many forms. The Stones used in Traditional Native healing are those found by river banks, along canyon walls and washes, which come to the surface through natural erosion. There is nothing wrong with taking from the Earth Mother if something is given back to her. It is always a good idea to offer Tobacco or to plant a tree in gratitude for that which was removed in another place.

The Stone People who come to the surface of our Earth Mother are record holders. Many will become soil in future generations due to erosion. These Stone People are considered common rocks by those not versed in the Language of the Stones. Every marking on a rock has a meaning and many times when intuition is used, faces of Two-leggeds and Creature-beings can be seen on the surface of the Stone. These faces are the connections that Stone has to the Children of Earth. For instance, if the face of Musk Ox is carved by nature in the face of a Stone, that Stone Person was around the area where the Musk Ox lived centuries ago and carries those historical records.

Nothing is ever put in our paths without a reason. When we are attracted to a certain rock and we pick that Stone Person up, it has a lesson for us. The Language of the Stones is a personal discovery with many messages for each individual. Since we are unique in our tastes, different Stone People will attract us. Grandmother Twylah of the Wolf Clan has written a booklet that covers the specific markings that teach the meanings of the Language of the Stones and is available through the Seneca Indian Historical Society. Anyone can learn what the Stone People are saying through the markings on their rock bodies by using this booklet as a guideline, making it easier to develop our intuition and hear the whispers of the Stone People as they ring in our hearts.

Each Stone Person can be a protecting and guiding force in life. The Sioux call their Protection Stones *Wo-Ties* and the Seneca call them Teaching Stones. In our Seneca Tradition, any Stone with a natural hole through it will bring protection to the holder. Stones have been used by Native Medicine People for divination purposes for centuries. In Ogalala Yuwipi ceremonies, the Yuwipi Men use the Stones to forecast the future of the recipient of the ceremony. The Stones are also used to assist the Yuwipi Men in finding lost items or missing persons. Although women are participants in these ceremonies, Traditionally all Yuwipi Medicine is reserved for a special society of Rock Medicine Men. These Medicine Men are growing more scarce as time passes; however, the few that still remain are very gifted and revered among the Ogalala, Lakota, and Dakota Sioux.

The role that Stone People play in the Tribes of Native America varies from Tribe to Tribe. Each Tribe has specific Teachings that were passed to them through the Stones over the past few centuries. Since these lessons are based upon trial and error, which then became Tradition, each Medicine Person has varying uses for the Stones. The Paiute Medicine People knew how to use an extract from the poisonous Stone Cinnebar in small quantities to heal certain illnesses among the People. The Tonkawas used Limestone with impressions of fossils to connect them to the Ancestors. The Comanches used certain types of Flint to make special arrowheads that were called Medicine Arrows and were used in Healing Ceremonies. The Apaches used certain colored Stones on a trail to divine the paths leading to Sacred Mountains. Each Tradition has found separate uses for the Language of the Stones and has revered the teachings of the Rock Nation as being messengers of the Earth Mother.

Every lesson of how to live in harmony on the Earth can be learned through connecting to the Stone People. The fact that each Rock is a part of the body of our Mother speaks for itself. When we seek to slow down our minds and feel the earthing influence that brings balance and serenity, a Stone Person is our tool. When nervous habits run us ragged, we are not feeling connected to the Earth Mother. Sure signs of being off balance are overeating, talking too much, addictions, compulsions, or erratic behavior. To calm the body, mind, or spirit, we need only to hold a Stone Person and breathe until the nervousness passes. This earthing influence is a way of anchoring the body to the Earth Mother and feeling the security of her nurturing influence. The impressions of every act of Creation from the moment our planet cooled until the present are contained in the bodies of the Stone People. This great fount of wisdom is ours as a gift if we are willing to connect with the Stone Teachers. The calming effect we receive is the wisdom of these Rock Elders who were the first historians for All Our Relations. Their mission is to be of service of the Two-leggeds. Now it is up to us to seek and accept their gifts.

The Application

The Stone People mark a time in which knowing will be revealed to you. Your personal records are held by these libraries of rock. Childhood memories may return and allow you to piece together a part of your personal puzzle. Memories of past lives or déjà vu could bring new awareness. Whatever the case, you are now in a position to know where you came from and where you are going.

A Stone Person can assist you in focusing your intent, dispelling confusion, changing habits, retrieving records from long ago, or getting grounded. Allow these teachers to become your Allies and discover a new world. Listen to the whispers of the mineral kingdom and your heart will know.

In all cases, the Stone People card asks you to open your mind because new understanding is coming your way. This knowledge is based on Earth-Records and may change the way in which you view life. These ancient friends are the oldest Children of Earth and only ask us to stop and listen.

≡ Great Smoking Mirror ≡

Through the smoke
 I see looking back
   Another reflection of me.

Mirror of my inner-self
 Who are you
   If I am me?

Mirror of my outer-Self
 What do others see?
Is it the truth in my heart
 Or human vanity?

≡ 40 ≡

Great Smoking Mirror

REFLECTIONS

The Teaching

Great Smoking Mirror is a widely used teaching of the Mayans and is sometimes taught by the Cheyenne and Pawnee. The Mayans say, "I am another one of Yourself." In this manner the Mayans stress that every life-form reflects every other life-form and that all originate from the same Original Source. The Smoking Mirror's concept of unity can eliminate all types of grandiose/elitist ideas that evolved in the Fourth World of Separation. If every Two-legged would see all other humans as unique expressions of oneself, we would have no basis for quarreling or war.

The Great Smoking Mirror speaks of the reflections of Self that are seen in others. Great Smoking Mirror allows the smoke screen of personal illusions to be pierced when the mirror, which is just beyond the smoke, is caught by a shaft of illuminating light or realization. In that moment, those who are willing to look at themselves, see the illusion of their personal myth. The part of Self that insists upon being the only one is shattered by the realization that every life-form holds an equal part to the solution of wholeness. Our criticism of other people holds no weight in the true light of self-reflection. We may have our opinions regarding others who continue to live with their own inner-division, but these opinions serve only as reminders of why we should strive for personal wholeness based in ideas of equality.

The Native American Teaching regarding "pointing our finger at another" applies here. When we point our finger at another person, three fingers are pointing back at us. In this context, the lesson may convey that others are merely reflecting what we need to recognize in the Self. Compassion for others who must learn difficult lessons on their personal paths is of the utmost importance. Lack of compassion results in an unforgiving coldness that consumes the heart. Life cannot quicken and grow inside a person who cannot forgive others or oneself. Some seekers in this time of awakening have adopted glib phrases that lack compassion. The phrase "They created their own reality," when spoken without understanding or compassion, reflects a lack of development in the seeker. When another person is treated in this callous manner, it is another one of ourselves who is being harmed.

Other seekers who look too deeply at themselves begin to demean the Self with the cold voice of the inner critical parent. The Great Smoking Mirror teaches balanced reflection that does not seek to lessen the value of the Self but rather to correct unhealthy attitudes that limit the growth potential. When we admire another's gifts, we are being asked to acknowledge the unique beauty of that esteemed person so we may see the similarities in ourselves. The Great Smoking Mirror is one tool we may use to create harmony in all our relationships through introspection and self-examination. When we are not at odds with the Self, the reflections we see in others will be ones of beauty.

When a mirror shatters into hundreds of pieces, each piece will give the viewer a complete picture just as the entire mirror did when it was whole. The Great Smoking Mirror is no exception. All of Creation can be viewed by seeing through the Smoke of physical illusion into the true nature of life. Worlds upon worlds can be discovered within each atom. Every part of Creation is interconnected and depends on all other life-forms within the whole. When any part of our world is thoughtlessly destroyed, many other interdependent parts suffer.

The Great Smoking Mirror teaches each person to look for similarity rather than difference when viewing others. The Red Race understands the Planetary Family and the value of learning the languages of all life-forms on the Earth Mother. Through the languages of all other life-forms, we are constantly given gifts of reflected knowing. People who use their creativity to find the personal answers that will assist their growth have discovered a part of the Great Smoking Mirror. Answers are reflected to every seeker in a different way. Each time the haze of an illusion clears and a bright new understanding appears on the horizon, we have shattered the lie that insists that we are too different to live in peace with other parts of Creation.

Mountain Rain was working as a healer in order to serve her people, the Mayans. As she grew in wisdom she saw strange things happen among the leaders of the Jaguar Priesthood. The priests began to insist that the gods of nature needed blood sacrifices and that these death rituals must be done with humans. Mountain Rain's heart was troubled for she knew that Sky God, the Ancient One, had never allowed such sacrifices in Tikal when he had come in his Solar Boat to teach the People.

Tikal was a huge city, teaming with inhabitants. Yet most of the people of Tikal seemed to accept the decree of the Jaguar Priests without question. Mountain Rain feared that this would be the beginning of the end for her people if the Jaguar Priests were allowed to complete their grisly plans. She searched her memory to see if anyone who remembered and honored Sky God's teachings was still living in Tikal. She began walking toward the Temple of the Double-headed Serpent, the healing temple, looking for an answer.

Suddenly as she neared the temple, her mind flashed upon the Ancient Grandmother who had taught the women of the

Double-headed Serpent Temple to use the Great Smoking Mirror. Mountain Rain cut through the jungle to search for the house of the Grandmother called She Who Sees. She Who Sees would be very old, if she still lived. At one time, this Grandmother inhabited a house where Mountain Rain had been taken during her early training.

After discovering the house of She Who Sees, Mountain Rain asked for permission to enter in the customary manner and went inside. She Who Sees was sitting with her son who was a Spotted Jaguar Priest discussing the turn of events. A blackened Medicine Bowl stood near the fire filled with water. The son, Toucan, was startled when Mountain Rain appeared. When Mountain Rain stated her reason for coming, Toucan relaxed and the three began to weave the magic of the Great Smoking Mirror, looking at their reflections in the Medicine Bowl and seeking answers.

Smoke wove a pattern over the reflection of the face of the Ancient Grandmother and her two students. The vision of hearts cut out and blood splattered across the alter of the Jaguar Temple made the three viewers wince in disgust and pain. The vision changed to the inner sanctum of the Jaguar Priests and the drugged seers who were eating the red mushroom of the Poppy tree. Mountain Rain and Toucan gasped in horror at the aberrant behavior of the drugged Seers as the men mounted each other and spent their frenzied energy sexually.

Suddenly the Void cleared the scene and Toucan was muttering his fear and outrage. "Look, my mother, at what they are doing!" he cried. "How can the Sacred Teachings be abused in this manner? How can I return to the temple and live among 'those People?'"

Slowly tears of a broken heart etched their way down the timeworn face of She Who Sees. "My son, they are but another one of ourselves," she whispered. Mountain Rain spoke, "But Grandmother, they are different. They are abusing the Medicine! They seek to destroy the teachings of Sky God. We are walking the Path of Beauty. How can they be another one of ourselves?"

She Who Sees looked deeply into the Medicine Bowl and as a tear from her ancient eyes hit the water, shimmering circles of light opened one upon another. Inside the concentric circles appeared the face of Sky God, the teacher from the Stars. "Be at peace my children, know that the crooked trail of these Jaguar Priests will end in folly. I taught the Mayans that the healing of the People would come through the heart and seeing all things as another one of themselves. I taught them that the remembering would come through the blood and their personal genetic memory. These priests have sought power over other Selves through the corruption of these truths."

Toucan asked Sky God how the corrupt Priesthood could be another one of themselves. Sky God answered, "The parts of yourselves that walk the crooked trail of those drugged Seers are merely your own shadows. These shadows have come to life through your refusal as a race to confront the greed and jealousy that surfaces in your thoughts. Beauty sees the feelings of the shadow as worthy opponents who insist on being conquered so that you may grow. Human fear sees those feelings as bad and in need of being repressed or denied. When you are afraid of feeling those shadow thoughts, they continue to rule you. Through your own fear you begin to believe that you are unworthy or evil. When the shadow is denied, it gains strength and will one day wake up with life-force of its own and eat the beauty inside you. Teach others to use the shadow parts of themselves as examples of the worthy opponent who can stir the growth of beauty inside the Self. You will see the beauty of balance come to the hearts of 'The People' as they remember."

The Application

The Great Smoking Mirror reflects the lesson of leaving the myth behind. You are what you decide you are. Remove the smoke screen that hides your natural talents or worth, and stand tall. Recognize the areas to be developed further and begin that process. Stop cowering before your potential and live your truth. There are millions of role models to choose from.

On another level you are being asked to be a good reflection for others. Encourage others to be bold through Walking Your Talk. The reflections you see in others may not make you happy if you are doubting yourself and your right to be. Jealousy on any level only inhibits growth and wastes energy. Shatter the mirrors that insist on self-importance, gloom, or failure so you can get down to what's really important.

On all levels, the Smoking Mirror asks us to accept light and shadow as equal. The reflections we dislike can be worthy opponents who teach us to grow into our potential. Even our shadow sides serve us by leading us through trial and error to the true image of Self.

≡ Shaman's Death ≡

Grandfather,
   I do ask for death,
      For the parts of me,
         That will not hear
            Or speak the truth,
               Which are too blind to see.

Grandmother,
   Give me birth again,
      With love as my guide,
         Truth and beauty as my path,
            With nothing left to hide.

≡ 41 ≡

Shaman's Death

DEATH AND REBIRTH

The Teaching

The teachings of Shaman's Death have many varied forms in the ceremonies of Native America. The idea of death as a means to experiencing new life is a common belief. Since all life is seen as movement on the Medicine Wheel, nothing is really ending without also being a new beginning. The Wheel of Life contains many spokes that mark the life-lessons and steps that every living creature will have to experience on the trail of physical life. These steps are called the Good Red Road and represent the spiral flow of life that comes to humans from Great Mystery. Native Americans have been taught that judging the steps another person must take in order to grow is foolish and unproductive.

As the Wheel of Life turns, all humans will reach the place where they will have to learn similar lessons. This is where Shaman's Death comes into play. If the lesson of each spoke on the Medicine Wheel is learned, the lesson of the next spoke is made available. The shadow side of Self, which inhibits growth, is constantly forced to die. These deaths occur on a daily basis, whether they be our fears, our doubts, our bad habits, our negative thoughts, or our self-importance. These deaths mark spiritual progress and speak of the ability of humankind to Walk in Beauty. Every death of a part of the shadow announces the birth of a new talent or gift contained in the Self. Each victory over a part of self that does not Walk in Beauty is a rebirth in itself. Every time a person reaches a crossroads and a decision must be made, that change in attitude marks the death of the old and the birth of the new.

A shaman is a person who is willing to confront the greatest fears and shadows of physical life. When I was working with Joaquin and the Grandmothers in Mexico, I was taught the difference between a healer and a shaman. A healer is a person who is able to use the forces of Good Medicine to effect a cure in the body, mind, or spirit of another. The healer, or *curandero,* does not use the forces of the shadow to effect cures. The shaman on the other hand, is a healer who has gone into the underworld and has unflinchingly confronted his or her own shadow as well as the evil of others and can successfully deal with those forces of darkness equally used with those of light. A shaman can do exorcisms and can reverse hexes and the results of black arts that have been used on a patient. The shaman, as well as the healer, can effect cures, but only the shaman is trained in dealing with any type of black arts that may have caused illness.

Many people in today's society are calling themselves shamans without any knowledge of exactly what this means. If the would-be shaman does not have the ability to look at his or her own shadow side, this person is not meant to follow the path of the shaman. This person would never be able to confront or handle the results and/or intentions of black shamanism. Among the people of Mexico and Central and South America, the black arts and the use of Good and bad Medicine together is very prevalent. Many shamans have died trying to protect others, thus invoking the wrath of those using the black arts. Although this type of bad Medicine among shamans is not as prevalent north of the Mexican border, it does exist. True Medicine People do not have to announce or brag that they are shamans or Medicine People at all. They work quietly and with humility because they know their worth in the eyes of Great Mystery. The opinions of others do not change the sense of Self held by a true healer or shaman.

A shaman has walked up to the gates of his or her personal hell and then walked in. The self-created demons of fear, insanity, loneliness, self-importance, and addictions have been confronted and conquered by the shaman who has gone through the gamut of Shaman's Deaths. The quality that always shines in a true shaman is compassion for the paths that others must walk. This comes from the fact that the shaman has also walked through the underworld of the shadow and knows firsthand the pain involved in breaking the stranglehold of inner darkness.

One such death/rebirth ritual is called The Night of Fear. This Tradition is practiced by many North American Tribes as a way to confront and conquer fear before going on a Vision Quest. The actual initiation involves going to a remote area and digging one's own grave. Then the seeker will lie in that grave alone all night. The opening to the grave is covered by a blanket. The sounds of the night and the nocturnal prowlers act as a catalyst that brings forth all of one's greatest imagined fears so that they may be confronted. Since the person cannot see through the blanket, the sounds, combined with imagination, are his or her worst enemy. The fears created by an active imagination can lead to the retrieval of inner-courage or the total paralyzation of the senses. After a person remains awake all night and confronts the shadowlike fears that stalk the imagination, he or she is eligible to go on a Vision Quest.

Another type of Shaman's Death ritual comes from the highlands of Mexico. In this ceremony, the initiate is stripped of clothing and is painted on the body with Bat symbols by members of his or her own gender. A hole is dug in the center of the village that will only allow the buried person's head to be above the Earth. Then the seeker is buried, standing up, for a twenty-four-hour period. All of the villagers call names, kick dust in the seeker's face, and urinate or defecate near the head of the buried and helpless person. The initiate is not allowed to answer any of the calls or actions verbally. The horror of what is happening destroys many of the notions one has of oneself. These indignities are a total surprise to the initiate and must be dealt with silently and with courage. The initiation is never explained beforehand except in the broadest terms.

After the twenty-four-hour ordeal, the initiate is removed from the hole and taken to a stream to be washed and perfumed. The members of the village dress the seeker and return him or her to the village draped in flowers and a new white garment. The final surprise is a feast that is held in the honor of the Bat god who stayed with the seeker and assisted the rebirth. Those who fail are lifted from the earth and washed and then looked after until the shaman's illness leaves. This illness is a borderline insanity that has broken the will of the shaman and can split the personality. Some villages have one or two initiates who lost touch with reality during the process and are cared for as people "touched by the gods."

The value of these types of Shaman's Deaths is that when a person succeeds in coming through the fire of insanity, the mind is strong and cannot be "thought adjusted" by sorcery. Thought adjusting is a telepathic invasion into the minds of the unaware. It is an ancient technique that involves the use of adjusting the attitudes or ideas of others for means of controlling their reason. Many black shamans seek to drive white shamans to insanity through invading their dreamscapes or using fear tactics to make their victims go crazy. In this way those who oppose the misuse of shamanism are removed from the gameboard. It is imperative for people studying to be shamans to study with a trained, tried and true Medicine Person. To unwittingly delve into shamanism without guidance, especially in those countries that regularly practice the dark arts, can be life-threatening.

Shamanism is also the ability to commune with all spirits dwelling on all levels of Creation. When a person has this ability from an early age it can be severely misunderstood. The natural shaman has usually had one or more major traumas between the ages of one and seven. These traumatic events cause a tear in the embryonic ego matrix that destroys the boundaries of the child. The sense of Self and one's Sacred Space is torn open and the communication between the Self and other voices begins. A small child is not able to discern which voices are helpful and which are harmful, and therefore may react to the direction of harmful earthbound spirits. In severe cases where the child is constantly abused by adults around him or her, the child may develop schizophrenia or split-personality syndrome.

In modern cultures, the treatment of these symptoms is tragic. In Mexican Tribal cultures, the child is taught how to eliminate the bad influences and accept the good voices that will lead to an adulthood as a gifted shaman. The series of Shaman's Deaths that must be conquered in the child's life is a natural path of discernment and strengthening of Self. These inner-battles are always fought with the assistance of trained healers and shamans of a Tribe. The finest shamans in our world today are those healed healers who have walked the path of death and rebirth destroying the shadows that have blocked their inner-clarity. Once a person has experienced the hard-fought road to wellness, it becomes easy to assist others in doing the same. When a shaman can recognize the shadow inside the Self, diagnosing similar darkness in others is possible.

The willingness to confront anything in the Self that is not serving The Sacred Path to wholeness and to go through the cleansing process of Shaman's Death is admirable. Shaman's Death is not just for shamans. Every time anyone wishes to change old habits and begin life again in a new and more productive way, there is a Shaman's Death. If old Corn stalks were not burned off and plowed under, the soil would not be fertilized and new Corn could not grow the next year.

Bat is the Mayan and Aztec symbol for rebirth. Bat hangs upside down in the cave just as humans make ready for birth, nestled upside down in their mothers' wombs. The darkness of the cave is safe for Bat, just as the darkness of the womb is safe for unborn children. In leaving the womb or the cave, each person is forced to look at light and shadow. Then one must make the decision as to which of these sides of the Self will allow further growth. The duality of the Universe will evolve into the Uniworld when each person is able to see both sides as equally contributing to the process of awareness. The Shaman's Death is one symbol of this growing understanding that leads to wholeness.

The Application

In choosing the Shaman's Death card, you are being put on notice that a death cycle or ending is in progress. Before the rebirth can occur, the habit, attitude, relationship, or part of Self that is dying must be looked at. Assist the process by consciously allowing the old to be removed. Let go and then make way for the new cycle of life to take hold.

Remember that you are creating fertile ground for new adventures when you are willing to let your old identities die. The rebirth cycle is always full of promise and growth when you allow the old patterns to die with dignity.

≡ Hour of Power ≡

Oh Sacred Hour that reconnects,
My spirit with the whole,
Mother Earth will fill me up,
Through my heart and soul.

I will sing my Spirit Song,
I will be at one,
I will share my energy,
Like Earth, Moon, and Sun.

≡ 42 ≡

Hour of Power

RITUAL OF JOY

The Teaching

All human beings have their own internal timing. Some are very quick to accomplish a daily task while others are more methodical. Some people have a slow metabolic rate and others have food seemingly run through their bodies. The thought processes of some are lightning quick and others are graced with the patience of examination. These examples of personal timing are some of the things that make us unique and different from one another.

So it is that each person also has an Hour of Power during a day's cycle. Every person feels more connection with a certain time of day or evening. For some it may be just before sunrise when the world is still and quiet and the fading darkness is about to greet Grandfather Sun. For others it may be at 3:00 or 4:00 A.M. when the stirrings of life are totally quiet and Entering the Silence is easier. For some it may be high noon when Grandfather Sun is at his peak and is flooding his love and warmth on all Creation. For others it may be sunset, the day's transition into starry wonder. For all people, their special time of day or evening is their Hour of Power.

Once again we need to look at the significance of power. When you feel powerful, you might feel happy, courageous, bold, ready to meet life, full of vitality, able to use your talents, connected to all life-forms, and/or balanced in who and what you are. These are all aspects of wholeness. The power that lives as truth is no more than our acknowledgment and proper use of all aspects of ourselves.

If you want to find your Hour of Power, notice when you feel at your best and when you feel at your weakest. The times are usually exactly opposite by twelve hours. These are your internal cycles. For instance, those that feel best at 3:00 A.M. are usually getting a dip in energy at 3:00 P.M. If you have never been up at 3:00 A.M., you may not have noticed how you feel at that hour. We all have that internal timepiece that sends us a splash of energy and vigor when we connect to the Earth at the peak hour of our personal cycle. When we are out of touch with our bodies or the Mother Earth from which they were made, we lose our sense of timing. Without that internal timing we tend to lose our balance.

I was taught the value of this internal cycle when I lived in Mexico. Joaquin was a master at teaching me how to touch that place that made me feel as if I was connected and electrified. One day he made me sit in the shade of a Jacaranda tree and be still for twelve hours. Joaquin was aware that my Hour of Power had to be near the evening since I had had my Vision Quest opening at midnight. So I began sitting at two in the afternoon. I had to notice the pulse of my body and how it harmonized with Mother Earth's heartbeat. At the time, I was unaware that our planet had a pulse. After an hour or so, I could feel the pulses and surges of energy coming from the Earth and how they entered my body or bounced off.

Just before sunset, the hills of San Luis transformed into the undulating sensuality of long shadows of lilac light highlighted with apricot and gold. Mother Earth's breathing female form was shown to me in the hills and mountains beyond. It was almost as if she was stretching and gently disengaging herself from the activities of the day. Then I felt the entry point of my Hour of Power as early evening donned a serene coat of pastel colors and the world stood still. It was as if the day was passing the baton to evening and the energy of the pulses of Earth totally changed.

My energy started to pick up and I could feel the life-force within me come into alignment with Mother Earth's pulses. The Jacaranda flowers blew in the gentle breeze born of total silence and in the stillness of the moment, day gave way to evening. The blue-violet blossoms matched the high heavens as my eyes traveled closer to the horizon, which sported the last rays of Grandfather's light. I could feel that dying light inside my middle as it gave birth to a new kind of Earth pulse. The new pulse was not as direct as the day pulse but was strong, while more feminine and sensual. My body was magnetizing the colors of sunset and was fueled and electrified with the new energizing force.

The empowerment of my internal timing and the energizing of my body was enough to let me know that this was my Hour of Power. I felt the buildup of energy as if my body was making ready for some great adventure. I had always known that I did my most creative work at night and now I fully understood why.

It is most important to be silent and to feel that Hour of Power in each day as it feeds and nourishes the body, heart, mind, and spirit. It is the zero-rest balance point, akin to the pause in between the in-breath and out-breath of the body, the place that is perfectly neutral just before the birth of a new phase of Creation. Our spirits come from the Wind, which is also our breath. The spirit pauses when our internal timing is shifting gears. Then the spirit fills the body with total joy and exuberance.

The Hour of Power is a ritual of joy. It is the time of day when each individual is filled with the essence of aliveness and pure connection to all Creation. As this time is unique with each person, it is a solitary time that invokes a sustaining flow of aliveness that will feed the person with Great Mystery's pure Manna, or life-force. The joy that fills you in this time period can be a Medicine you may call on at any other time of day when there is need. To call on the Medicine of the Hour of Power, you need only to close your eyes and breathe in the pulses of Mother Earth's heartbeat and recreate the joy through remembrance. Remember how it felt during your Hour of Power, firmly plant your feet on Mother Earth, and as you breathe in the joy, feel it coming up the soles of your feet from Mother Earth's molten heart center. This Earth-Connection is pure sustenance and will allow you to ride out any storm.

Due to the lack of Earth-Connection in the modern urban world, many have disconnected from their personal rhythms. The Hour of Power has no connection to your birth time; it is your internal rhythm. The changing of body structure caused by surgery, trauma, shock, etc., can change the internal timing as a result of the interrupted connection to the heartbeat of the Mother Earth. If a person were to stay connected to the Earth and allow the body to be healed through Earth-Connection, there would not be any change in the internal timing. When there has been a growth period, change in consciousness, or healing, the Hour of Power may change. We are constantly evolving and our internal timing will also regulate to the new growth. Then the body's original Hour of Power can take on a new rhythm or different timing due to its new state of health.

The Application

The Hour of Power speaks of Rituals of Joy. No matter what your present situation, you are being asked to do what gives your heart the greatest joy. Drop any activity that is taxing and focus on connecting to the Earth and being fed with the energy you need to maintain happiness.

This card signals the zero-rest balance point that will keep you from becoming out of harmony if you realign body, mind, and spirit by doing something that gives you joy. This little happiness break is what will keep you from breaking apart if you are stressed out.

Life-force is available to you in this moment. Be reminded not to leak this precious Manna on regret or indecision. The keynote here is celebrating life. Find the blessings that give you joy, discover your Hour of Power, and feed the talents that allow you to develop your greatest potential.

≡ Give-Away Ceremony ≡

Aho Child of Earth!
  Do you know the secret

               of the Give-Away?
The more you release,
        The more you receive,
           For that is nature's way.
Aho Child of Earth!
  Do you believe

        in reaping what you sow?
A drop of wisdom

       Will bring the truth
         And you will truly know.

≡ 43 ≡

Give-Away Ceremony

RELEASE

The Teaching

One of the most important ceremonies in Native American teachings is the Give-Away, or Potlatch, Ceremony. In this ritual, giving away of useful or loved possessions is a form of sharing with others. It is also a sign that the giver is willing to make a sacrifice and surrender a gift to another person without attachment or regret. The Native understanding of sacrifice originally meant "to make sacred." To make any act or any gift sacred, one has to complete that action with a joyful heart and a humble attitude. Giving is only one step of the process and allows the giver to look within so that he or she may examine the growth potential associated with the Give-Away.

Many years ago among the Tlingit Indians of the Northwest, the Raven Clan and Eagle Clan held Potlatch Ceremonies. These Clans would gather all they could to give those in need. Each time the Potlatch was held, the Clan on the giving end would distribute an even greater amount of goods than they had received at a previous Potlatch in order to show their appreciation. The United States Government put a stop to this ritual in the early 1900s. The government believed that the Potlatches were getting out of hand because people were

313

giving too much away. The government agents could not conceive of how people who were seemingly poor could take what little they had and give it to others, then live with practically nothing. These agents thought the Potlatch Ceremony was a kind of competition that brought shame and poverty to the People. This was far from the truth.

In Native Tradition, no one is ever abandoned, orphaned, or left without food, dwellings, or help. The understanding among Native people is that when one shares all that one has, in order that the People may live, honor and abundance is brought to the giver. Indians have extended families who adopt many relatives and care for one another. Those who are blessed with possessions and food have always shared with those who are lacking. The Medicine Wheel may turn tomorrow and the ones who are in need today, may be blessed with abundance that they may share.

The purpose of the Give-Away is sharing. The lessons connected to this ceremony teach the People how to release possessions and to let go the ideas of importance connected with those belongings. The more prized the possession and the greater the sense of ownership, the more potent the lesson. The Give-Away Ceremony is never used to get rid of belongings that are no longer functional or badly in need of repair. Some gifts of the Give-Away may be made especially for the occasion. To give cast-off items is a disgrace to the giver and shows a lack of respect for the receiver.

If one cannot give without strings attached, there is no true release and the sacredness of giving without expectations has been destroyed. The idea of envy and coveting the possessions of another was an alien concept before the invasion of Turtle Island by the White Eyes. Among the Tribes of Native America, if everyone was not taken care of, the People lost face. There was never any justification for some to live in luxury while others of the same Tribe starved.

In Native Tradition, a gift is never thought of as an obligation or used as a means of controlling the person who receives the gift. The obligatory giving concept came with the Boat People whose ideas were based in European thought, which was that if a person gave a gift, the giver expected something in return. When this manner of giving is experienced, there is no true Give-Away or release. When the attachment to material possessions is strong in a person, the favors given to others are heavily laden with expectations or demands. The Red Race knows that giving is a way of releasing the People's spirit from the attachment to the physical world. In releasing possessions we love dearly, we are able to open our lives for future abundance.

Wealth is measured in many different ways by Two-leggeds across our planet. In Native Tradition, one important measure of wealth is a person's ability to assist others. Developed talents and the willingness to use them to aid those in need, set a person apart from others who seek self-gratification. This type of individual is the symbol of a potential leader in a Tribe. Selflessness is a sign that the giving individual is able to stand apart from the attachments of the physical world. The spiritual life of this person is usually well developed and carries the Medicine of the Ancestors.

The concept of Indian Giving came from a misunderstanding when a Boat Person received a Give-Away and the Indian who gave the gift later reclaimed it. This manner of taking back a gift is done for a reason. If any item is given to someone who has no use for it, the giver has the right to reclaim the gift and give it to another who will use it. Every substance in our world has a role in Creation. We Two-leggeds have the ability to assist every part of Creation by honoring the particular missions of each one and allowing them to be used.

If a clay pot sits on a shelf and is not used, the mission of that pot has not been honored as sacred, and therefore, should be passed to someone who will allow it to complete its mission of service. When anything is made by human hands, the Medicine of the maker is a part of the object created. To wantonly destroy the object would be to dishonor the Medicine of the maker along with that tool's ability to be of use. The Ancestors say that if an object is carelessly broken by a human, the spirit of that object has been killed. To make fun of, criticize, or break anything that another has created is to dishonor one's Self. The idea that gifts should be used to their fullest potential has sustained the Red Race for centuries. In this manner, everyone acknowledges the gifts Great Mystery gives through the Field of Plenty as well as the purpose of not accumulating more than one can personally use.

The teachings of the Give-Away are basic to Native understanding. Many other lessons are learned each time one has the opportunity to share and is faced with personal feelings that arise when a decision to Give-Away is made. As we free ourselves from the need to give with strings attached or the regret that sometimes follows, we are able to release our spirits and allow them to soar beyond the limited understanding of our former Selves.

The Application

The Give-Away card spells relief through release. Don't get stuck holding on to anything that no longer serves you. Associates, ideas, habits, and belongings may need to go at this time. Attachment to attitudes like needing to be needed or liked may no longer serve either.

You are being asked to share what you can, give away something that can help someone else, or just let go. Don't hold on so tight. The natural flow of life is squelched when you insist on total control.

In all cases, the Give-Away card tells us to release any bond that makes us captives of our own creation. In so doing, we can spread our wings and fly. Remember that generosity is a talent and a virtue that comes from dropping the fear of scarcity and from trusting Great Mystery.

≡ Sacred Space ≡

Great Mystery,
   Teach me to honor
      The laws of Sacred Space,
   The customs and Traditions
      Of every creed and race.
Great Mystery,
   Teach me to develop
      The talents that I own
   And to behave with reverence
      In another's home.
Great Mystery,
   Teach the child in me
      To accept with grace
   The part of Sacred Mystery
      Found in every space.

≡ 44 ≡

Sacred Space

RESPECT

The Teaching

The idea of Sacred Space has been one of the foundations of Native American philosophy throughout time. We see all life-forms as having their own Medicine Wheel or life-cycles. Each life-form from a Stone Person to a Cloud Person to a Standing Person has a space that deserves respect. Every Creature-being has its own territory and respects the territory of other animals. Two-leggeds also have a personal space that, if respected, becomes Sacred Space.

Nature teaches us how to know ourselves in the purest way possible. If we listen and watch, every lesson of human living is given by the animals, the changes in the Wind, Father Sky, Mother Earth, and All Our Relations. Each aspect of our world has its own space in which to create. If that space is respected by others, growth continues in harmony.

For instance, in the forest each Standing Person is naturally seeded by the Wind. Many trees may grow close together until one among them becomes stronger and needs more room. The others will naturally respect the space of the one who has the best chance of maturing and seeding others of its kind. The weakest ones sometimes uproot and use their bodies to fertilize the stronger one. When these Standing People were smaller, they served each other as protection, and later they served the whole Tree Tribe by allowing the stronger one to survive. This is an act of selfless love. The spirit of every Standing Person who contributed to the survival of the strong one is still alive in the forest even though the trunk, branches, and roots may have changed form. The decay of the body in service has allowed that Standing Person's spirit to grow and evolve.

Other Creature-beings also respect Sacred Space by marking the area of their territory with their urine. They will not cross another animal's border unless they are looking for food when it is scarce. If food is plentiful, even a Two-legged can mark a campsite with urine and have the marked area respected. There is no reason for an animal to invade another's space unless that Creature-being is hunting or is physically attacked.

In humankind, Sacred Space extends to our habitat, belongings, and feelings as well as our bodies. We Two-leggeds may feel invaded if our car or home is broken into. We certainly feel invaded if violence is done to our bodies, but we don't need to feel mauled if someone else has different beliefs or ideas. If another person states her Point of View and our internal knowing says, "This idea does not feel like it fits into my personal knowing," there is never any need to defend our personal right to be.

The concept of Sacred Space is more than a belief in the Native American way of thinking. From the earliest life-lessons, Indian children are taught to listen and respect the words of others, especially their Elders. These children are taught the value of their possessions and no one touches their things without permission. Consequently, through example, children do not touch the belongings of others without consent. Adults allow the children the right to have their own ideas, their own possessions, their own play and work areas, as well as their own rights and respect. Just because a child is not fully developed does not mean that their Sacred Space should not be respected. If a child learns the ideas of Sacred Space through example, that child will always respect the ideas, belongings, homes, and bodies of others.

This practice of teaching respect gives humans the understanding of how other life-forms have their own Sacred Space and individual mission to accomplish in this Earth Walk. A Traditional Medicine Person would never cross a forest without asking permission from the Chief Standing Person (tree) or the Creature-beings that lived there. A Tobacco offering would be made and if the request was denied, the decision would be honored by the Indian seeking permission to enter.

How conceited is it for a Two-legged to believe that humans are the only creatures Great Mystery created with their Sacred Space attached? Is it possible that the Heyokah, or Trickster, part of Great Mystery has played a cosmic joke on everyone? Is it only the Two-leggeds who don't understand Sacred Space? Are all of our plant, animal, stone, cloud, and natural element counterparts here to serve as Guardians for us until we wake up? Sometimes it seems so. If we could laugh at the joke without crying, we might make some progress in the areas of self-respect and the respect of others.

Defining our boundaries is important. For instance, if we have a house guest and we don't give the ground rules we expect to be maintained in our home, we will certainly be angry if unspoken rules are broken. The anger is usually at ourselves for not discussing the ground rules in the beginning.

The damage done to a child when his or her Sacred Space is invaded at an early age may require a lifelong healing process. This damage can be created through physical or emotional abuse, the destruction of belongings, the refusal to allow the child an opinion, favoritism of one child over another by parents, not honoring the child's freedom of choice when selecting clothing or toys, neglect, or constant Mother-smothering. These instances teach a child, through example, that nobody is to be respected and in turn that child may become self-destructive. When a child believes that his or her space, belongings, and persona are not held in high regard by others, he or she often carries that legacy of abuse into future life situations.

Many times Indian children will be encouraged to find their favorite place to be by themselves. This is a lesson in choosing for oneself as well as a way to teach the child to enjoy the company of Self. Of course the child will also be in the company of nature's creatures and will find a connection to the Earth Mother through making a shelter or playhouse. Children grow when they are allowed to use their own creativity, imagination, intuition, and self-reliance. This special place is not visited by the parents without an invitation from the child. All materials the child needs are provided along with answers to the child's questions regarding the use of these materials. The child is urged to use her or his own talent to complete the Sacred Space. It is very important for the parents to praise a job well done and not to criticize the child's efforts.

One of the most important elements in instilling the understanding of Sacred Space is to allow children to develop the talents they have through posing questions that will allow them to think for themselves. If Indian children act silly or can't get an answer for themselves, their Grandparents may just ignore them and speak as if the child is not present. For instance, one Grandparent may say, "I wonder why Blue Heron wants to be so silly? He must not want to hear his own answers." Then the other Grandparent may reply, "No, I think he got stung by Bumble Bee and is buzzing around his own head." The child may be sitting two feet in front of the Grandparents, and being treated as if he is not there gets his attention. This may go on for days until the child works out his own answer to the question posed. When the child uses his thinking process and finds the answer, he is rewarded through becoming visible again. The child feels a sense of accomplishment and worthiness. The lesson further instills respect for the Grandparents and the value of their wisdom.

Every inch of our Earth Mother is the home of one life-form or another. We are guests in another's space when we leave our own. We share air, food, soil, water, and sunlight with all living things. We only have one Mother Earth and by her grace we are given the Guardianship of our Sacred Spaces during our Earth Walk. We must clean our personal Sacred Spaces in order to learn respect for others. The time is NOW and the power is in understanding the validity of each life-form's right to life.

The Application

The Sacred Space card insists on respect for the possessions, ideas, homes, and persons of others. This also applies to demanding it for the Self. Mark your territory. Respect yourself so that others will see that reflection in themselves and in how they deal with you. Be willing to say no.

Sacred Space means that you consider your body, feelings, and possessions sacred and will not allow others to abuse them. Only invite those who have earned the right into your Sacred Space. You are the one who sets up how other people treat you through how you treat yourself.

In all cases the respect you show yourself and other life-forms determines how you relate to the Planetary Family. If you allow others to be destructive in your Sacred Space, on some level you don't have the guts to be disliked. It is not important to be liked by others, but it is important to be able to live with yourself. Happiness begins within.

Just One Arrow

Oh the road is long and narrow,
And I'm down to just one arrow,
And my old paint, he can hardly stand.
But you can point me toward the battle,
Put me back up in my saddle,
It's time for me to take my *own* last stand.

I've been looking for a way to cross the Rockies in my mind,
Tryin' to decide about my own Great Divide.
There's a mighty Mississippi ragin' somewhere in my soul,
I've got to cross this desert, before I reach my goal.

'Cause the road is long and narrow,
And I'm down to just one arrow,
And my old paint, he can hardly stand.
But you can point me toward the battle,
Put me back up in my saddle,
It's time for me to make my *own* last stand . . .

John York

Author's Note

The faith and trust that allow the human spirit to continue the growth process are qualities that are discovered and rediscovered within the Self. Like the Sacred Water Bird who dives into its watery reflection and through the crack in the universe only to become a new Self, each person faces the point of total transformation many times. The decision is always our own. Will we have the courage to enter the Void where Future lives, or will we forget that we have as many alternatives as our creativity allows?

My friend John York, one of the Byrds, is a brilliant songwriter. He has touched my heart with a song he wrote called "Just One Arrow." When John came to a transition point in his life, he wrote this song. It has given me the personal courage to carry on when I thought I was too weary to continue. I want to share the words with you because I feel they are the spirit of the Ancestors who walked the Wind and carried the wisdom through hard times so that these Teachings would live forever.